THE MIRACULOUS ELEMENT

IN THE

GOSPELS.

THE

Miraculous Element

IN THE

Gospels

A Course of Lectures on the "Ely Foundation"

DELIVERED IN
UNION THEOLOGICAL SEMINARY

BY

ALEXANDER BALMAIN BRUCE, D.D.

Professor of Apologetics and New Testament Exegesis in Free Church College, Glasgow. Author of "The Parabolic Teaching of Christ," etc., etc.

HODDER & STOUGHTON
NEW YORK
GEORGE H. DORAN COMPANY

PREFACE.

THESE Lectures on *The Miraculous Element in the Gospels* were delivered by appointment on the foundation established in the Union Theological Seminary by Mr. Zebulon Stiles Ely, of New York, in the following terms:

"The undersigned gives the sum of ten thousand dollars to the Union Theological Seminary of the city of New York, to found a lectureship in the same, the title of which shall be, 'THE ELIAS P. ELY LECTURES ON THE EVIDENCES OF CHRISTIANITY.'

"The course of Lectures given on this foundation is to comprise any topics that serve to establish the proposition that Christianity is a religion from God, or that it is the perfect and final form of religion for man.

"Among the subjects discussed may be,—

"The Nature and Need of a Revelation;

"The Character and Influence of Christ and His Apostles;

"The Authenticity and Credibility of the Scriptures, Miracles, and Prophecy;

"The Diffusion and Benefits of Christianity; and

"The Philosophy of Religion in its Relation to the Christian System.

"Upon one or more of such subjects a course of ten public Lectures shall be given at least once in two or three years. The appointment of the Lecturer is to be by the concurrent action of the directors and faculty of said Seminary and the undersigned; and it shall ordinarily be made two years in advance.

"The interest of the fund is to be devoted to the payment of the Lecturers, and the publication of the Lectures within a year after the delivery of the same. The copyright of the volumes thus published is to be vested in the Seminary.

"In case it should seem more advisable, the directors have it at their discretion at times to use the proceeds of this fund in providing special courses of lectures or instruction, in place of the aforesaid public lectures, for the students of the Seminary on the above named subjects.

"Should there at any time be a surplus of the fund, the directors are authorised to employ it in the way of prizes for dissertations by students of the Seminary upon any of the above topics, or of prizes for essays thereon, open to public competition.

"ZEBULON STILES ELY.

"NEW YORK, *May* 8, 1865."

This work, though constructed on a different method, may be regarded as a companion to my work on *The Parabolic Teaching of Christ*, published a few years ago. In the fifth and sixth Lectures I have considered from my point of view at considerable length a large number of the miraculous narratives, and made observations on nearly the whole of the narratives of this character contained in the Gospels. My object in these portions of the work is not to expound homiletically the whole narrative in which a miracle is recorded, but to enquire whether the event recorded be indeed a miracle.

To prevent misapprehension readers are requested to note that throughout the discussions in this volume the Gospels are regarded, not from the viewpoint of a strict doctrine of inspiration, but from that of substantial historicity. It is not dogmatically the highest point of view, but it is that which is most germane to apologetic enquiries.

To facilitate reference an index is attached at the end. For the preparation of this I am indebted to Mr. C. R. Gillett, librarian to the Union Theological Seminary.

A. B. BRUCE.

CONTENTS.

VI.—The Gospel Miracles in Relation to Exegesis —The Miracles Wrought on Nature.

VII.—The Gospel Miracles in Relation to the Worker.

VIII.—The Gospel Miracles in Relation to the Christian Revelation.

IX.—The Great Moral Miracle.

X.—Christianity without Miracle.

THE

MIRACULOUS ELEMENT IN THE GOSPELS.

I.

MIRACLES IN RELATION TO THEORIES OF THE UNIVERSE.

I PURPOSE in the following lectures to consider under various points of view the miraculous element in the Gospels. It is but a fragment of a larger subject, the miraculous element contained in the Records of Divine Revelation. It is, however, the part around which the main apologetic interest revolves. The Gospel miracles are at once intrinsically the most important of all the Bible miracles, and the best attested. They therefore form the key of the position. If we fail here in establishing the reality of a breach in the continuity of nature, we fail all along the line. If we succeed here we can regard with comparative equanimity assaults at other points. So long as the miracles of Jesus remain, the question as to the reality of the miracles of Moses or of Elisha, though important, is only of secondary moment.

The alleged occurrence of a single miracle raises the question as to the possibility of the miraculous. To that weighty question I must therefore first address myself. I do so under a certain feeling of discouragement. The advocate of miracles is very conscious in these days that he goes against the current of contemporary opinion. The oracles, literary, philosophic, and scientific, pronounce against them. Mr. Arnold declares that the human mind is turning away from miracles.* Dr. Strauss decrees that miracle must take itself off.† M. Renan announces that the whole body of modern sciences yield the immense result, that there is no supernatural.‡ It seems as if miraculous narratives must henceforth be relegated from the realms of fact to those of art; their proper place not the page of history, but the cathedral window; capable still of yielding us pleasure, but only because we are no longer expected to believe them.§

Why do we cling to Bible miracles, and especially to those related in the Gospels, against the potent voices of the time? Is it that we fear church censures, or clutch conservatively old creeds? No! we could part with both church and creed, if need were, without breaking our heart. It is because our faith in God and in Christ is involved. All the miraculous must go, if any goes on speculative grounds. The moral miracles must be sacrificed to the Moloch of naturalism not less than the physical; Christ's stainless character as well as His healing ministry. It has been said that Christ was perhaps as incapable of working a physical miracle as He was of sinning.‖ The implied position is philosophically inconsistent and untenable. It is not unphilosophical to say Christ could not sin and *did* not work miracles. But it is unphilo-

---

* *Literature and Dogma*, p. 129.

† *Der alte und der neue Glaube*, p. 180.

‡ *Etudes d'Histoire Religieuse*, p. 206.

§ Such in effect is the view of Pfleiderer as expressed in *Religionsphilosophie*, p. 621, in these terms: "As the sensible expression of faith, the eternal spiritual miracle, the miracle-legend, its dearest child, will ever hold its place there where the religious spirit unfolds and enjoys its mystery through the senses; in the symbolism of religious art and the worship which through it speaks to the heart."

‖ So Dr. Abbott, in Preface to *Oxford Sermons*.

sophical to say Christ could not sin and could not work miracles; for sinlessness is a miracle in the moral sphere, and speculative grounds against the miraculous, if valid at all, are equally valid in all spheres. An eclectic half-way naturalism is irrational.

It is because we clearly perceive this to be true that we earnestly enquire whether miracle be indeed ruled out by philosophy or science. For the same reason indeed, even if we failed to discover any way of adjusting the idea of the miraculous to our speculative views, we should still hold on to the Gospel miracles with the heart, walking by faith where sight failed. Such a position, however, that of one in whom speculative reason and religious faith are in conflict, is essentially weak and unstable. It is therefore desirable for our own confirmation, as professed believers in Christ, to institute the preliminary enquiry now proposed, in the hope that antichristian philosophic prejudices bred of the spirit of the age, lurking in our minds, may thereby be dispelled.

The enquiry proposed is important also for apologetic purposes. It affords an opportunity of pointing out that much unbelief in the supernatural has its root in a priori speculative reasoning. This is in truth the simple fact Philosophic bias, not strict science, is the mother of much current unbelief. It is easily possible to occupy such a philosophical attitude that no amount of evidence will convince of miracle. This is evident in the extreme cases of the Materialist and Pantheist. Neither can rationally believe in miraculous breaches of the continuity of nature, because for neither does a God exist distinct from nature through whose agency such breaches can take place. To the Materialist the notion of the supernatural is absurd; nature for him is the All. For the Pantheist the term supernatural is not a word without meaning. But his supernatural is not distinct from nature; it reveals itself in nature, it is nature viewed ideally. To the one nature is the only reality, and God an idle expletive; to the other God is the ideality of nature, and nature the reality of God. Whichever of the two theories of the universe we adopt, the miraculous is effectually excluded.

In making these remarks I do not mean to insinuate that all unbelievers in miracle may legitimately be stigmatised as Materialists or Pantheists. I do not forget, I will rather hereafter carefully point out, that such unbelief is compatible with certain forms of theism. I remember also that the scientific spirit, not less than philosophy, is sceptical in its attitude towards the supernatural. Nevertheless it remains the fact that much existing unbelief is largely due to philosophy alone. And such unbelief becomes less imposing when it is considered that there are other things besides miracles which cannot be made credible to a certain speculative bias, even when science is on the other side. I mention as outstanding instances, the eternity of matter, the origin of life, and the nature of consciousness.

On all these three questions materialistic philosophy and science look in different directions. Recent science argues from the phenomena of the existing world that it must have come into existence so many millions of years ago. This inference of science, religious faith gladly accepts as most in harmony with Scripture teaching. At the same time it ought to be said that it is not essential to our position as theists to maintain that matter must have been created, and that the world must have had a beginning in time. Faith in a Divine Maker and Sustainer remains intact even if the eternity of matter be conceded. Though as believers in God and in Scripture we have our bias on the question, we do not need to dogmatise on it; and the less we have to dogmatise on such topics the better. But what I wish here to point out is that Materialism, and I may add Pantheism, does need to dogmatise on the subject in question. These theories cannot afford to leave the question as to the eternity of matter open. Matter must have existed eternally, for if it had a beginning, a God must be postulated as its cause.

As to the origin of life the state of the case is the same. The verdict of science, after the most careful investigation, is decidedly adverse to Abiogenesis. With oracular confidence the microscope declares: no life is found except where a parent life has been before. The bearing of the result on the inquiry as to the first beginning of life in the world is as obvious as it is important. It is universally admitted that there was a time when no life in any form existed. Whence then did the first rudimentary forms of life come? Did they spring into being spontaneously on the principle of Abiogenesis, contrary to present experience; or did they owe their origin to a Divine creative initiative? The materialist, in absence of all evidence and contrary to such evidence as is available, decides dogmatically for the former alternative. If, says Mr. Huxley, whose pardon I ask for citing him, contrary to his wish, as a Materialist, "If it were given me to look beyond the abyss of geologically recorded time to the still more remote period when the earth was passing through physical and chemical conditions, which it can no more see again than a man can recall his infancy, I should expect to be a witness of the evolution of living protoplasm from not living matter. I should expect to see it appear under forms of great simplicity, endowed, like existing fungi, with the power of determining the formation of new protoplasm from such matters as ammonium carbonates, oxalates and tartrates, alkaline and earthy phos phates, and water, without the aid of light." * Mr. Huxley candidly confesses that he has no right to call this opinion anything but an act of philosophical faith. Faith philosophical, as distinct from scientific, it certainly is, having its ground not in scientific evidence, but in speculative unbelief in the possibility of any new phenomenon appearing in nature which does not owe its origin to purely natural conditions. In the hands of Strauss this philosophic faith degenerates into a bold philosophic dogmatism. "Though," he remarks, "the occurrence of spontaneous generation at the present time cannot be proved, this proves nothing in regard to the premundane period with its entirely different conditions. As we in the course of the earth's development see life emerging for the first time, what must we conclude thence, but that under wholly unusual conditions, in the time of great revolutions of the earth, the wonder of life took place, of course in its most incomplete form. This most incomplete form has actually been discovered. Huxley has found the *Bathybius*, a slimy gellatine mass at the bottom of the sea, and Haeckel the *Monera*, structureless lumps of a white carbonaceous combination, which, without being composed of organs, yet take nourishment and grow; whereby the cleft may be said to be filled up, the transition mediated from the inorganic to the organic." †

With reference to the phenomena of mind, materialism dogmatises with equal confidence, in defiance of all scientific testimony. That thought is not resolvable into motion is the unanimous opinion of physicists of authority. The circle of physical change in nerves and brain is declared to be complete without thought, and consciousness in relation thereto is described as a "bye product." Nevertheless

---

* *Critiques and Addresses*, p. 239.

† *Der alte und der neue Glaube*, pp. 171–174.

Strauss, to select him again as the representative man, cheerily affirms that thought is a mere mode of motion. "It is not long," he remarks, "since the law of the conservation of force was discovered, and it will take long to clear up and define its application to the conversion of heat into motion, and of motion into heat. But the time cannot be far off when they will begin to make application of the law to the problems of feeling and thinking. If under certain conditions motion changes itself into heat, why should there not also be conditions under which it changes itself into sensation? The conditions, the apparatus for the purpose, we have in the brain and nervous system of the higher animals, and in those organs of the lower animals which take their place. On the one side the nerve is touched and set into internal movement; on the other a feeling, a perception takes place, a thought arises; and inversely the feeling and the thought on the way outwards translate themselves into motion of the members. When Helmholtz says 'in the generation of heat through rubbing and pushing the motion of the whole mass passes over into a motion of its smaller parts; inversely in the production of driving power through heat the motion of the smallest parts passes over into a motion of the whole mass'—I ask, is this anything essentially different, is the above account of the connection between the movement of the body and the thought of the mind not the necessary continuation of that law? One may say I speak of things I don't understand. Good—but others will come who do understand, and who have also understood me." * The man who thus jauntily dogmatises on the most difficult of all problems is the same who invented the mythical theory of the Life of Jesus with a view

---

* *Der alte und der neue Glaube*, pp. 211-2.

to the elimination of the miraculous element from it. The speculative identity is easily recognisable.

Passing from these observations on the dogmatic unbelief of materialism, I go on to consider the attitude towards the miraculous of the Theistic theory of the universe. It is a common remark of apologetic writers that at least the abstract possibility of miracle is involved in Theism. This general statement, however, does not carry us far. As Baden Powell reminds us, it depends on the nature and degree of our Theism whether we can, or cannot, regard miracles as credible or possible.* Those who believe in a God in the sense of a Power above the world, not identical with it as Pantheism affirms, or otiose, a view virtually equivalent to Atheism, are a mixed multitude, many of whom for various reasons are hostile to the miraculous. Among the theistic deniers of miracle fall to be classed the Deists. Their position was not that miracles are impossible, for they believed in Divine Omnipotence, and recognised in the creation of the world a miraculous manifestation thereof. Their denial of miracle had reference to the course of nature after it had been established, and was based on an optimistic view of the world as the best possible. God, it was admitted, could alter the course of nature by a miraculous interposition, if He chose, but He could not rationally choose when change could only be for the worse; therefore in His wisdom He could only let the frame of nature alone, or sustain it in its fixed, orderly course.

A second class of theistic unbelievers in miracle is found in the more modern school of Deists of the type of Theodore Parker, who prefer to call themselves Theists, feeling

---

* *Study of the Evidences of Christianity*, in *Essays and Reviews.*

eighteenth century Deism to be a system out of date and discredited, and therefore not unnaturally exhibiting a nervous anxiety to draw as broad a distinction as possible between themselves and their predecessors. To a great extent the difference is in tone rather than in principle, as may be gathered from the words of an English adherent of the recent school: "The Deism of the last century," says Miss Cobbe, "with its cold and dry negations of Christianity, has passed away forever, and given place to a Theism which in the writings of Newman and Theodore Parker may vie for spirituality and warmth of religious feeling with any other faith in the world." * The claim thus advanced is on the whole well founded. Modern Theism is at once warmer and more reverent in its religious tone than the Deism it replaces. Its God is not the Great First Cause dwelling remote above the world, but the Father in heaven who, while transcendent, is also immanent in the world, and ever near His children. It learns God's Being and Nature not merely from the outward world, and through elaborate arguments from design, but from the heart and the moral consciousness. Towards Christianity and its sacred writings its attitude is more sympathetic and appreciative than that of the older school. While denying to the Bible all claim to be, in a strict or exclusive sense, a divine revelation, and the literary product of an inspiration limited to its writers, modern Theists are effusive in their eulogy upon the Holy Scriptures, as being, so far as known, the most excellent of all productions of human genius working on the great theme of religion. Of Christ, too, while not admitting His Divinity, or even His absolute moral perfection, they are warm admirers, professing themselves unable to find

* *Broken Lights*, p. 175.

words to express their sense of the unsurpassed, if not un surpassable, wisdom and goodness revealed in His teachings and life. Therefore they despise not the name "Christian," but call themselves "Christian theists," and even claim to be more truly Christian than the believers in the creed of Christendom.

To a certain extent the denial of miracle by modern Theism rests on the same ground as that of Deism, viz., on an optimistic view of the world. It asserts, with effusive eloquence, that all things in nature and in Providence work together for the good of all sentient creatures, beasts and birds not less than human beings, and therefore it can conceive no rational ground for a change in the fixed order of the world by miraculous incursion. But, besides this reason for denial of miracle common to it with Deism, modern Theism has another peculiar to itself. This it finds in its conception of God's relation to the world as one of immanence. At this point the contrast between it and the older system of thought becomes one not of mere sentiment, but of principle. The God of the Deist was outside the world, the God of the modern Theist dwells within it. Immanence is the philosophic watchword which he has in view when he assigns to his system of thought the designation of *Speculative Theism.** And the watchword implies not only the inutility of miracle, but its impossibility. For the divine immanence signifies that the Divine activity is restricted to the fixed order of nature. God acts through the laws of the universe; we have no evidence that He ever has acted in any other way, no right to think that He can act in any other way. That is to say, immanence is not a matter of volition, but of necessity. The world is not only

* *Vide* Theodore Parker's Discourse: *Of Speculative Theism regarded as a theory of the Universe.* Works, vol. xi.

God's dwelling-place, but His prison; a prison in which He has been immured from eternity—for the world, according to the modern theist, was not created, but is co-eternal with God—and in which He must remain a prisoner eternally. Miracle is thus forever excluded by the doctrine of immanence as asserted by this system. "The law of nature," says Parker, "represents the modes of action of God Himself, who is the only true Cause and the only true Power· and as He is infinite, unchangeably perfect, and perfectly unchangeable, His mode of action is therefore constant and universal, so that there can be no such thing as a violation of God's constant mode of action." * He affects, indeed, to treat the question of miracle as one of fact and evidence; but it is clear enough that a miracle, except as an unusual phenomenon, whose cause is as yet unknown, is for him a thing which no evidence whatever could establish. Thus, with reference to the Resurrection of Christ, he asks: "Is the testimony sufficient to show that a man, thoroughly dead as Abraham and Isaac were, came back to life, passed through closed doors, and ascended into the sky? I cannot speak for others, but most certainly I cannot believe such monstrous facts on such evidence." † The term "monstrous" shows plainly that to one of Mr. Parker's sentiments it does not matter what evidence is adduced for such an event as the resurrection of Christ, and that the detailed examination of existing evidence is only a farce, serving to give an aspect of judicial impartiality to a foregone conclusion.

A yet more recent type of theism, more completely antagonistic to miracle than either of the foregoing, remains to be noticed. It is based on the synthetic Philosophy of Mr. Herbert Spencer; it accepts, without reserve, the evo

* *Vide* Discourse referred to in previous note.

† *A Discourse of Religion*, chapter iv. Works, vol. i.

lutionary theory of the origin of the universe; its appropriate name is *Cosmic Theism*, and its principal expounder I may say its promulgator, is Mr. Fiske. One could not desire a more competent and genial interpreter of a new type of speculative religious thought, and in anything I may say in the way of criticism I desire to show the respect I feel for the spirit of a writer in whose work on the *Outlines of Cosmic Philosophy* I have found both intellectual entertainment and moral stimulus.

Mr. Fiske's attitude on the theistic question, like that of his master, is agnostic, but his agnosticism is carefully defined. "Deity," he says, "is unknowable just in so far as it is not manifested to consciousness through the phenomenal world,—knowable just in so far as it is thus manifested; unknowable in so far as infinite and absolute,—knowable in the order of its phenomenal manifestations; knowable, in a symbolic way, as the Power which is disclosed in every throb of the mighty rhythmic life of the universe; knowable as the Eternal Source of a moral Law which is implicated with each action of our lives, and in obedience to which lies our only guarantee of the happiness which is incorruptible and which neither inevitable misfortune nor unmerited obloquy can take away. Thus, though we may not by searching find out God, though we may not compass infinitude or attain to absolute knowledge, we may at least know all that it concerns us to know as intelligent and responsible beings." * At the first blush this description of the God of Cosmic Theism may seem to give us all we ask or need—an intelligent Maker and moral Governor of the Universe. But Mr. Fiske objects to ascribing intelligence and volition to God as Anthropomorphism. He offers his

* *Outlines of Cosmic Philosophy*, vol. ii., p. 470.

new Cosmic Theism as a substitute for the anthropomorphic Theism of unscientific ages, believing "that the process of deanthropomorphisation which has from the first characterised the history of philosophic development must still continue to go on, until the Intelligent Will postulated by the modern theologian shall have shared the fate of the earlier and still more imperfect symbols whereby finite man has vainly tried to realise that which must ever transcend his powers of conception." * While holding that the phenomenal universe is the manifestation of a Divine Power that cannot be identified with the totality of phenomena, he maintains that we can learn nothing as to the nature of this power from the qualities of the phenomena. The ultimate Cause of the world cannot be known through its effects. Even if the competency of this method of knowing God were conceded it would prove more than the anthropomorphic theist desires to establish. Since the universe contains material as well as psychical phenomena its First Cause must partake of all the differential qualities of these phenomena. If it reasons and wills, like the higher animals, it must also, like minerals, plants, and the lowest animals be unintelligent and unendowed with the power of volition, thus requiring in the First Cause "a more than Hegelian capacity for uniting contradictory attributes." † Mr. Fiske further contends that a Deity who thinks, contrives, and legislates, is simply a product of evolution. Intelligence consists in "the continuous adjustment of specialised inner relations to specialised outer relations"; therefore to represent Deity as intelligent is to surround Deity with an environment, so destroying its infinity and self-existence. "The eternal Power whereof the web of

* *Outlines of Cosmic Philosophy*, vol. ii., p. 410.

† *Cosmic Philosophy*, vol. ii., p. 388.

phenomena is but the visible garment, becomes degraded into a mere strand in the web of phenomena; and the Cosmos, in exchange for the loss of its infinite and inscrutable God, receives an anomalous sovereign of mythological pedigree." * To the hypothesis of a moral Governor the author objects that a moral government necessarily implies an immoral government.† The vast evils that afflict mankind create no difficulty from the evolutionist's point of view; they are simply the inevitable accompaniments of the onward march of the universe destined to be eliminated more and more as the process of evolution approaches its goal. But a Personal Governor of the world becomes responsible for these evils; if He leaves them unremedied it must be either from lack of power or from lack of goodwill, either alternative being fatal to traditional theism.

Such in very brief outline is the argument by which it is attempted to upset the throne of the so-called anthropomorphic God in the interest of his new rival, the Cosmic Deity, whom or which we may not conceive as possessing intelligence or will or personality. It is unnecessary to remark that under the reign of the new Divinity miracles are not to be looked for. These belong to the old régime. Belief in miracle is one of the weeds which spring up in minds uncultivated by science. To combat such belief by argument is a waste of time; it will pass away of itself with the night of ignorance, as the light of Cosmic Philosophy is diffused over the world.‡

While not insensible to the fascinations of the new Divinity I cannot admit that his claims to our allegiance are beyond question. In the first place, we are not to be

---

* *Cosmic Philosophy*, vol. ii., p. 395. † Ib., vol. ii., p. 407.

‡ Ib., vol. ii., p. 380.

scared from faith in the old God of Christendom by the word anthropomorphism, which I cannot help thinking is as much a bugbear to our evolutionary friends as, according to them, is the term materialism to orthodox apologists. There is nothing to be ashamed of in a man-like God, any more than there is in a God-like man. Then it is a fair question whether when you strike off all the attributes which form the basis of the charge of Anthropomorphism, the God which remains can in any proper sense be represented as the object of a *theistic* belief. An acute critic of the "Cosmic Philosophy" has asserted that Mr. Fiske carries the process of deanthropomorphisation so far as to remove the theistic element, and in effect purifies the Deity altogether out of existence.* The assertion is not without ground. Undoubtedly the term theism has hitherto been associated with the distinctive conception of God which ascribes to Him an intelligent Will and therefore Personality and it can only lead to confusion when its range of meaning is so extended as to include a conception from which these attributes are omitted. At the same time I have no wish to deny to the distinguished author of the Cosmic Philosophy the title of Theist if he desires to wear it. The critic already referred to affirms that Mr. Fiske's view is not essentially different from Atheism. Belief in a mere self-existent something, if not a-theism, is at least, he thinks, non-theism. But it is invidious to charge what is repudiated; and it will be at once more agreeable and more profitable to note what is admitted in the direction of theistic belief. In his various works Mr. Fiske makes several very important statements concerning God. We are told that God is a Power, that He is a Spirit,† that He makes for

* *A Candid Examination of Theism*, by Physicus, p. 138.

† *Cosmic Philosophy*, vol. ii., p. 449.

righteousness,* that He cares for man, cares so much that when the planet on which he now lives perishes by falling into the sun He will provide that His fairest work shall not perish along with it.† These propositions, it is true, are given only as symbolic utterances and private opinions possessing no authority or absolute validity. They are the kind of things a man may rationally believe and say concerning God if he is to believe and say anything, and does not prefer to maintain an austere attitude of nescience and silence. It appears to me that Mr. Fiske, under the impulse of a warm poetic temperament, has said more than his philosophy, strictly applied, would admit, approaching very closely to the theistic position, and that having gone so far he need not have hesitated to go further and join with the theist in ascribing to the Deity, by way of symbolic utterance and private opinion, the human attributes of reason, will, and personality. His argument for the incompetency of such ascription is by no means invincible. In the first place, it is not a scientific, but only a philosophic argument. The whole system of modern agnosticism has only a philosophical, as distinct from a scientific, basis. Though it is associated in the writings of Mr. Spencer with the scientific theory of evolution, it is quite separable from that theory. The attitude of Mr. Fiske towards the theistic problem is really not radically different from that of Mr. Mansel. He, too, taught that we can think of God only in symbol, and that our utterances concerning Him have only relative and subjective value. And his reasoning in support of this agnostic position was much the same as that of the author of Cosmic Philosophy. It consists largely in both cases of metaphysics, and, as many

---

* *Excursions of an Evolutionist*, pp. 301–5.

† *Man's Destiny*, pp. 115, 116.

competent judges think, very weak metaphysics.* Both writers assure us that we can know only through likeness, difference, and relation, and that therefore the absolute is unknowable. Both declare that an absolute personality is, from the philosophical point of view, unthinkable. These abstruse reasonings must be taken for what they are worth. And they must stand by themselves, as philosophical reasonings, and not be allowed to derive prestige from any supposed connection with science, or even with scientific hypotheses capable of verification, such as that of evolution. We may entertain these philosophical views without being evolutionists, and we can be evolutionists and treat them with supreme indifference.

It is very important to grasp the truth now stated, viz., that modern agnosticism and the doctrine of evolution, though often associated in fact, are by no means inseparable. An impression to the contrary might readily mislead the advocate of Christian Theism into a precarious policy of uncompromising antagonism to prevalent scientific views concerning the origin of the world, as if to refute these were a matter of life and death. I for my part have no sympathy with such a view of the apologist's present duty. I feel no jealousy of the doctrine of evolution, and see no occasion for cherishing such a feeling. I do not profess competency to pronounce on the scientific pretensions of the doctrine; but I am very sensible of the grandeur of the view which it presents of the universe, and I am not indisposed to accept it as truth, and to acknowledge the obligation thence arising to adjust our whole mode of thinking on religious questions to the new situation. I believe that the

---

* *Vide* Martineau's *Essays Philosophical and Theological,* pp. 171-243, for a trenchant exposure of the weakness of Agnostic reasonings.

old religious faith can live with the new scientific faith.* Evolution, so far as I understand it, excludes neither God nor the knowledge of God.

The authoritative expounders of the new scientific theory, indeed, think otherwise. Their view is that there is a Power at work throughout the universe, the real ultimate cause of all that happens, to which we may give the familiar name of God. Of this Power all phenomena are manifestations. Yet by none of them is its nature revealed. We know only from the phenomena *that* it is; we cannot know *what* it is. But without presumption it may be asked how we know so much if we cannot know more. Is it not a more consistent and rational position to say that from the existence of the universe we know that the Power is, and from the character of the universe what it is? This position doubtless requires guarding to exclude Pantheism, which makes God like all parts of the universe indifferently, therefore substantially at once matter and mind, and in character possessing the attributes of both substances, extension and thought. Mr Fiske contends that you must admit both or neither; that the only alternatives are Spinozism or Agnosticism. And we must face this dilemma, not evade it by misrepresenta-

* For a spirited attempt to justify this position in detail, vide *Can the old Faith live with the New?* By Dr. Matheson, of Edinburgh. An Evolution in some sense may be said to be now universally accepted by men of science. But some scientists of good name decline to admit an indefinite, aimless evolution promoted by chance variation, and involving change without limit in all the lines of development of forms. Thus Dr. Cleland, of the University of Glasgow, contends for a definite evolution issuing in "terminal forms," and guided by morphological design. He conceives of the animal kingdom not as an indefinite growth like a tree, but as "a temple with many minarets, none of them capable of being prolonged, while the central dome is completed by the structure of man." Vide *Evolution, Expression, and Sensation*, Chapter I, and *Terminal Forms of Life* in Journal of Anatomy and Physiology, vol. xviii.

tion, as is done when the charge of anthropomorphism brought against current theism is met by a counter charge of physico-morphism.* It is not correct to say that the Agnostic in denying an anthropomorphic divinity sets up in his room a physico-morphic divinity, possessing the attributes of the material, inanimate, or infra-human portion of the universe. The position of the consistent agnostic is to deny both types of Divinity and to maintain that they must both be either denied or united into one protean pantheistic deity. The question precisely is whether these are indeed the only alternatives. I think not, and for the following reasons.

The universe is not a miscellaneous collection of existences, stars, rocks, plants, apes, men, all on an equal footing, in like relation to the ultimate Cause, and all equally fit or unfit to reveal his character. In some such way Spinoza conceived it. Distinction between perfect and imperfect higher and lower, good and evil, had no meaning for him In his view all things are alike perfect, because real; reality and perfection are the same thing. Even bad men and fools are not less perfect than saints and sages, simply because they exist; and they exist because there was not wanting to God matter wherewith to make all things, them included, and whatever is possible is necessarily and eternally actual. The two great divisions of nature,—*res extensæ*, and *res cogitantes*,—have equal claims to consideration. They are two parallel streams of being flowing out of one fountain—the absolute substance, and showing different aspects of the Divine nature, the one exhibiting God as a *res extensa*, the other as a *res cogitans*, the two attributes of extension and thought being recognisable by the intellect as distinct, but

* So Wace in *The Gospel and its Witnesses*, p. 103.

not otherwise to be contrasted. On this theory the world ceases to have any rational or moral significance, and becomes a mere monotonous waste of being. It gains meaning and interest only when we introduce into our conception of it the notion of gradation, and think of it as the result of a process in which there has been a steady advance from lower to higher forms of being. And just such is the view which the modern doctrine of Evolution has taught us to entertain. We have learned therefrom to think of the world, as we now behold it, as the product of a process which began with a fiery cloud and passed thence through many successive stages in an ever ascending scale, from star-vapour to stars, from dead planets to life, from plants to animals, from apes to men; humanity being up to date its latest and highest achievement. And is it not in keeping with the spirit of this magnificent conception when we see in the final stage of the process a key to the meaning of the whole? Because every successive stage of being rises in a silent, stealthy way out of the one preceding, are we required to regard all stages as alike significant, and to accord to the fiery vapour out of which planets were formed the admiration we bestow on the phenomena of Consciousness? Ought we not rather to see in the process of the universe a grand drama of self-revelation, on the part of the Unknown Power who is the cause of all, which does not become intelligible until it reaches its culmination in the highest product—man? The last result of evolution being reason, is not the legitimate inference that its source is rational? Strauss has said that the world does not proceed from the highest reason, but moves on towards the highest reason. This is all that can be expected from a materialist, but better things may be looked for from a system which teaches that the true cause of all that exists lies beyond the phenomenal. The appropriate motto for it is rather this: the world process ends in reason because it begins in reason.

The view just enunciated, if not strictly demonstrable, is to say the least most reasonable. It is reasonable to attach to man a significance which belongs to no other part of the creation, and it is equally reasonable to see in man on that account a specially clear revelation of the nature of God. The former of these two propositions is acknowledged by some who demur to the latter, and by none more frankly than by Mr. Fiske. In his charming little volume on the Destiny of Man, he states that "so far from degrading Humanity, or putting it on a level with the animal world in general, the doctrine of evolution shows us distinctly for the first time how the creation and the perfecting of man is the goal towards which Nature's work has been tending from the first. We can now see clearly that our new knowledge enlarges tenfold the significance of human life, and makes it seem more than ever the chief object of Divine care, the consummate fruition of that creative energy which is manifested throughout the knowable universe." * How far this concession as to man's importance goes in settling the other question as to the rationality of the Great Power through which the universe subsists, may be guessed from the fact that the author whose words have just been quoted, feels himself constrained to believe in the immortality of the soul, "as a supreme act of faith in the reasonableness of God's work." † He is fully aware that man's immortality is not a demonstrable truth of science, but he cannot believe that the crowning result of the grand drama of evolution, humanity, is destined to perish with the planet on which it lives.

* p. 107.

† *Man's Destiny*, p. 116; *vide* also the more recent work, *The Idea of God*, p. 161.

It would stultify the whole process; it would make the Unknown Power appear as unreasonable as a child, "who builds houses out of blocks, just for the pleasure of knocking them down."* But why not, if the Power who made the world be not endowed with Reason and also with Goodness? Why otherwise should the bright and hopeful view of man' future be preferred to that of the pessimist? Why should not the great unconscious power, as it is called by Hartmann, which works as if it had conscious ends in view, but really has not, first by a slow evolutionary process blindly produce a world, and then set itself wantonly or with sublime indifference to destroy it along with all its inhabitants? It is admitted that science points to the destruction of the physical worlds as a probable or even certain event of the distant future. Why should there be any exception in favour of man? Why should humanity be rescued from the wreck of matter and the crash of worlds? No reason can be given except that the Power that made the universe is himself a reasonable Being, for whom a rational creature like man has an exceptional value, because possessing a nature in affinity with His own.

I conclude, therefore, that the modern doctrine of evolution does not rob the Christian theist of his God. In so far as it exalts man to an exceptional place in the universe, it justifies us in regarding him as not only the interpreter of nature, but "also its interpretation," "the highest revelation of its creative power."† The theist has no cause in this new scientific era to be ashamed of believing in a Divine Being possessing the attributes of intelligence, goodness, and Personality. If these attributes only partially and im-

---

* *Man's Destiny*, p. 114.

† Fairbairn, *Studies in the Philosophy of Religion and History*, p. 100.

perfectly express the truth, it is for reasons having no special connection with the theory of evolution. And as we may still believe in a so-called anthropomorphic God, so may we also continue to believe in his gracious thoughts towards man. The crown of creation and interpreter of the creator may rationally be regarded as the object of Divine Love. If a scientific philosopher on the ground of God's care for his fairest work may without prejudice to his philosophic reputation believe in human immortality, we may without laying ourselves open to the charge of ignorant superstition believe in human redemption and in whatever divine activity may be necessary to that end. Even miracles may continue to be credible.

It must be confessed, however, that to find a niche for the miraculous in the new world of evolutionary philosophy seems by no means easy. Yet let us clearly understand why. It is not because of any modification in the idea of God. Evolution, we have seen, leaves us a God with theistic attributes, therefore capable, if needful, of working miracles. If therefore miracle be excluded it must be on the ground, not that it exceeds Divine Power, but because it is out of harmony with the ascertained *method* of Divine action. A well-known writer says: "Science discloses the method of the world, but not its cause; Religion its cause, but not its method." * The saying is true, and applying it to the subject on hand I remark, that evolution cannot claim to negative miracles on the ground that no cause exists adequate to work them; it may, however, more plausibly rest such a claim on the ground of method. God's method of working, it may be argued, proceeds by insensible progression. In the process of evolution there

* Martineau, *Essays Philosophical and Theological,* p. 178.

are no catastrophes, no leaps, only minute steps onwards The process always begins at the beginning of each new stage. There were star-clouds before there were stars; life appeared first in the most rudimentary forms; intellect showed itself first in the dimmest glimmerings of thought civilisation began in the family through the prolongation of infancy, then spread to the tribe, then slowly passed into the larger aggregates of nations. What room is there in a world evolved in this way for miraculous incursions?

Such in effect is the position taken up by Pfleiderer in discussing the subject of miracles in his work on the Philosophy of Religion. Replying to the argument in behalf of the miraculous drawn from the analogies presented in nature by the entrance of higher forms of life into the lower, he says that "these analogies strictly considered prove nothing for the miracle proper, viewed as a suspension of law. For these so-called 'new beginnings' are always completely grounded in the totality of the order of the world; they were latent as germs in the preceding development, and they make their appearance with infallible regularity so soon as the necessary conditions have been prepared; fitting themselves in harmoniously to the general order. Of contradiction with the general system of law, or breach of the natural connection of cause and effect, there is no trace; therefore we cannot in this connection speak of miracle in the absolute sense, but only in the relative sense of the *mirabile*. What relatively to a lower department of nature is a wonderful higher may yet be a necessary member in the development of nature, contemplated from the first and duly mediated by law, and as such it is no real miracle." * The practical effect of this statement is the reduction of

* *Religionsphilosophie*, pp. 617–8.

admissible miracle to an infinitesimal minimum. Divine initiative at critical turning-points in the course of natural development, as at the first entrance of life, and the later entrance of the higher life of consciousness, seems to be admitted at least for the sake of argument. It is not asserted that without such creative initiative life could have made its appearance, as the purely natural result of certain chemical conditions. But it is maintained that the divine activity was so conditioned by and adapted to the contemporary state of nature, that the result—the new phenomenon of life—was not a miracle, but only a marvel. And the implication is that such marvels are the only miracles possible, and that as matter of fact have ever happened. In other words, the method on which the Creator works, even when exerting his Power with exceptional emphasis, is to proceed as noiselessly and as naturally as possible. What Christ said of the Kingdom of God holds true of the Power of God exhibited at critical epochs in creative initiative. It cometh not with observation; but silently, stealthily, unobtrusively. All you can notice is something that you had not seen before: a new phenomenon, yet a most minute innovation—the phenomenon of life, say, in its most rudimentary form. The new thing makes its appearance so modestly that the imaginary spectator may not be much surprised, or have the question urgently forced on his mind: what can be its cause? The hand of the Creator does not thrust itself upon his astonished view. He may quite readily regard the novel phenomenon of life as a case of what philosophers in our time call *spontaneous generation.* Were life to appear first in a highly developed form, as in that of a horse or even of a bee, one seeing it might exclaim, Behold a miracle, the hand of God is here. Kant said: "Give me matter and I will show you how a world can spring out of it, but I cannot say, give me matter and I will show you how a caterpillar can be generated." But God does not begin with creating a caterpillar, not to speak of a bee or a horse, but with something so little in advance of inanimate matter that, in absence of special reasons for thinking otherwise, we, if we had been there to witness, would almost as a matter of course have regarded it as the natural product of the dust of the earth.*

Such, in free paraphrase, appears to be the theory suggested by the foregoing quotation from Pfleiderer. The general principle involved is that the divine initiative is always just enough to originate a new departure; whereby miracles, not only in the sense of events contrary to nature, but also in the sense of events much in advance of a contemporary state of nature, seem to be utterly excluded. We may conceive the principle as coming into play at four crises, at the creation of matter, at the first dawn of life, at the commencement of self-conscious life in man, and at the introduction of the higher spiritual life in the new Christian humanity. The application of the principle to the first stage demands that matter should be brought into being not in composite masses, but in isolated particles—a chaos of atoms "without form and void." At the second stage, as already indicated, the principle requires that life should

* Vide *Can the Old Faith live with the New?* pp. 180–1. If, says Dr. Matheson, "The entire life of the universe should at a certain moment of time impart a portion of its being to one of the physical forms of nature, and if the eye of a spectator could be imagined to have witnessed the creative ceremony, what would he see? he would see only the appearance of a *spontaneous generation*. . . . . At that early time we should not have had any data for affirming that it was not the nature of life to spring up spontaneously; it has been reserved for modern science, by the result of those experiments which have denied this power to nature, to convert the act of simple faith into an assured affirmation of reason."

first appear in the most rudimentary form, leaving all higher forms of plant and animal life to develop naturally out of a few vital germs. At the third stage the same law would dictate that the phenomena of human intelligence should manifest themselves in the form of a faint dim dawn in the mind of a savage man some steps higher in the scale of being than the ape—leaving the early dawn to advance slowly on through the long ages to the perfect day of cultivated Reason. And what will the law signify as applied to the last and highest stage that ushers in the Kingdom of Heaven, and the era of a regenerated humanity? In other words, what will constitute a sufficient initiative in this sphere? Is a Christ who is the realised ideal of humanity and endowed with miraculous grace and power necessary, or will less suffice?

A full answer to this question must be reserved for a future lecture, in which we shall consider what is to be expected from a Christianity without miracle. Meantime, I remark that our conception of what might constitute the necessary and sufficient outfit for the inaugurator of the new era will largely depend upon the strength of our conviction as to the need for a new departure in the moral history of humanity. The mission of Christ is ever represented in the New Testament as having its reason of existence in the moral condition of the world. He came, He himself declared, to seek the lost, and to be a Physician to the sick. No one can rightly estimate His fitness for these functions who fails to realise the import of the pathetic terms He employed to describe the objects of His care. Here, Deism was grievously at fault, through its rose-colored optimism. In the moral state of man it saw no cause for grave concern. Human nature is essentially good; even in its worst phases it is not wicked, but only weak; and the weakness springs from the body, the seat of appetite and desire. The soul is pure, and death, which severs soul and body, will deliver from all evil habits; no other redeemer is needed. With these sanguine sentiments of eighteenth century Freethinkers, modern Theists of the type of Parker generally concur. Moral evil, in their view, is but the pardonable aberration of freedom, sin but the stumbling of a child learning to walk. In falling, man falls upwards towards perfection and heaven, to which at last a benevolent Deity will bring every human soul, in payment of the debt of felicity which the Creator owes to all His sentient creatures.

These forms of sentimental optimism are now things of the past. The current type of philosophic thought entertains views of man more in accordance with fact and with Christian doctrine. The evolutionist knows full well how very rude is the condition of humanity in the early stages of its development. He does not, with the theologian, regard that moral rudeness as a fall from a primitive state of integrity; but, in the description of the state itself, he would probably not seriously dissent from the terms employed by an orthodox Christian. He is not an optimist, by any means, with regard to the past, or even with regard to the present, condition of the human race. He is an optimist only, as has been remarked of Mr. Spencer, for the far future! * He expects that, after long ages have elapsed—when the slow, secular process of evolution has culminated in a perfect civilisation—humanity will at length realise the ideal of wisdom and goodness towards which it has from the first been tending. And what is to come of the generations whose lot it is to live in ages when the evolutionary process is yet far from the goal? Are they to pass out of existence as mere abor-

* Graham, *The Creed of Science*, p. 89.

tions? It is at this point that the evolutionist and the Christian are apt to part company. Agreeing as to the state, they may differ as to the fate of rude specimens of humanity. Taught by modern philosophy, the one may say: Nature cares only for the type, not for the individual, or only for the individuals in which the type is realised—the picked samples of the race. Heaven, eternal life is for them alone, if it be in store for any human souls; all others must perish like blossoms that are nipped by the frost—all in whom the spiritual nature remains an undeveloped germ. Taught of Christ, the other says: God cares for the weak, the morally rude, the savage and uncivilised; there is hope in Him for them also; "it is not the will of the Father in heaven that one of these little ones should perish."

If we heartily receive this doctrine, we shall probably have no difficulty in believing in the Christ presented to us in the Gospels, with all his miraculous endowments, personal or functional. But is not such a doctrine wholly incompatible with the teaching and spirit of modern evolutionary philosophy? How utterly unlike this God who cares for the weak and the bad, to the God who presides over the process of evolution—the awful, mysterious Cosmic Deity. The difference, on first view, is certainly great enough, yet second thoughts go far towards bridging the gulf. We have seen that it is in accordance with the view of the universe suggested by the theory of evolution, to assign to man an exceptional significance, as revealing the nature of God. But, if it is competent to regard man as a revelation of God, it is not only justifiable, but incumbent, to take man at his best as the medium of revelation. In any man, however ignorant, vicious, or uncivilised, we may discern some rudiments of the Divine Image; but, only in the finished product of human culture, can we expect to see the fair, undistorted face of Deity. And what are the leading features of the charac ter thus revealed? Foremost among them is love. In savage man the prominent moral characteristic is selfish ness, developed by the struggle for existence. In perfectly civilised man the prominent characteristic, we are told, will be sympathy, care for others, self-sacrifice. In the golden age to come, according to Mr. Fiske, "the development of the sympathetic side of human nature will become prodigious. The manifestation of selfish and hateful feelings will be more and more sternly repressed by public opinion, and such feelings will become weakened by disuse, while the sympathetic feelings will increase in strength as the sphere for their exercise is enlarged."* And, according to the same authority, the blessed process of training in sympathy and self-sacrifice, of which this is to be the consummation, had its origin in the prolongation of infancy, giving occasion for the formation of family affections. With the genesis of the family, man ceased to be a mere brute, and became human. Through the helplessness of babyhood man, so to speak, entered the kingdom of heaven. "The latest science now shows us," says the eloquent author of the Cosmic Philosophy, "that, unless we had been as babes, the ethical phenomena which give all its significance to the phrase, 'kingdom of heaven,' would have been non-existent for us. Without the circumstances of infancy, we might have become formidable among animals through sheer force of sharp-wittedness; but, except for these circumstances, we should never have comprehended the meaning of such phrases as 'self-sacrifice,' or 'devotion.' The phenomena of social life would have been omitted from the history of the world, and with them the phenomena of ethics and of religion."†

* *Man's Destiny*, p. 102.

† *Outlines of Cosmic Philosophy*, ii., 363.

Here, many thousand years ago, were the beginnings of God's care for weakness—the first revelations of His loving-kindness, faintly foreshadowing a more complete revelation in a humanity perfected in sympathy. After all, the features of the Cosmic Deity are not so different from those of the Father-God proclaimed by Jesus. If the gospel of infancy preached by Mr. Fiske be true—and to me it appears both credible and worthy of all acceptation—then it ought not to seem incredible that Jesus Christ was sent by God into the world, to seek and save all, of whom a child in its helplessness is an appropriate emblem—the weak, the fallen, the degraded.

This being the God-worthy end of Christ's mission, certain means of attaining it are at once seen to be appropriate. A Saviour of the morally weak can become a beneficent power over them in at least two ways. First, by presenting in his own character the realised ideal of humanity; second, by bringing to bear on the objects of his care in maximum intensity the spirit of love. By the former means a Saviour may benefit men in a morally rude condition in a twofold manner. He can awaken in them admiration of and aspiration after the ideal goodness exemplified in himself. He can also confer on them a certain vicarious goodness. The unholy may have just enough affinity for holiness to see in him one as unlike as possible to themselves, with whom they are not worthy to claim brotherhood; and receiving him in the name of a righteous man, they, though unrighteous, may receive a righteous man's reward.* By the other means—the manifestation in a superlative degree of gracious love—the Saviour of the lost can establish His claim to be regarded *par excellence* as the

* For a striking statement of this truth, see a paper by Dr. Matheson on *The Three Christian Sympathies*, in *The Monthly Interpreter* for March, 1885.

Friend of sinners, the one great Philanthropist, so making Himself the object of a passionate devotion which transforms into saints the most depraved.

Both modes of influence involve miracle. In the former case the miracle is one of character, consisting in the exhibition in an individual who lived many centuries ago of the perfect ideal of human goodness. A perfect man is doubly miraculous; *first*, because he realises in absolute form a moral ideal which in the natural course of things can never be more than asymptotically approximated, the actual always being more or less imperfect; *second*, because he antedates by ages moral attainments which according to the theory of evolution can be reached only in some yet far distant future epoch. Miraculous or not, the supposed anticipation seems actually to have taken place in the person of Jesus. Love, altruistic feeling, being the element in which man has most need to grow, it may truly be affirmed that the ripe fruit has already appeared in the ungenial soil of Judæa. The best evidence of this is the imperfect degree in which up till this hour even the Christian Church has been able to comprehend, not to say imitate, the spirit of its Founder.

To the category of active philanthropy belong the miracles of healing. These miracles benefited physically only a single generation, but they are a symbol of sympathy to all generations. In this view they possess, like the Passion, perennial efficacy. The death of Jesus, though a long past event, is endowed with endless virtue because therein He offered Himself a sacrifice by an *eternal spirit* of holy love. Even so there is perennial virtue in the healing ministry, because therein an eternal spirit of humane sympathy embodied itself, and Jesus of Nazareth stands in view of the world, and for all time, the Friend of Man.

II.

MIRACLES IN RELATION TO THE ORDER OF NATURE.

In the previous lecture I gave no formal definition of miracles, but went on the assumption that they are events out of the common course of nature, and not explicable by natural laws. It was a sufficiently definite conception for the purpose then in hand. It is, however, an important enquiry how a miracle is to be conceived of in relation to the fixed order of the physical universe. Such an enquiry is prescribed by the spirit of an age in which the study of science has bred a profound sense of the reign of law everywhere. The apologist of the present time has an interest in minimizing the miraculousness of miracles, and making them appear as natural as possible. The time has long past when the crude conception, which satisfied Hume, of a miracle as a violation of the laws of nature, can be offered with any hope of acceptance. But indeed contemporary apologists do not need to be compelled to present miracles under an aspect better adjusted to the scientific view of the world. Their own bias is in full sympathy with the aversion of men of science to the notion of any irregularity in the action of natural law, or any disturbance of the fixed order. Some seem inclined to give miracles the go-by as things of the past which might serve a purpose in a pre-scientific age, but are now of little use and hardly credible. Others, while accepting loyally miraculous facts, call in question their miraculousness, and suggest hypotheses by which they may be made to appear more or less natural. On all sides the tendency is to naturalize the miraculous. Nay, the present temper of the religious public would seem to be to naturalize not only miracles, but the whole spiritual world. "Natural law in the spiritual world" has almost become the watchword of faith. The phenomenal popularity of a work bearing that name shows how widely acceptable the attitude it expresses is to religious minds. The position of the gifted author is itself full of significance. On the one hand a man of science, on the other a man of intensely religious spirit, he is the meeting place of two interests often supposed to be hostile, which in his person imperiously demand reconciliation. He believes that he has discovered the principle of reconciliation in the identity of law in the two spheres. Like Abraham he is willing to follow whithersoever the principle will lead. Whether it will lead to the promised land is a question on which many are in suspense.

My remarks on the present topic may conveniently take the form of a statement and discussion of the various attempts which have been made at adjustment of the idea of miracle to the fixed order of nature.

I begin with a view which seems to breathe the spirit of defiance rather than of accommodation to present modes of thought, that of the Bampton lecturer for 1865. Dr. Mozley takes up the bold position that our belief in the fixity of the order of nature, however necessary for the purposes of practical life, is one for which no rational account can be given, but is on the contrary an unintelligent impulse common to men with the lower animals. All conceivable reasons for the expectation that the future will be like the past, which is what is meant by the order of nature, resolve themselves on examination into mere statements of the belief itself. Our first impulse is to say it is self-evident: which is simply not true, for that only can be called self-evident of which the opposite is self-contradictory; for though the fact that the sun rose to-day would be contradicted by the fact that it did not rise to-day, it is in no way contradicted by the fact that it will not rise to-morrow. If it be said that repetition of a fact of nature shows that a permanent cause is at work, we are driven from that position by the reflection that the effects produced show a cause at work only to the extent of these effects. If next we take refuge in the mystic term *experience*, we are told that the term on being analysed means that from what we know to have happened, we expect something to happen in future, which is not an explanation of our expectation, but simply a statement of the fact to be explained. If in despair we seek the solution of the problem in the reflection that though no man has had experience of what *is* future, every man has had experience of what *was* future, the ready reply is that the expectation to be accounted for relates not to what was future, but to what is future, and the consideration that every man has had experience of what was future is a reason for his confidence in what is future only on the assumption that the future will be like the past; that is, the reason given for the belief does not account for it, but assumes it. The conclusion is that no reason for it can be given; practically indispensable to human life, it has no more producible reason than a speculation of fancy. The apologetic use of the conclusion, in connection with the subject of miracles is obvious enough. If the belief in the constancy of nature is itself not founded on reason, it cannot be adduced as an argument against the rationality of miracles. "The logic of unbelief wants a universal. But no real universal is forthcoming, and it only wastes its strength in wielding a fictitious one." *

---

* Lecture ii., On the *Order of Nature.*

The argument is certainly as ingenious as it is bold, yet it belongs to that class of arguments which silence rather than convince. In the first place the apologist of miracle finds himself in suspicious company, Hume, as he is aware, having said very much the same thing. It does not, of course, invalidate a process of reasoning that it has been used by a sceptic, but it does raise a legitimate doubt whether such reasoning can be of much service to faith. And accordingly the truth seems to be that this attempt at unsettling the fixity of nature's order, while rendering miracles more credible as events, robs them of their significance as miracles. In absence of a fixed order anything may happen, a centaur may turn up, or a dead man come to life. But what then? Why should we be surprised? Why think that a miracle, something very wonderful has taken place? Why imagine that a supernatural cause must be called in to account for the occurrence? All we have to do is to recognise an addition to our experience, and to include the new fact in our conception of nature as defined by Mr. Huxley to mean "neither more nor less than that which is; the sum of phenomena presented to our experience; the totality of events past, present, and to come." * In this totality Mr. Huxley has no objection to include "miracles." He recognises the force of Dr. Mozley's argument as previously stated by Hume, and on the ground thereof frankly admits the abstract possibility of miracles.† But then they are not miracles for him in the sense of events demanding a supernatural cause, but simply very unusual occurrences proceeding from some unknown natural cause which it is the scientific man's business, if possible, to discover. The author of *Supernatural Religion* has not failed to detect the

* *Vide* his *Hume*, p. 131.

† *Hume*, pp. 131–3.

weak point in Dr. Mozley's armour. He pronounces the argument fatal to the cause it is meant to defend. Miracles can have no evidential force unless they be supernatural. But unless there be an order of nature, how can there be any exception to it? If belief in it be not based on any ground of reason, how can it be asserted that miracles are supernatural? If we have no rational ground for believing that the future will be like the past, what rational ground can we have for thinking that anything which happens is exceptional, and out of the common course of nature?* These questions, it must be admitted, have force. There must be a fixed order of nature, otherwise the term supernatural is without meaning. When we speak of the supernatural we assume that the belief in the fixed order of nature, however originating, is according to truth, and we cannot afford to kick away the foundation from beneath our own position merely because it happens to be the ground on which our adversaries also stand. The author of *Supernatural Religion* asserts that an order of nature is at once necessary and fatal to miracles. That is the position of our opponents on the question. Our proper position, on the other hand, is that an order of nature is necessary but not fatal to miracles.

Dr. Mozley places the miraculous element of a miracle not in the mere event or material fact, but in what he calls the prophetical principle. "A miracle is the material fact as coinciding with an express announcement, or with express supernatural pretensions in the agent. If a person says to a blind man 'see,' and he sees, it is not the sudden return of sight alone that we have to account for, but its return at that particular moment."† It is this correspond-

* *Supernatural Religion,* p. 59.

† Bampton Lectures. Lecture vi., p. 148.

ence of the fact, with a foregoing notification, that distinguishes miracles from mere marvels. But if the fixed order of nature be unsettled it is open to a sceptic to suggest that the correspondence alluded to, while very remarkable, is only a marvel in a higher degree resolvable into an unmeaning casualty. In a world without order why should not a man now and then appear possessing magical endowments—able to fly, to walk on the water, to give the blind their sight, to raise the dead?

From this eccentric attempt to confound unbelief by an assault on the natural order of which it makes an idol I pass to consider a hypothesis which may be said to go to the opposite extreme of an excessive respect for nature and its laws. I refer to the hypothesis that miracles are effects due to the action of some unknown physical law, sometimes called a Higher Law. The language of those who advocate this view is apt to be vague and to run into rhetorical phraseology, as when we are told that a miracle is to be regarded "as a point of intersection between some vast outer circle of God's ways and the small inner circle to which we ourselves are better accustomed."* The expressions "unknown law" and "higher law" are somewhat indeterminate. Of the former Dr. Mozley remarks that it may mean either unknown law or unknown connexion with known law. The second of these alternatives points to a mode of conceiving certain miracles of which I shall have occasion to speak further on. Taken in the other sense the expression unknown law declares the belief that every miraculous event happens in accordance with some physical law, though from the nature of the case we are in

* Curteis, *The Scientific Obstacles to Christian Belief*, the Boyle Lectures for 1884, p. 76.

ignorance what it is. The phrase higher law means, or ought to mean, something more than this, viz., that the unknown law according to which a miracle happens stands in some unknown connexion with known physical laws, the supposed higher law being a generalisation embracing within itself both the known and the unknown laws, the known law of ordinary events and the unknown law of miraculous events. The physical order of the universe, according to this view, resembles Mr. Babbage's calculating machine, which was so constructed as to show successive numbers, 1, 2, 3, 4, 5, till the one hundred million and first term, and at the next term changed so as to show a sum higher than the last, not by a unit, but by ten thousand and one; the law of the machine thus embracing a law yielding successive numbers up to that point, and another law yielding divergent numbers at and after that point.*

On this hypothesis, much in favour with some recent apologists, three remarks may be made. In the first place, it has all the appearance of an apologetic device for the legitimate enough purpose of making miracles less offensive to scientific minds. These so-called miraculous facts which seem so strange, do not, it is virtually said, necessarily occur without law; there may be a physical law according to which they happen, though we have not the least idea what it is; and there may also be a secret connexion between that unknown law and the laws we do know, in virtue of which it happens now and then that a man rises from the dead, just as it happens ordinarily that dead men lie still in their graves. Such a purely conjectural scheme could suggest itself only to a mind drawn in opposite directions by two conflicting interests; desirous on the one

* Vide *The Ninth Bridgewater Treatise*, p. 33.

hand to retain faith in miraculous events recorded in Scripture, and on the other inclined to concede the absolutely unbroken reign throughout the universe of physical law.

The second remark is that this imaginary unknown law of miracles presupposes that miracles, however rare, are, nevertheless, periodically recurring phenomena. It is idle to speak of a law unless there be such phenomena to be accounted for. If there be indeed a law of miracles there must be facts regularly recurring similar to those recorded in the Gospels; blind men recovering their sight, dead men rising from their graves. In the words of Dr. Mozley: "A law of miraculous recoveries of sight without such recoveries of sight, a law of real suspensions of gravitation without such suspensions of gravitation, a law of miraculous production of material substances without such productions, a law of resurrections from the dead without resurrections from the dead—these laws are absurdities."* With reference to the topic last mentioned a more recent Bampton Lecturer has pled that though up till now such an event as the resurrection of Jesus has been, or seemed, anomalous it may hereafter be seen to be in accordance with law. That event, says Bishop Temple, "foreshadows and begins the general resurrection; when that general resurrection comes we may find that it is, after all, the natural issue of physical laws always at work."† But it is difficult to conceive of the same physical laws being so intermittent in their action; producing first a single resurrection, then after protracted ages, the simultaneous resurrection of millions. Are we to suppose that the Divine Will meantime counteracts these laws, so as to make them lie dormant? In that case the miracle

* Bampton Lectures, p. 153.

† *The Relations between Religion and Science;* The Bampton Lectures for 1884, p. 197.

is simply shifted, and made to consist in the fact that dead men do not rise. Instead of thus lowering the Resurrection of our Lord to the supposed natural level of the general resurrection, it would be more fitting to raise the latter event to the supernatural level of the earlier. The apostle Paul does indeed represent the risen Christ as "the first-fruits of them that slept,"* a mode of expression which brings both our Lord's resurrection and the general resurrection into analogy with the course of nature. But his language is the warm utterance of religious feeling, not the cold precise statement of scientific truth; not to say that it had an appropriateness in the mouth of one who expected the speedy end of the world, which it has necessarily lost in part through the delay of the final consummation.

I remark, lastly, that this hypothesis, equally with the attempt to base the defence of miracles on the irrationality of the belief in the fixed order of nature, saves miracles as events by the sacrifice of their miraculous significance. The extremes meet at this point. The extraordinary event which happens through the intermittent action of some unknown physical law, far from indicating the presence of special Divine Causality, may be believed in by an atheist, provided only he be satisfied that the alleged law has a place *in rerum naturâ*. It no more calls for the interposition of Divine Power than the sudden appearance at rare intervals of a meteor or a comet within the terrestrial orbit, for that, too, is a case of intersection between the wide outer circle of unknown physical law and the narrow inner circle with which we are acquainted. If it be said that the miracle consists in the intersection being of set purpose, arranged

* 1 Corinth. xv. 20.

to act as a sign and a moral force upon certain observers, it may be replied that substantially the same thing has been affirmed of meteors and comets.*

I now proceed to consider the less ambitious suggestion that miracles, or a certain number of them, may be the effects of obscure natural causes with whose action we are partially acquainted. The suggestion has reference more especially to the healing miracles recorded in the Gospels, and in that connexion it has found favour both with the friends and with the foes of miracles; with the former from a desire to meet objectors half-way, with the latter from the wish to do homage to the historicity of the Gospels without compromising their naturalistic philosophy. Mr. Arnold, who may be taken as the spokesman of unbelief, remarks: "In one respect alone have the miracles recorded by the evangelists a more real ground than the mass of miracles of which we have the relation. Medical science has never gauged, perhaps never enough set itself to gauge the intimate connexion between moral fault and disease. To what extent, or in how many cases what is called illness is due to moral springs having been used amiss, whether by being over-used, or by not being used sufficiently, we hardly at all know, and we too little enquire. Certainly it is due to this very much more than we commonly think, and the more it is due to this the more do moral therapeutics rise in possibility and importance." † On this view it is conceivable that medical science may yet penetrate the secret of Christ's healing

---

* Such is the view of Mr. Curteis, vide *The Scientific Obstacles to Christian Belief*, p. 76. The metaphor of the meteor or comet is actually employed by him to illustrate the notion of a miracle. "It (miracle) is as though a meteor or a comet of vast orbit abruptly came and went within our terrestrial orbit."

† *Literature and Dogma*, pp. 143–4.

ministry, just as it is possible, and we may hope probable, that the causes and cures of such fatal diseases as cholera and consumption will yet be discovered. When that day comes moral therapeutics will be a recognised branch of medical art, and many of the evangelic "miracles" of healing will be miracles no longer, but natural cures; or at most it will be recognised that Jesus possessed in a remarkable degree powers over diseases having their roots in men's mental and moral nature, which in kind were common to Him with other men. Against this theory apologists desirous of keeping truth with the spirit of the age offer no serious objection, contenting themselves with the position that Christ's healing acts were at least *relative miracles*, miracles if not for the purposes of science, at least for the purposes of revelation—arresting attention on the Agent, as crediting Him as God's messenger, singling Him out from other men and proving Him to be in possession of credentials deserving serious consideration; miracles for Christ's own time if not for ours, and having for that time the function and value of genuine miraculous deeds.*

This theory of relative miracle cannot be summarily dismissed like the baseless hypothesis of higher law. The alleged law of cure in the case of the healing miracles is not, as in the theory previously considered, purely imaginary. Moral therapeutics are not a mere invention of naturalistic critics or liberal apologists. Facts resembling the miracles of healing have been recurrent; by many they are believed to be happening at this hour. That they are really facts of the same kind is not to be taken for granted, but neither is it to be scornfully denied; it is a question for grave con-

* So Bishop Temple in *The Relations between Religion and Science*, pp. 201–2.

sideration. There are at least superficial resemblances: moral power in the healer, faith in the healed, and apparent recovery of health as the result of the combined action of the two forces. Neither is it a matter of life and death for the apologist that he should repudiate the suggestion that the cure of disease by Jesus was to a certain extent natural. Though only relatively miraculous His healing ministry might perform some functions of miracles if not all, for the age in which He lived if not for all ages. Whether miraculous or not that ministry serves a very important permanent purpose as a manifestation of Christ's sympathy with human suffering. It is not necessary to prove that the cures wrought by our Lord were miraculous, in order to vindicate the appropriateness of the citation by the evangelist in reference to these of the prophetic oracle: "Himself took our infirmities and bare our sicknesses." * In any case He did His utmost to alleviate woe. If what He did was not miraculous, it was in one sense only the better evidence of His love. If other men had His power to help, they lacked His will; for He stood alone in the extent of His beneficent activity. If He was not unique in virtue of miraculous charisms, He was certainly unparalleled in the enthusiasm of His humanity. We can therefore afford to regard the attempt to reduce the miracles of healing to the level of the natural with considerable equanimity. If that view were established these "miracles" would lose their value as signs annexed to a doctrinal revelation—the function on which the older apologists laid so much stress, but they would retain and even in some respects increase their value as a very important integral part of revelation—as a revelation of the infinite depths of compassion in the heart of the Son of Man.

---

* Matth. viii. 17.

The view of miracles we are now discussing, according to which they were miraculous only in reference to the age in which they were wrought, is analogous to Lessing's theory of Revelation, according to which revelation consists in communicating to men certain religious ideas which they might ultimately have discovered for themselves, but much later and with greater difficulty. In either case the hypothesis is abstractly legitimate. It is not incredible that God should endow one entrusted with a mission of great importance to human well-being with powers of healing disease far in advance of the medical skill of his age, in order to enhance his influence. Neither is it incredible that God for the religious education of the human race should anticipate the slow result of a purely natural process of development by communicating at an early stage, through inspired recipients, the leading truths relating to things divine. But the weak point in either hypothesis is the difficulty of verification. If the truths communicated by revelation were ideas ultimately discoverable by reason, how can we be sure that they were not arrived at in a natural way by some one of exceptional religious insight—the intuitions of a spiritually gifted mind? In like manner, if the healing powers of Jesus were such as medical science is destined one day to attain, how can we be sure that these powers possessed any special significance, and were not simply the natural endowments of a remarkable man who was before his time both in the healing art and in religious thought?

I cannot pass from this topic without remarking that, while conceding the claims of "moral therapeutics" to be something more than an invention of critics or apologists, I do not share the sanguine expectations of Mr. Arnold. I should be only too glad to believe that a time will come when physicians or saints will be able to give the blind their sight, to make the deaf hear, to restore to palsied limbs their strength, and to confer sanity on diseased minds. Again and again we find it written in the Gospels that multitudes suffering from all sorts of diseases gathered around Jesus, and that He healed them all. How happy will the world be when in every great centre of population there will be men of medical skill or saintly character, or say a single man, who can become such a centre of life and health for suffering millions! But, alas! I am not able to rise to the height of this great hope! I believe that there are ample resources for the healing art remaining yet undiscovered in nature's bosom; for I am optimist enough to think that there are rudiments of a gospel of mercy to be found even there. I do not despair of a time when specific cures for diseases hitherto incurable will be discovered. But I do not expect a time when physicians will be able by a touch to heal leprosy, by a word to open the eyes of one blind from his birth, or to restore to reason a raving maniac, or to enable a palsied one to rise and walk. The theory of moral therapeutics will not apply to such cases, and in all time coming it will probably be necessary for unbelievers in the supernatural to have recourse to the alternative method for getting rid of the miraculous element in the Gospels, that of mistake on the part of the reporters.

To a certain class of Gospel miracles the hypothesis of relative miraculousness is not applicable—those wrought on Nature, such as the multiplication of the loaves, and the change of water into wine. If miracles at all, these were very great miracles, as inconceivable and impossible to ordinary men to-day as they were eighteen centuries ago. All that can be done, in this class of miracles, towards conciliating naturalism is to insist on the analogy between the miraculous processes and the ordinary processes of nature.

Thus in the case of the two miracles just referred to, it may be said that in changing the water into wine and multiplying the few loaves so as to make them suffice for the wants of thousands, Jesus only did quickly what nature does every year by her slow, gradual processes; in every vineyard transforming water into grape-juice, and in every harvest-field multiplying the grain sown in spring an hundredfold.* But this analogy is edifying rather than serviceable for apologetic purposes. It gratifies the believing mind, but it does not tend to convert unbelievers to faith. The acts of Jesus, is it said, differ from those of nature only in the rapidity with which they are effected? Yes, but what a difference is there! The momentary character of the transactions presents a startling contrast to the habit of nature in which gradual growth is the universal law.

Among the various attempts whereby it has been sought to evince the naturalness of miracles mention may here be made in a sentence of a line of thought based on the graded order of being. The universe consists of various kingdoms ranged one above another. First there is the kingdom of inanimate matter, then above that there is the kingdom of vegetable life, which in turn rises into the animal kingdom. Next comes the kingdom of human intelligence, and highest of all is the kingdom of God. The point insisted on is that the phenomena of each of these

* So Augustine, and after him Trench in *Notes on the Miracles.* On the miracle at Cana Augustine remarks: Ipse fecit vinum in nuptiis, qui omni anno hoc facit in vitibus. Illud autem non miramur, quia omni anno fit: assiduitate amisit admirationem. In Ev. Joh. Tract. 8. Steinmeyer observes that the same key suits other miracles, as, *e.g.*, the cursing of the fig-tree in so far that the tree would at last have withered of itself or the many accounts of healing in the Gospels, as an illness which is not fatal is gradually mitigated by the healing power of nature. Vide *The Miracles of our Lord*, p. 11.

kingdoms in succession, while natural and normal viewed from within, are supernatural when viewed from the kingdom below. Life is a miracle viewed from the level of the mineral kingdom, human thought from the level of the lower animal world; and in like manner the phenomena peculiar to the kingdom of heaven are a great mystery to the uninitiated members of the human family; yet in each case that which is miracle seen from below is natural contemplated on its own plane. An eloquent expositor of this view puts it thus: "What to one being is supernatural, because it exceeds the powers of his nature, to another being is natural, because it lies within the powers of his nature. This may be taken to hold good in an ascending gradation, till what is supernatural to the mightiest angel becomes natural to the Power whence spring all powers. According to this view, natural and supernatural run along side by side, from the lowest order of agents up to the highest, until every degree of might reaches its central point in Him from whom finite forces originally sprang, and within the powers of whose nature they all lie; in Him who, seated above all rule, and authority, and power, looks down upon them all, like the sun looking down on his own beams." * There is a grandeur in this wide generalisation which captivates the imagination; but whether it is fitted to yield much help in solving the problem of miracles is a question on which one may reasonably cherish doubts. It seems rather to transform the idea of miracle than to contribute to the defence of what we are accustomed to call miracles. On this view all things are at once natural and supernatural. The life of a plant is from the

---

* Arthur: *On the Difference between Physical and Moral Law.* The Fernley Lectures of 1883, pp. 183–4.

mineral point of view as miraculous as the raising of a dead man, and on the other hand the highest mysteries of the kingdom of heaven are to the children of the kingdom as natural as the growth of a tree in the vegetable world. But suppose we accept this conception of the miraculous, the question arises: What are the normal phenomena of the kingdom of God? Should we not expect these to be purely spiritual, consisting in peculiar mental experiences, not in outward events like the miracles recorded in the Gospels? Or if these be included, the further question arises, to whom are they normal? To all the children of the kingdom? That would mean that it is natural to all men partaking of the life of the kingdom to work such miracles as Christ wrought, as it is natural to all ordinary men to think, to all animals to eat, and to all plants to grow.

The manner in which the relation between miracles and nature is viewed by Rothe is well deserving consideration. Rothe's special aim is to combat the idea that miracles necessarily involve collision with the fixed order of nature. He cannot understand why an advanced insight into the laws of nature should be thought an objection against miracles, seeing that natural law and miracles are correlative ideas, and only where a clear conception of the former is entertained can a proper idea of the latter be formed. In absence of the idea of a course of nature, there can be no idea of a miracle, simply because all is miracle. There is, therefore, no reason why we should be afraid of this great word of modern science, "laws of nature"; we may look the Medusa-head quietly in the eye, without any superstition. We can recognise, in the most unreserved manner, the fixed order of the world, and yet maintain along with it the possibility of miracle. For, in truth, the so-called collision between the two is only imaginary. To make this clear, Rothe distinguishes different kinds of miracles, according to the measure in which the absolute causality of God comes into play. The maximum of miracle is found there, where a certain effect is produced by the divine causality without the intervention of any creaturely second causes. The miraculous conception, the change of water into wine, and the multiplication of the loaves, are cited as examples, and with reference to these the question is asked: Where is the conflict between them and the order of nature? There is not, it is affirmed, even contact, not to speak of conflict. In this class of miracles the creature is not a concurrent cause. The thing produced is simply added to the sum of things by the creative power of God, and once brought into existence it forms a part of nature and is subject to its laws. From this class of miracles Rothe distinguishes another, in which God, by the medium of creaturely causality, produces certain results, which the creature and its laws, by themselves, could not have produced. This class is divisible into two. God may bring forth an effect exceeding the native power of earthly causality by a direct activity, by bringing about a combination of the activities of natural forces exceeding both our knowledge and our power. This sort of miracle stands in analogy to the kind of effect which the human will can produce upon nature, only that the particular effects exhibited in the miracle are beyond our power. We, as well as God, can make experiments on nature by combination of her forces, but we are only bunglers in comparison with the divine artist. He can manipulate the organism of nature, disposing all its forces with such infinite skill and unlimited power of control, that miracles of power become transmuted into miracles of providence. Here, also, there is no collision with nature. It is a mere case of using nature's forces, already existing, in order to bring about by new combinations new results; a kind of influence upon nature analogous to that which man exercises in physical experiments, only far higher in degree. The other subdivision of the second class of miracles embraces those cases in which God brings about new effects by new combinations of nature's forces, indirectly by the instrumentality of angels, whose power of control, exceeding that of men, is adequate to effects which, to our view, are miracles. Neither of these classes of miracles, any more than the first, it is maintained, involves any collision with nature's laws. Miracle comes into collision only with the pretended absolutism of natural law, and the idolatry with which Atheism regards it; testifying that natural law is not the highest power in the world, but that over it He reigns who made it, the living, personal God; that He, in making nature, did not produce a thing which was to limit and hem in His absolute, holy freedom, but rather a thing which should be a pliant instrument in His hands, serving His ends.*

According to this representation miracles resolve themselves either into acts of creation or into acts of control upon already existing nature, using its laws by new combinations for the production of new effects. In either case the idea of collision seems to be eliminated. Of course it is not to be supposed that the mouths of objectors to miracles must therefore be stopped. Against miracles of creation it may be alleged that the sum of being and of force is eternally a maximum which cannot be added to; and against miracles of control that nature is an organism so perfect that its powers cannot be used in new ways without detriment to the whole. These, however, are not scientific truths, but only opinions. No one is entitled to assert dog-

---

* Vide *Zur Dogmatik*, pp. 106–7.

matically that the sum of being and of force can neither be increased nor diminished, or that no combinations of force are possible save those which nature spontaneously brings about, or none save those which are effected in the laboratory. In absence of miraculous occurrences we might incline to think both these positions correct, but we are not entitled to advance them *in limine* as objections to alleged miracles. We must hold ourselves open to the idea of a possible exertion of the Divine will in the direction either of creation or of control, adding to nature's sum of being or disposing her forces to new effects. Of such manifestations of Divine Power it may be difficult to form any clear conception. It is, indeed, not merely difficult, but impossible. We can form no idea of the feeding of the thousands. How should we be able to conceive it, if it be indeed an instance of direct divine causality without the intervention of second causes? But inconceivability is no valid objection to a miracle. How our will acts on physical nature is beyond our power of conception, yet we know it does so act. In like manner a miracle, in which the will of God acts on physical nature, may be utterly inconceivable and yet be an undeniable fact.

In close affinity with the views of Rothe are those of Bushnell, as set forth in his great work on *Nature and the Supernatural.* The statement in this treatise on the subject in hand is one of the best considered to be found in the whole range of apologetic literature. The points of special interest for us are these three: the way in which the relation between nature and the supernatural is conceived; the use made of the human will to illustrate the supernatural, and the sense in which miracle is represented to be in accordance with law. Bushnell avoids the opposite extremes of the idolatry and the disparagement of the fixed order of nature, and regards nature and the supernatural as together constituting the one system of God. Conceiving of nature as not a final end for God, but as ordained to be played upon by higher powers, by God Himself and by free agents under Him, he remarks that "To serve this intent two things manifestly are wanted, and one as truly as the other: viz., nature and the supernatural; an invariable, scientific order, and a pliant submission of that order to the sovereignty of wills, human and divine, without any infringement of its constancy. For if nature were to be violated and tossed about by capricious overturnings of her laws, there would be an end of all confidence and exact intelligence. And if it could not be used, or set in new conjunctions by God and His children, it would be a wall. a catacomb, and nothing more. This latter is the world of scientific naturalism, a world that might well enough answer for the housing of manikins, but not for the exercise of living men."* This is the true position for defenders of the supernatural to take up. We must posit a nature to be acted upon, so fixed in its course that when any departure therefrom takes place we can be quite sure that it is not a mere random variety in the order of phenomena, but the result and proof of the action upon nature of higher, spiritual powers. On the other hand, while positing a nature thus fixed in its course, we must bear in mind that this course was meant to be acted on by a class of powers altogether different from physical forces. These forces are wills.

The action of will Bushnell regards as essentially supernatural, whether it be the will of God, of angels, of devils, or of men. "That is supernatural, whatever it be, that is

---

* *Nature and the Supernatural*, pp. 257–8.

either not in the chain of natural cause and effect, or which acts on the chain of cause and effect, from without the chain. Thus if any event transpires in the bosom or on the platform of what is called nature, which is not from nature itself, or is varied from the process nature would execute by her own laws, that is supernatural by whatever power it is wrought. If the processes, combinations, and results of our system of nature are interrupted, or varied by the action whether of God, or angels, or men, so as to bring to pass what would not come to pass in it by its own internal action, under the laws of mere cause and effect, the variations are supernatural." * From this general definition of the supernatural, it follows that the action of man on nature is supernatural, because man is a free being, not a part of nature, but above it, while closely connected with it. "The very idea of personality is that of a being not under the law of cause and effect, a being supernatural." † It is easy to see what advantage is gained by the inclusion of human agency within the scope of the definition. If in the will of man we have an instance of a power not belonging to nature producing effects upon nature, which could not be produced by nature herself, there is no difficulty in conceiving analogous effects produced by wills other than human, divine, or it may be angelic or diabolic. Whatever mystery is involved in the supernatural action of a free cause upon nature is already present as a matter of fact in the agency of men. When linen cloth is made out of flax a sort of miracle is wrought, for nature never produced linen cloth, and never will. The only question that can be raised regarding the supernatural action of other free agents besides men, is as to their existence. We may doubt, *e. g.*,

---

* *Nature and the Supernatural*, p. 37. † Ib., p. 43.

whether there be such beings as angels, but assuming their existence, we have no reason to be sceptical as to their exercising some control over nature, or as to the effects produced by their agency surpassing those flowing from the activity of human wills. It is a mere question of degree. The kind of effect is already given in man's action upon nature, and the whole stress of the difficulty lies in the kind, not in the degree.

Miracles Bushnell conceives of as happening according to law, in the sense that they are wrought in accordance with a purpose, what he calls the law of one's end. "We do not," he says, "immediately conceive what is meant by the fact that the supernatural works of God are dispensed by fixed laws till we bring into view a third kind of law (distinct both from physical and moral laws), viz., the law of one's end, or the law which one's reason imposes in the way of determining his end." He ascribes to God an end never varying, based in perfect reason, towards which all His supernatural acts, providences, and works tend. Because God's end never varies and His reason is perfect, His world plan, comprehending the supernatural, will be an exact and perfect system, centred in the eternal unity of reason about His last end. In accordance with this principle it is asserted that a supernatural event, known to occur but once—such, for example, as the miracle of the Incarnation—takes place under an immutable universal law. Under the same conditions the same miracle would recur, just as a stone falls when for the millionth time its support is taken away.*

This phrase, "the law of the end," employed by Bushnell to describe the sense in which miracles happen according to

---

* *Nature and the Supernatural*, pp. 264–9.

law, seems to be equivalent in import to the well-known phrase used by Bishop Butler for the same purpose—"general laws of wisdom." * Attempts have been made, on the ground of this expression, to make the author of *the Analogy* appear as the patron of the hypothesis of Higher Law.† But there can be no reasonable doubt that by laws of wisdom Butler did not mean physical laws, but reasons by which the Divine mind is guided in the performance of miraculous acts.‡ And with all deference to the advocates of the hypothesis alluded to, I think that Butler and Bushnell have indicated the true sense in which it can be said that miracles are subject to law. Miracles are not the effects of partially or wholly unknown physical causes; they are produced by immediate divine causality. But they are not on that account lawless or unnatural. They are wrought for a worthy end, and in accordance with a wise plan. They are natural in the sense that they are congruous to the nature of God, falling within the compass of His power, and subject to the direction of His wise, holy, loving will. They are natural further, I may add, in the sense that they do not wantonly interrupt or upset the order of nature, but rather put it to higher uses, which from the first it has been fitted and destined to subserve.

The most assailable, and the most frequently assailed point in Bushnell's theory is the conception of the human will as supernatural. The materialist, of course, disposes at once of the pretension, by the sweeping assertion that free

* *Analogy of Religion*, Part ii., chap. iv., § 3.

† Baden Powell, *e. g.*, speaks of this hypothesis as derived, perhaps, from the philosophy of Leibnitz, and suggested by Bishop Butler. Vide *Order of Nature*, p. 297.

‡ Such is the interpretation put upon the phrase by Mozley. Vide *Bampton Lectures*, note 4 to lecture vi.

will is a delusion, and that man is simply a part of the physical universe, an automaton imagining himself to be a voluntary agent. But even where there is no sympathy with this position, and where there is conceded to the human will a power of initiation as an efficient cause acting among the forces of nature, it may be contended that its action is not supernatural in any sense which can form the basis of a theory of miracles. The will of man though free, it may be said, is nevertheless hemmed in on every side by physical nature, acts through and in accordance with the laws of nature, and may be considered a part of nature as much as a plant or a crystal. From its action you cannot legitimately argue to a miraculous action of the Divine will, but only to action of a similar kind. Man's will keeps within the course of nature, and in like manner the will of God may be expected to do the same. All, therefore, that is gained by making the human will supernatural is a *natural* supernatural, not a miraculous supernatural, in which the laws of nature are superseded.* It cannot be denied that such criticism is not without force. We cannot establish the reality of strictly miraculous agency by the short-cut method of calling the action of our own will supernatural. Not that this use of the term is arbitrary or unjustifiable, or that it yields us no help whatever. There is a sense in which our will is supernatural, as there is also a sense in which it belongs to nature. We are above nature inasmuch as we are free agents; we are a part of nature, not merely in the sense that we are included in the universe of being, but in the more definite sense that our will acts through nature's laws, and in its actings along these channels forms a familiar part of the established order of things. The aid to faith we re-

* So in effect the author of *Supernatural Religion*, vide p. 45. Also Pfleiderer, vide *Religionsphilosophie*, p. 618.

ceive from emphasizing the supernatural aspect of our will-force is not any immediate proof of miracles, but emancipation from the thraldom of a purely mechanical conception of the universe. Through the consciousness that we ourselves are something more than mechanism, we rise more easily to the thought of a Supreme Will reigning above the universe. How that will acts, whether always and only through the physical laws which it ordained, or also for special ends, and on sundry occasions, after another manner, is a question for which an answer must be sought from a different quarter.

Bushnell's chief merit lies in the manner in which he states the relation between nature and the supernatural, assigning to each its own sphere, and yet conceiving of both as forming in combination one Divine system. This view avoids not only the opposite extremes of the disparagement and the idolatry of the fixed order of nature, but other forms of one-sidedness in conceiving the universe to which I have not yet very particularly alluded, but of which some notice may here conveniently be taken. We are accustomed to speak of two worlds, the natural and the spiritual. Now we may conceive of these two worlds as mutually independent, exclusive and inaccessible, having each its own laws, and its own evidence, the one an object of investigation to reason, the other revealing itself and its mysteries only to faith. Or we may go to the other extreme, and conceive of these two worlds as one; one in substance, one in law, one in evidence merging the natural in the spiritual, or the spiritual in the natural. The former is the way of contemplating the universe advocated in the works of Baden Powell. The order of nature as therein described is an absolutely fixed, inviolable uniformity. Through that order is revealed Divine Intelligence—a supreme reason, ultimate source of a cosmos which is interpretable by reason, but not certain other attributes ascribed by theologians to Deity, such as personality, omnipotence, righteousness, love. Such conceptions "can originate only from some other source than physical philosophy," and fall not within the sphere of cosmo-theology. The reality of these attributes is not denied; they are simply relegated to revelation, and regarded as objects not of knowledge, but of religious faith. The order of nature not only supplies no proof of divine omnipotence, it excludes manifestations of it in the shape of miracles which interrupt its uniformity. There can be no miracles in the physical sphere; such miracles may indeed be believed in by devout minds, but they exist only for faith, not *in rerum naturâ*. There may, however, be spiritual miracles such as those involved in revelation, inspiration, or regeneration, for these belong exclusively to the spiritual sphere, and in no wise interrupt nature's fixed order.*

This dualistic scheme cannot be accepted. It is difficult to conceive how it could satisfy the author except on the explanation offered by Dr. Martineau that he had thought out only the one side of the question which was congenial with his intellectual habits and pursuits, and that his imagination "left alone with the astounding revelations of modern science, was not simply possessed, but overpowered by the conception of all-comprehending and necessary laws." †
A similar explanation is probably to be given of the crudities with which some more recent speculations on religion emanating from physicists have made us familiar. The cosmos must teach less of God or more. If it reveal a Divine Reason, it also reveals Divine Character. Even Strauss ad-

* Vide *The Order of Nature.* Essay ii. on *Nature and Revelation.*
† *Essays Philosophical and Theological,* p. 132.

mitted that there are traces of a moral order not less than of a rational order in the universe. The distinction between reason and faith is much too broadly drawn. It virtually relegates spiritual things to the region of dreamland. Then as for miracles, they cannot easily be retained in the spiritual sphere, when they have been excluded from the material, and that because of that very reign of law which forms the plea for exclusion. For the spirit has its laws as well as matter, and the difficulty of reconciling the Divine causality with the natural order confronts us in the one region not less than in the other. Hence a consistent naturalism does not think of admitting miracle into the spiritual sphere after excluding it from the material. Deniers of Christ's resurrection deny likewise the miraculousness of Paul's conversion. Once more, the natural and the spiritual worlds are not so far apart as this author asserts. The spiritual can descend with its influences into the physical, and the physical can become the instrument of the spiritual. They are made for each other, and both glorify the One Maker.

But, though closely related, the two worlds are not one; to say that they are is simply to go to the opposite extreme. Perhaps no one has ever made the affirmation in plain terms, except such as deny the spiritual outright. But the present tendency is in that direction. Identity, to an indefinite extent, is suggested by some recent utterances: as when it is spoken of as at least possible that gravitation operates in the spiritual world, implying a conception of spirit as very thin matter;* or when the formula, "nature *in* the

---

* *Natural Law in the Spiritual World*, p. 42. A similar view of the spiritual world is implied in the opinion expressed by the authors of *The Unseen Universe*, that the available energy and possibly, also, the matter of the visible universe will ultimately pass into the invisible, "so that we

supernatural," is proposed as a substitute for Bushnell's "nature *and* the supernatural";* or when it is claimed that by the application of this principle, theology can be placed on a strictly scientific basis, and become a statement of spiritual facts "in terms of the rest of our knowledge."† Here is virtual identity in essence, law, and evidence. The theory is, however, as yet avowedly little more than a suggestion. In a spirit equally loyal to science and to religion a problem is tentatively thrown out for solution, rather than actually worked out. Whatever the results of the new departure may turn out to be, they are certainly expected by the originator to be, in the main, conservative, and it has been hailed by many as giving promise of a most triumphant vindication of old orthodoxy by the most advanced science. One may, therefore, consider the import of the theory, without embarrassment arising from fear of being supposed to impute opinions not avowed or expressly repudiated. In my student days, the professor of mathematics propounded this question for discussion to his class: Assuming that the three angles of a triangle are not equal to two right angles, what consequences follow? I desire to discuss the new metaphysical problem as dispassionately as, in bygone days, I discussed the mathematical one.

The new theory, then, seems to me open to some serious objections:

1. It involves, in the first place, an ominous limitation of the spiritual world. One is inclined, indeed, to ask why there should be any spiritual world at all—why all should

---

shall have no huge, useless, inert mass existing in after-ages, to remind the passer-by of a form of energy and a species of matter that is long since out of date and functionally effete. Why should not the universe bury its dead out of sight?" Chap. iv., at the end.

* *Natural Law in the Spiritual World*, p. 14. † Ib., p. 25.

not be given up to nature; God being regarded as the ulti mate cause, and the whole universe as the product of evolution. The existence of a distinct spiritual world cannot, of course, be asserted on the mere authority of Scripture, for the method of proof is to be scientific, and authority, whether of Church, creed, or sacred Book, must be discarded. The appeal must be to observation. Accordingly, the ground for asserting that such a world exists is found in the peculiar facts of religious experience, especially those connected with the beginning of religious life. As these appear most obtrusively in connection with the popular religious movements familiarly known as revivals, it may be said that the fact basis of the thesis—there is a spiritual world—is largely supplied by the phenomena of the enquiry meeting. Thus the spiritual world, so far as man is concerned, consists in the portion of the human race which undergoes "conversion." The remaining, and much the larger, part is handed over to evolutionary science, recognisable by it simply as animal, "sub-kingdom vertebrata, class mammalia, order Bimana,"* explicable by it in its whole past history and present attainments, intellectual and moral. These attainments may, in some respects, be very remarkable; nevertheless, their possessor, with all possible talents and virtues, is only animal—as distinct from the spiritual man as a stone from a plant. This definition of the spiritual reminds one of a remark somewhere made by Strauss that the sphere of religion is being narrowed by science as the territory of the Red Indian is being narrowed by civilisation. Natural law not only invades, but, to a large extent, swallows up the spiritual world. One cannot help thinking that, if evolutionary processes can account for so much, there is a pre-

* *Natural Law in the Spiritual World*, p. 99.

sumption in favour of their being able to account for all. If, through these processes, the scientist can explain the genesis of mind, will, and conscience, is he likely to despair of explaining, on purely natural principles, the phenomena of religious experience? Already, indeed, cosmic philosophy has made a beginning by conceiving of religion as consisting in that adjustment to the Divine environment wherein, we are told, the very essence of spiritual life lies. Neglect to adjust ourselves to that environment is, we are taught, sin, and to charge ourselves with the sin is to repent, and to be on the highway to spiritual improvement.*

The spiritual world has a much wider area than the "converted" Christianised portion of mankind. It embraces the whole of humanity "converted" or "unconverted." Reason, will, and conscience are essentially spiritual; every human being, as possessing these, is at least potentially a spiritual man, and has it for his task to become such actually.

2. The theory under consideration must affect injuriously our idea of God, especially in its moral aspect. In forming a judgment of the character of God we cannot but attach much significance to the initial creative act through which He brings into existence the new spiritual world. But what does that act signify? The arbitrary election of a certain number of the human family to participation in spiritual life, and the abandonment of all the rest to whatever fate the evolutionary process may have in store for them. The Being who is capable of doing this is an inhuman Deity whom the Christian consciousness, taught by Christ to regard all men as brethren, must disown. The theology which teaches such a God is as objectionable as

---

* Vide *Outlines of Cosmic Philosophy*, vol. ii., Part iii., Chap. v., on *Religion as Adjustment*.

the companion anthropology which regards the natural man as a mere animal. It is, I may add incidentally, as contrary to Scripture as it is to Christian feeling. There is, indeed, a doctrine of election in Scripture, but it is not a doctrine of arbitrary selection and heartless abandonment; though it has sometimes, I must admit, been supposed to be. The elect of the Bible are not chosen to a monopoly of Divine Favour. They are chosen not so much to privilege as to function. Their vocation is to be the light, the salt, the leaven of their race, and they neglect their duty at the peril of being cast out as savourless salt to be trodden under foot of men.

3. The theory in question, having begun with greatly narrowing the spiritual world, ends with virtually robbing it of distinctive character by insisting on the identity of law in the two worlds. One expects every world, like every land, to have its own laws. The kind of law should determine the kind of world. Accordingly the alleged identity cannot be maintained without overlooking a radical distinction between the natural and the spiritual worlds, this, viz., that the one is the sphere of necessary physical determination, and the other the sphere of freedom.* This distinction duly recognised, will be found to carry many other points of difference along with it. So far from being true that law in the two spheres is absolutely identical, it may turn out to be nearer the truth that there is not a single law of nature which, on passing into the spiritual world, does not undergo modification or transformation due to the distinc-

* This point is well stated in an excellent critique of Professor Drummond's work entitled *Natural Law in the Spiritual World, by a Brother of the Natural Man.* In this "brother of the Natural Man," I am happy to recognise my esteemed friend and former pupil, the Rev. James Denney, now minister of East Free Church, Broughty Ferry.

tive character of that world. That there should be resemblances, often striking, between the laws of the two worlds is to be expected, from the fact that they are but two departments of one universe whose Maker is God. And it is well that these resemblances be noted and that generalisations based thereon should be made, yielding statements of laws common to both spheres. Thus, *e. g.*, in reference to growth, it is well to point out that there *is* growth in spiritual life not less than in natural life, a fact very imperfectly realised by many religious people; and likewise that in both departments growth proceeds by stages, passing successively in the lower world through blade, green ear, ripe corn, and in the higher, through analogous stages. These are wide generalisations concerning life common to the two worlds. But the law of growth is not in all respects identical in these worlds. In the lower forms of life growth is entirely passive, proceeding without effort or consciousness on the part of the subject. Even of the growth of the human body this holds true. But in the spiritual life it is otherwise. Here there may be, and ought to be, conscious expenditure of effort towards growth, on which account it is rational to address to spiritual subjects exhortations to grow, though as against a fussing, unbelieving activity, it is also rational to remind them that in the kingdom of God, as in nature, growth is to a considerable extent automatic. The subject of election, already referred to, supplies an example of a law not only modified but even reversed in passing out of the natural into the spiritual world. There is an election in the lower kingdom of nature, as well as in the higher kingdom of grace. A law of election or selection runs through the whole domain of life. But in the lower provinces the law is that the possessors of certain advantages prevail in the struggle for existence. The same law prevails largely in human society; in the competi tion of life the strong thrive at the expense of the weak. But in the kingdom of God the law undergoes transformation. There the privileged care for the unprivileged, the fit for the unfit. Whereas elsewhere the weak are involuntarily sacrificed to the strong, here the strong freely sacrifice themselves for the weak. The change is due to the fact that in this sphere the agents act on higher impulses than the blind instinct of self-preservation. They are free men, and their wills obey the law of love.

Even in the palmary instance of the origination of life the law is not strictly identical in the two spheres. The subject of regeneration does not occupy the same position in reference to the Divine activity as that of inanimate matter when life was first introduced into the world. Doubtless the theory requires that the parallelism should be complete, for only on that assumption can it be made to appear that there is such a thing as a spiritual world. But the comparison of the natural man to inanimate matter is an exaggeration, whether proceeding from modern science or from antique theology, based neither on a careful observation of facts nor on a discriminating interpretation of texts. The natural man is in the first place a man, having humanity in common with the spiritual man. He is next a man who is not living in accordance with his true nature, really an unnatural degenerate man; therefore blameworthy, which he would not be if his life were normal for one who had reached his particular stage of being in the onward march of evolution. Therefore, when he becomes spiritual, he does not rise into a region of being with which he had formerly nothing in common, but rather becomes truly natural, returns to himself. Finally, he is a rational being who becomes spiritual chiefly through the influence of truth ad dressed to his spiritual faculties—reason, heart, conscience He is not regenerated magically through the mysterious immediate causality of the Divine Spirit. A Logos, a Christ, is necessary to the process. The Spirit takes of the things of Christ and shows them to the soul, and the natural man becomes a Christian by the free intelligent reception of Christ thus exhibited as an object of faith and love.

What place may be found for miracles under the theory one can only conjecture. One thing is certain, they must be naturalised somehow. Obviously spiritual miracles, in the form of conversions, come into prominence, presenting instances of immediate Divine causality, yet natural while miraculous, because in analogy with the first introduction of life by creative energy. But how the Gospel miracles are to be disposed of is not so clear. It is not inconceivable that the passion for naturalising, once it had taken a firm hold of the religious mind, might end in indifference to and unbelief in miracles within the physical sphere. These miracles signify an influx of the spiritual into the natural; but the current in the case supposed would run strongly the other way, threatening to sweep away the miraculous on its swelling flood. But it is also conceivable that a basis for faith in the Gospel miracles might be found in the modern phenomenon of faith-healing conceived to be essentially similar facts. The theory of miracles would then be that they are natural as falling within the ordinary powers of spiritual men. The miracles of Christ would be accredited by their resemblance to phenomena of frequent recurrence in the spiritual world, and open to observation. This mode of verification might claim to be in accordance with scientific method. On the same principle Christ Himself, the great moral miracle, might be verified. The line of argument would be: such a Christ as the Church believes in must have been, because he is required to account for the phenomena of conversion. It would be a repetition under a new form of Schleiermacher's construction of Christology from the data of Christian consciousness. In fact we may say that the whole method of constructing theology advocated by the propounder of the new theory is in principle identical with that pursued by the gifted author of the *Christliche Glaube*. One can only wish that some one possessing equal learning and genius may be found to work out exhaustively the method in our altered circumstances. We shall then be better able to estimate its value by a comparison of results.

III.

THE GOSPEL MIRACLES IN RELATION TO THE APOSTOLIC WITNESSES.

In the foregoing lectures we have been considering the subject of miracles in general in relation to speculative philosophy and scientific views of the order of nature. We come now to the special topic with which we are directly concerned, the Gospel miracles, which I shall consider under various aspects in succession. In the present lecture I propose to treat of these miracles in relation to the apostolic witnesses.

The credibility of the Gospel History is a wide field of enquiry into which I have neither occasion nor space to enter at length in this course. A slight reference to it, however, cannot well be avoided. For it is the miraculous element in the Gospels that chiefly raises the question as to their historical trustworthiness. Eliminate that element and hardly a doubt would remain: the residuary words and deeds of Jesus would be welcomed as proof that in Judæa there once lived a sage and philanthropist of unparalleled wisdom and goodness. It is therefore a very urgent question: on whose authority do these miraculous narratives rest? are the men who had been with Jesus—the apostles, responsible for them? can the testimony of the twelve, or of any of their number, be cited in their favour?

Of all the replies to Hume's famous argument against the credibility of miracles, that of Paley is the most forcible, and the one which has been most noticed either by way of approva. or as a subject of criticism. The case is put of twelve men of known probity concurring in an account of a miracle wrought before their eyes, in which it was impossible for them to be mistaken, and enduring martyrdom in evidence of their sincerity, and the question is asked whether even in such a case Hume's theorem will hold that no testimony can be received which contradicts a uniform experience.* The hypothetical case is a roundabout description of the twelve apostles and their situation as witnesses for the *memorabilia* of their Master's history, and especially for His resurrection. The case is highly coloured, but justifiably so, the purpose being to test the sceptic's reasoning by an extreme instance.

Two questions may be asked in reference to this test case. First, a speculative one: suppose such an ideal case, combining all the highest requirements of trustworthy testimony, to be realised, would the evidence supplied suffice to attest the raising of Lazarus, or say the resurrection of Christ Himself? Second, a historical one: how far does the ideal case correspond with fact; how far is the testimony of the twelve available for the two miracles referred to, or for the Gospel miracles generally?

It is the latter of these two questions which now chiefly awakens interest. Men have grown tired of chopping logic on Hume's puzzle, and of weighing the comparative credibility of testimony and experience of nature's constancy. Nor do we now sympathize altogether with the demand for an excessive amount of testimony of first-rate quality for the miraculous occurrences reported in the Gospels. Instead of insisting on all the twelve bearing witness, we should be content to be perfectly assured that the Gospel miracles, or

* Paley, *Evidences of Christianity*, pp. 7–8.

a large proportion of them, rest on the authority of a single member of the apostolic band. If any one of the four Gospels were as indubitably apostolic in its authorship, as the four Epistles to the Galatian, Corinthian, and Roman churches are indubitably Pauline, how little we should trouble ourselves about Hume's ingenious reasonings!

But before passing to the practical question it may be right to say a few words on the speculative one. Hume's argument has been variously regarded by recent unbelievers in the supernatural. Mr. Huxley, for example, finds it in some respects weak and unsatisfactory. He pronounces it irrefragable, in so far as it amounts to a demand that for all alleged interruptions of the known order of nature very strong evidence shall be produced, but accounts it mistaken in so far as it implies that an event contrary to uniform experience cannot happen, or if it happened, would be a violation of the laws of nature. The truth he takes to be that "If a dead man did come to life, the fact would be evidence, not that any law of nature had been violated, but that those laws, even when they express the results of a very long and uniform experience, are necessarily based on incomplete knowledge, and are to be held only as grounds of more or less justifiable expectation." * No event is too extraordinary to be possible. At the same time we owe it to the well-ascertained course of nature to be very incredulous in our attitude towards the extraordinary, and Mr. Huxley confesses that hardly any testimony would satisfy him as to the existence of a live centaur; and it would probably be doing him no injustice to assume that he would make a similar remark with reference to the Gospel miracles.†

---

* *Vide* his *Hume*, p. 133. † *Hume*, p. 135.

The author of *Supernatural Religion* thinks Paley's "simple case" utterly without cogency against Hume's doctrine. "No assertion," he affirms, "of any twelve men would be sufficient to overthrow a law of nature, which is the result of a complete induction." * The position is borrowed from Mr. John Stuart Mill. In his observations on Hume's argument Mr. Mill says that "Hume's celebrated doctrine that nothing is credible which is contradictory to experience, is merely this very plain and harmless proposition that whatever is contradictory to a complete induction is incredible. We cannot admit a proposition as a law of nature, and yet believe a fact in real contradiction to it. We must disbelieve the alleged fact, or believe that we were mistaken in admitting the supposed law." † But he explains that by a fact in real contradiction to a law he means a case in which the cause A took place and yet the effect B did not follow without any counteracting cause, and he points out that the assertion in the case of miracles is not of this sort, the effect being supposed to be defeated not in absence, but in consequence of a counteracting cause—the will of a being who has power over nature. Mr. Mill's position, therefore, is not that miracles are incapable of being established by testimony; he rather tacitly admits that miracles may rationally be believed on sufficient evidence by any one who is not on other grounds convinced that no cause exists whose interposition between A and B could prevent the usual result from taking place.‡

Mr. Baden Powell virtually endorses Hume's scepticism, but he expresses his opinion in a new and plausible way. "No testimony," he says, "can reach to the supernatural;

* *Supernatural Religion*, p. 211.

† Mill, *A System of Logic*, vol. ii., p. 184.

‡ Mill, *Logic*, ii., p. 186.

testimony can apply only to apparent sensible facts; testimony can only prove an extraordinary and perhaps inexplicable occurrence or phenomenon: that it is due to supernatural causes is entirely dependent on the previous belief and assumptions of the parties." * The statement, as has been pointed out by Dr. Mozley,† is ambiguous. In one sense it is undoubtedly true. Testimony can attest only the miraculous fact; it cannot reach its supernatural cause; that we arrive at through a process of reasoning. But the important question is: can testimony establish a fact for which no other than a supernatural explanation can be suggested? That Mr. Powell would have answered this question in the negative may be gathered from the significant expression, "sensible fact," as also from the following remark occurring in the same essay: "The proposition that an event may be so incredible intrinsically as to set aside any degree of testimony, in no way applies to or affects the *honesty* or *veracity* of that testimony, or the reality of the impressions on the minds of the witnesses so far as it relates to the matter of *sensible fact* simply. It merely means this: that from the nature of our antecedent convictions, the probability of *some* kind of mistake or deception *somewhere*, though we know not where, is greater than the probability of the event really happening in *the way* and from the *causes* assigned." ‡ Two doors are thus open to the sceptic who wishes to escape from the supernatural. The one is: this fact admitted to be as reported, may have had a natural cause. The other is: this fact for which as reported no natural cause can be conceived, may not have happened as reported. The reporters, doubtless, have recorded honestly

---

* *Essays and Reviews*, p. 107. † *On Miracles*, p. 128.

‡ *Essays and Reviews*, p. 106.

the effect produced on their senses, but their senses may have been deceived. Thus in the case of Christ's resurrection: there were doubtless visions which suggested to the disciples the idea that their Lord was risen, but who shall guarantee that they were not mistaken in their interpretation of the appearances? It thus appears that the aphorism: testimony cannot reach to the supernatural, really means: there is no supernatural to reach. Miracles as such have no place in history: they exist only for faith.

Passing now from the theoretical to the practical question, I observe that the history of opinion among unbelievers with reference to it is very instructive. The general fact is that when it has been thought possible to admit apostolic authority direct or indirect for the Gospel narratives without accepting the miraculous element as true it has been admitted; when the contrary has been thought to be the case it has been denied. Beginning with the free-thinkers of the eighteenth century, we find that they showed no great zeal in calling in question the ancient tradition respecting the origin and authorship of the four Gospels. The truth is that they had no interest in denying whatever connection between the evangelic history and the apostles as the ultimate source of information believers might be disposed to assert, for they had such a poor opinion of the apostles that even if it had been certain that each Gospel had one of them for its author, and that all the rest concurred in the statements made by their brethren, they would not have felt under any obligation to believe in miracles on their word. Optimistic in their general estimate of human nature, they deemed nothing too wicked to be perpetrated by the founders and functionaries of positive religions. Therefore they could dispose of the whole question of miracles by a single word—*fraud*. According to Reimarus, who may be taken as a type of the German school, Jesus and His companions were simply a band of tricksters. The former he deemed capable of arranging with certain persons that they should feign themselves lame, blind, dumb, insane, that He might have the credit of curing them. The latter he accused of stealing the dead body of their crucified Master and then giving out that He had risen from the dead.* Men that could do that were of course capable of telling any number of lies for the honour of their hero. What value could be attached to miraculous narratives vouched for by such persons? Woolston, the member of the English deistical fraternity who made the miracles the subject of special attack, deemed it convenient for personal safety to have two hypotheses. The miracles were either frauds or allegories conveying under the guise of miraculous histories hidden spiritual truth.†

This coarse brutal method of treating sacred persons could not fail to engender disgust, and to prepare men for welcoming a theory which would relieve them from the necessity of believing in the miracles without imputing dishonourable conduct to those on whose authority they were reported. Such a theory was furnished by *Paulus*. In his critical views the founder of the Rationalistic school of interpretation was in the main conservative. He believed that Matthew wrote a Gospel of which the substance is given in the Gospel which bears his name; that the second Gospel contains

---

* *Vide* Strauss, *Hermann Samuel Reimarus, und seine Schutzschrift für die Vernünftigen Verehrer Gottes*, pp. 193, 214.

† *Vide* Woolston's *Letters on the Miracles*. An account of Woolston's views is given by Trench in the introduction to his *Notes on the Miracles*, by Lechler in his *Geschichte des Englischen Deismus*, and by Strauss in the introduction to his *Leben Jesu*. The chief contemporary reply to Woolston was by Bishop Smalbroke in *A Vindication of the Miracles* in two vols.

a faithful report of apostolic preaching as gathered specially from the lips of Peter; that the third contains accounts taken from written collections of evangelic incidents compiled by hearers of the apostles, carefully corrected by first-hand information derived from the eye and ear witnesses of Christ's ministry; and that the fourth Gospel had John for its author. The Gospel history, that is to say, according to Paulus, is apostolic in its source. And as such it is, in his view, entirely trustworthy. The apostles were thoroughly honest men whose statements may be implicitly believed. That, however, does not mean that we are to accept as miraculous the so-called Gospel miracles. In point of fact no miracles really took place. In some instances, where miraculous occurrences are usually found, the evangelists do not even intend to relate miracles. In the case of the feeding of the five thousand, *e. g.*, reported by all the four evangelists, and in particular by Matthew and John, who were eye witnesses, close attention to the narrative will show that it does not represent five loaves as alone sufficing for the wants of thousands. The honour of two apostles requires us to be very careful not to import our notions into their words, because it was a case in which it was possible to know exactly what happened. It was a matter of simple eyesight. Had the apostolic evangelists said that the multitude was fed by the few loaves alone, they must either have seen this, or they must have wished to deceive their readers.* Another instance in which there is no intention to relate a miracle is the narrative concerning the tribute money related by Matthew. It is simply a stupid mistake of miracle-loving interpreters to imagine that the piece of money needed to pay the tax was found in the mouth of

* Paulus, *Exegetisches Handbuch über die drei ersten Evangelien*, vol. ii., p 205.

the fish. It was found by as much fish being sold as would raise the needed sum. So Jesus meant, and so the evangelist well understood, and it never entered into His mind to guard against any other construction.* In other cases, however, the reporters of Christ's deeds did believe that something miraculous had occurred. Though perfectly honest they were still comparatively ignorant men, who shared the false superstitious notions of their time, believing in demoniacal possession, angelic appearances and the like; and they had an unbounded admiration of their Master's powers. Therefore there are many narratives in the Gospels, in which, in the opinion of the evangelist, and of those from whom he derived his information, a supernatural element is involved. But in such cases the utmost care must be taken to distinguish between the fact as it actually happened and the inference or judgment of the reporter. And happily it is always possible to do this, for the reporters had no intention to deceive, and therefore have taken no pains to obliterate the features in the story that go to show that what occurred was a purely natural event. Thus, in the instance of the woman with the issue: the fact was that the woman, sharing the popular belief in Christ's wonderful healing power, approached His person in the hope that an unobserved touch of His garments would suffice to heal her, and after touch felt a sensation which led her to conclude that she was really healed, though that could only be ascertained by time. She tried then to retire unnoticed, but Jesus suddenly asked: Who touched me? It was *inferred* that Jesus put the question because He had felt a healing virtue go forth from Him, and so the matter is reported in Mark's narrative.† The next step was that one of the collectors from

* *Handbuch*, ii., p. 497.

† Mark v. 30.

whom Luke drew his materials, deeming this the only possible explanation of Christ's question, in perfect good faith put it into Christ's own mouth, whence it comes that in Luke's version the story runs: "Jesus said, Somebody hath touched me; for I perceive that virtue is gone out of me."* Here, as so often, fact and judgment get mixed together without any intention to deceive, but by a little care in comparing narratives we may easily extricate the one from the other.† And even so in all cases it is possible to eliminate the supernatural, and reduce the miracles to the level of the natural. The fever suddenly attacked Peter's mother-in-law after he had left for the synagogue; it was of an intermittent character, and a fever of that sort may be subdued by a mental impression, such as that produced on the patient by the word of Jesus. The stilling of the storm on the lake of Gennesaret by the rebuke of the wind, amounted to nothing more than a declaration in dramatic form that the gale would soon blow past. The walking on the waters of the same lake was really a walking on the land, which from the ship appeared like walking on the sea. The palsied man laboured under the depressing belief that his disease was incurable on account of his sin. Jesus disabused his mind of the prejudice by assuring him that his sins were forgiven; and perceiving that his physical strength was not wholly gone, said in effect: let him only try his powers: "Arise, take up thy bed and go unto thine house." The lepers were not cleansed in the sense of being healed, but only pronounced clean, Jesus having skill enough to ascertain that the disease in the particular cases was not contagious. In the case of the three raisings from the dead, the persons were not really dead. In the case of the ruler's

* Luke viii. 46.

† *Handbuch*, i., 524.

daughter, Jesus himself said so expressly. In the case of the widow's son, a person supposed to be dead was being buried by mistake; a mistake which might easily happen where interment took place very soon after decease. Jesus saw that it was a case of this kind, and said to the apparently dead one, "Arise!" The feeding of the multitude took place in the simplest possible way. The generous spirit of Jesus spread through the crowd, and all who had brought provisions with them willingly made them available for the wants of those who had none. The withered hand and the case of dropsy were minor forms of disease easily curable without miracle. The woman bowed down with infirmity was afflicted with chronic melancholy, aggravated by the imagination that the trouble was due to demoniac influence. Jesus delivered her from this fancy, and with the return of cheerfulness she naturally recovered her erect position. Jesus touched the eyes of the blind man of Jericho to remove the hindrance to sight. As He found this possible, there can have been no miracle. The cure of demoniacs was quite an easy affair. The disease was imaginary, a form which insanity at that period assumed; and the cure consisted in making the patient believe that the devil, by which he fancied himself possessed, had gone out of him. For this it was necessary to treat the sufferer as if he were possessed, which accordingly Jesus did, partly by way of humouring diseased hallucinations, but probably also because he shared the erroneous opinions of his age in reference to the causes of certain forms of disease.

All this is very ingenious; indeed, quite too ingenious. For after perusal of the laborious attempts of Dr. Paulus to eliminate the supernatural from the evangelic history, the conviction remains that much of that history is miraculous in warp and woof. Some of the explanations may be so plausible as to produce temporary half-persuasion, but many more strike one as far-fetched, and the final impression is that the theory is a failure. And so one can understand how men at length grew very weary of Paulus and his exegetical devices, and felt the need of a theory proceeding on entirely different lines, frankly admitting the miraculous character of the Gospel narratives, but striving to account for the origin of the narratives, without assuming that events like those reported ever happened, or were ever said to have happened by those who, like the apostles, had the best means of knowing. This want was met by the mythical hypothesis with which the name of Dr. Strauss is chiefly associated. According to this theory the miraculous narratives in the Gospel were simply myths: pure myths, in some instances, without any fact basis—embodiments of Christian ideas, above all of the Messianic idea; in other cases myths with a slender basis of fact, say some word of Jesus such as that concerning His disciples becoming fishers of men, shaping itself ultimately into the story of the miraculous draught of fishes. Thus the healing ministry of Jesus was to a large extent simply a group of myths which had grown out of the prophetic description of the Messianic age as one in which the eyes of the blind should be opened, and the ears of the deaf unstopped, and the lame man should leap as an hart, and the tongue of the dumb sing.* If Jesus was the Messiah such things must have happened through the forth-putting of his Messianic power; so reasoned the believing mind, and so these Gospel legends grew up noiselessly, unawares, without intention or set purpose of invention on the part of individuals, sprouting out of the faith of the Church as germs break through the earth. A theory of this sort applying to the Gospels a method of in-

* Isaiah xxxv. 5, 6.

terpretation, which had previously been used with success in profane history, could not fail to be welcome to men of naturalistic views and philosophic proclivities. It has so much that is reasonable and convincing to say for itself. There are myths in all religions. It is the way of faith thus to crown its hero with a garland of marvels. It is the way of mankind in the infancy of thought to embody ideas in myths, to express abstract conceptions in the form of concrete events. This happens, doubtless, chiefly in prehistoric ages before civilisation has dawned; but though Jesus lived in a historic age, it is not necessary to suppose that the historic spirit had penetrated into all corners of the world. The sun does not rise in the valleys as soon as on the hilltops; the mental condition of the people of Galilee and Judæa at the beginning of our era was very different from that of highly cultured Greece and world-ruling Rome. Then while the theory has these *a priori* considerations in its favour, do not the facts correspond? Do we not find in the Evangelic narratives, comparing one account with another, just such discrepancies as we should expect to meet with in stories having their origin among an ignorant people inspired by an intense religious enthusiasm? Finally, with this theory one has the great comfort of being relieved from the unwelcome necessity of charging the twelve, or indeed anybody, with fraud or folly. Myths are not the deliberate products of individual invention; they are the impersonal outgrowths of faith. As for the twelve, they are to a very small extent responsible for the contents of the Gospels. The miracle tales grew up without their knowledge, in all probability after they were dead and gone; for the formation of myths demands time.*

* For Strauss' exposition and defence of the mythical hypothesis, vide *Das Leben Jesu*, Einleitung.

The late origin and non-apostolic authorship of the Gospels is a necessary postulate of this theory. To admit that the evangelic records could lay claim to apostolic credentials would be fatal, as it would involve either that these records with all their marvels are true, or that they are fabrications. Strauss, however, made no elaborate attempt to establish the views as to the dates and authorship of the Gospels which his theory required. He was content to prove by internal evidence that the Gospels cannot have originated in the apostolic age, and to point out that there is nothing in the patristic tradition which shuts us up to an opposite conclusion. The result of his criticism was thus purely negative, and as such was deemed unsatisfactory. The enquiry was raised, Can we not know more about these Gospels, so important to the Christian religion, than that they must have been of comparatively late origin, patristic tradition to the contrary notwithstanding? Hitherto we have been engaged, under the guidance of Dr. Strauss, in criticising the history contained in these writings; suppose we now examine the writings themselves and try to find out from their characteristics under what circumstances they were written, and with what aims their authors came to their tasks. Such was the attitude assumed by the succeeding phase of unbelief. Dr. Baur was the most famous representative of the new departure, under which the negative criticism of Strauss gave place to the historical criticism of the Tübingen school.

Baur's aim was a much wider one than that of Strauss it was not to get rid of the evangelic miracles, but to account for Christianity on naturalistic principles and in connection therewith to explain the genesis of the New Testament. The chief value of Strauss's work he took to be that it delivered men from undue reverence, and set them free to carry on critical enquiries concerning sacred books with as little embarrassment as scholars feel in conducting similar enquiries respecting profane literature. Such liberty he certainly used to the uttermost. And the conclusion at which he arrived concerning the New Testament books was this. These writings are all, without exception, dominated by *tendency;* the writers intend to serve a certain purpose, theological or polemical. The tendency in each case depends on the part which each book was designed to play in the great controversy which formed the most outstanding phenomenon in the history of Christianity during the first century of our era and part of the second; that between the *Judaists* on the one hand and the *Paulinists* who contended for a gentile, universal Christianity, on the other. Some books are devoted to the maintenance of either extreme, some to reconciliation of opposing parties, some express the sentiments characteristic of the period of completed reconciliation and union. Those which belong to the first class date from the apostolic age and proceed from apostolic authors. They include five books—the four Epistles to the Galatian, Corinthian, and Roman churches by Paul, and the Apocalypse by John. These apostolic writings represent the antagonism in its unmitigated form. The writings devoted to conciliation are, of course, post-apostolic, because the spirit of conciliation did not begin to work till the men who were irreconcilably opposed to each other—Paul on the one hand and the eleven on the other—had gone to their rest. This class embraces, among many others, the Synoptical Gospels. The writings representing the union period are necessarily later still. And of course the later the less historical. On this principle the fourth Gospel, the chief writing of this group, is the least trustworthy of all the historical books. The interest in it is purely ideal; the historic narratives are mere inventions to serve as framework for theological conceptions. The writer, a gentile gnostic, has no knowledge of the evangelic history except through the Synoptical Gospels, of which he makes as free use as a novelist makes of old chronicles in constructing a work of fiction. The miraculous narratives in his pages have no historic value; they simply embody mystic truths. The opening of the eyes of the blind man sets forth Jesus as the Light of the world; the raising of Lazarus exhibits Him as the source of Life. The Synoptics, being dominated also by tendency, "Matthew" conciliatory on the Judaistic side, "Luke" on the Pauline, "Mark" ignobly neutral—are also more or less unreliable; but by comparison with the fourth Gospel they are historical. The greatest measure of historic trustworthiness belongs to *Matthew*, which is also the earliest of the three.

Such in hasty outline is the Tübingen theory of the New Testament writings.* In its bearing on the Gospels it leaves time for the growth of myths, and supplies motives for conscious inventions. How far the "miracles" were real natural occurrences, myths, or inventions Baur does not very clearly indicate, his purpose, as already stated, being rather to deal with the whole question of the genesis of Christianity and its documents than to consider the miraculous element in the Gospels. He discerned in the narratives a mixture of all three; real occurrences where such were possible on naturalistic principles, legends or myths springing up spontaneously out of the fertile soil of faith, inventions as in the case of most of John's miracles.† In the first class of narratives, but in them alone, an apos-

* For a connected view of this theory, *vide* Baur's *Geschichte der Christlichen Kirche*, 1st Band.

† Vide *Die Kanonischen Evangelien*, p. 603.

tolic source might consistently be admitted. With this view Strauss in his second *Leben Jesu* substantially concurs, acknowledging himself convinced by Baur's investigations that invention has played a greater part in the evangelic history than at an earlier period he was prepared to believe.

Strauss and Baur represent the high-water mark of scepticism. In their writings the amount of historical matter to be found in the Gospels resting on the reliable authority of the men who had been with Jesus, is reduced to a minimum. Since their time opinion, even among theologians of the naturalistic school, has been tending steadily towards earlier dates and higher degrees of historicity. The fourth Gospel is indeed still a subject of serious dispute, and cannot be put on the same platform with the Synoptics in estimating the critical consensus. Keim, author of the well-known learned and genial work on the *History of Jesus of Nazareth*, may be taken as the representative of more recent critical views. While not absolutely negativing the Tübingen theory of tendency with concomitant invention this writer regards it as chargeable with gross exaggeration. The Gospels, he thinks, were all in existence very shortly after the close of the first century; the earliest, *Matthew*, before the destruction of Jerusalem in A.D. 70; the latest, *John*, between A.D. 100 and A.D. 117; both dates being some fifty years earlier than those assigned to the same Gospels by Dr. Baur. The wholesale conversion of the miracle-histories into myths by Strauss he by no means approves, though he believes that a legendary element is not wanting in the Gospels. To this category he relegates certain groups of miracles, such as the *duplicates*, of which the feeding of the four thousand is a type; the miracles which are to be regarded as *transformed parables*, including the cursing of the fig-tree, and the miraculous draught of fishes; *picture histories* in miraculous form arising not, like the two just mentioned, out of any special word or action of Christ, but out of the general impression made by His work as a whole—the story of the Gadarene demoniac being cited as an example of this kind and described as "a witty, in the literal sense impossible history"; and lastly *imitation miracles* which arose out of the desire to make Jesus as a miracle-worker equal or superior to Moses and Elias. After all these deductions and a few more, such as the feeding of the five thousand, the stilling of the storm, and the change of water into wine, rejected for no very definite reason except that they were not the kind of miracles to which Jesus referred in proof of His mission or which were wrought afterwards by His apostles, there remain the miracles of healing, which taken as a whole Keim regards as real histories. Speaking generally, this writer goes as far in recognising the historicity of the evangelic records as is possible for one holding a naturalistic theory of the universe, and the impression left by a perusal of his work is that he would have gone further had he not been prevented by a philosophy which lays it down as an axiom that the miraculous in the strict sense is impossible.*

In a still more recent work on the Life of Jesus, that of Dr. Bernhard Weiss, an ampler homage is done to the historical trustworthiness of the Gospels by one who, while not naturalistic in his philosophy, handles critical questions with considerable freedom. Yet, curiously enough this last step in the onward progress of opinion brings us back to *Paulus*, of course in a very modified form. In this new *Leben Jesu* the Gospel records are regarded as on the whole historical, and based on reliable apostolic tradition; but some narratives generally deemed miraculous are consid-

* *Geschichte Jesu von Nazara*, ii., p. 127.

ered resolvable by exegesis into non-miraculous histories. Among these is included the feeding of the multitude. An opportunity will present itself hereafter for considering how far this reversion to the exegetical results of Paulus is justifiable. Meantime I may remark that one conspicuous feature in this recent work is its defence of the authenticity and credibility of the fourth Gospel. One weighty line of argument brought to bear on the question consists in the endeavour to show, that in this Gospel, as compared with the Synoptics, is displayed in connection with important epochs of our Lord's life, such as the Galilean crisis and the Passion, an exact knowledge such as could be possessed only by one who, like John, was an eye-witness. According to Weiss it throws a light on the events connected with the Capernaum desertion which we look for in vain in the Synoptical accounts; and, in reference to the time of the last passover and the crucifixion, distinctly corrects the inexact representations of the first three Gospels. This is a method of argumentation which is not available for one bound by strict views of inspiration. But the apologist will think twice before he allows himself to be debarred from its use by merely dogmatic considerations. It is of much more importance to the interest which the apologist has at heart, the defence of the Christian faith in its essentials, that the Gospels should be shown to be historical than that they should be held to be absolutely free from such errors as creep into the best histories. If it should be found that a solid argument for the authenticity of John's Gospel can be based upon the discrepancies between it and the Synoptical Gospels, we gain much more than we lose by the admission that in the pages of the latter comparatively slight inaccuracies may be discovered. In the hands of Strauss and others, discrepancy has been pressed into the service of unbelief. Why should it not be boldly applied to the establishment of the faith?*

The foregoing historical review has shown the close connection subsisting between the views entertained by critics on the question how far the Gospel history flows from apostolic sources, and their speculative opinions concerning the miraculous. I have now to direct attention to a different line of enquiry bearing on the subject of this lecture suggested by recent investigations into the literary connections of the first three Gospels. The critical problem presented in the resemblances and differences observable in the Synoptics, when compared with each other, is a wide and difficult one, into which I cannot here go at length; but it has a bearing on the miraculous element in the Gospels and its attestation, which I desire briefly to explain.

The phenomena connected with the Synoptical problem have been accounted for on various hypotheses: such as mutual use, use of common documents, common dependence on the oral tradition of apostolic preaching. The document theory and the tradition theory still divide the suffrages of scholars. If common documents were employed in the construction of the Canonical Gospels, the important question arises: what was the earliest form of the written

---

* It may be well here to explain, once for all, that in these lectures the subject of inspiration is left on one side, and only substantial historicity is claimed for the Gospels, as sufficient for the purposes of the argument. It follows from the adoption of this point of view that the legitimacy of all critical procedures compatible with substantial historicity is recognised. This remark must be specially borne in mind in connection with some of the points touched on in the next lecture. How far inspiration is reconcilable with any measure of historical inexactitude is a question I do not here pronounce on. I only contend that no one is entitled to start with the *a priori* assumption that the admission of errors as to matters of fact, however few or minute, is fatal to inspiration.

tradition—the primitive gospel to which all the three Evangelists had recourse for the material which reappears in very similar form in all their pages? Three hypotheses have recently found influential support. One is that *Mark*, either as we have it or in an earlier form of which the Canonical Mark is a recension, was the first written Gospel, and the source of the matter common to the three Synoptists. This view has been ably advocated by Holtzmann in his work on the Synoptical Gospels. Another view is that not Mark, either as we have it or in an earlier form, was the primitive written Gospel, but an apostolic document to be identified with the *Logia* compiled, according to the testimony of Papias, by the apostle Matthew. This book of *Logia* was, it is believed, a source for all the three Synoptical Evangelists, the second gospel by Mark being an additional source for the first and third. Such is the view of Weiss. According to the third hypothesis we are to find the primitive Gospel, source of the triple tradition in the Synoptics, by extracting from these those portions in which there is exact verbal agreement. What results is a sort of skeleton gospel consisting of unexpanded notes, such as a student might take in a class of a professor's lecture, or a hearer in church of a preacher's sermon. This is the view advocated by Dr. Abbott in his article on the Gospels in the Encyclopædia Britannica. All three hypotheses imply that none of the Synoptical Gospels is of apostolic authorship, but that all of them have apostolic authority behind them, and represent faithfully on the whole the oral tradition of apostolic preaching.*

---

* The Synoptical problem has been still more recently handled in an able manner by Wendt in his work, *Die Lehre Jesu*, Erster Theil, 1886. Wendt holds a position intermediate between Holtzmann and Weiss. Mark, as we have it, he regards as a source for our first and third

I do not propose here to discuss the comparative merits of these hypotheses, or to express any decided preference for one more than another. My purpose rather is to point out to what extent the miraculous element in the Gospels can claim apostolic credentials on any one of the rival views. Meantime I may briefly indicate a modest opinion on the question at issue between them. It is intrinsically probable, then, that the work of the apostles took the form chiefly, if not exclusively, of preaching, their great theme being the person and work of Jesus Christ, their Lord. Out of this preaching would soon grow an oral tradition, likely to be tolerably uniform, because the ministry of the eleven for a considerable time at least, was confined within a narrow area, being exercised among the Jews only, a fact for which the apostle Paul is voucher.* This oral tradition could not fail, ere long, to assume a written form. Many hearers, evangelists themselves possibly, might write down what they had heard for their own benefit or for the use of others, and in this way a group of rudimentary gospels might arise such as Luke refers to in the preface of his Gospel. There is nothing improbable in the supposition that a written account of the public ministry of Jesus was prepared even by one of the apostles whose previous habits fitted him for the task, say by Matthew. Or such a work might be written at the request of an apostle, say Peter, by a companion, such as Mark. Or, finally, any disciple might on his own responsibility make copious notes of what he had learnt from the lips of one or more of the apostles, and so prepare a document of sufficient extent and value to form a foundation for an evangelic literature. That the

Gospels. The *Logia*, according to his view, was a source only for the Canonical Matthew and Luke; not, as Weiss holds, also for our Mark.

* Galatians ii. 9.

notes would be as elliptical and laconic as Dr. Abbott supposes I hardly think likely. Dr. Abbott, indeed, thinks that by the hypothesis of such an elliptical document, easily liable to be differently read or interpreted, may be satisfactorily explained certain discrepancies occurring in the Synoptical reports of the same words or incidents. He gives some ingenious samples in his work on *The common tradition of the Synoptical Gospels*, and promises more,* and if such solutions could be multiplied, they would certainly amount to an argument of no small weight in favour of his view.

But, as I said, I am not concerned to argue for or against any of these rival hypotheses. The point I wish to make is that with any one of them we should get a primitive Gospel which was to a greater or less extent a *miracle*-Gospel. To begin with the hypothesis favoured by Holtzmann, viz., that an earlier form of Mark was the source of the matter common to the three Synoptics. On this view the primitive Gospel must have contained at least eleven miracle-histories. The list, taken in the order in which they occur in Mark, is as follows:

1. The healing of Peter's mother-in-law—Mark i. 29–34; Matt. viii. 14, 15; Luke iv. 38–39.
2. The healing of the leper—Mark i. 40–45; Matt. viii. 2–4; Luke v. 12–16.
3. The healing of the paralytic—Mark ii. 1–12; Matt. ix. 2–8; Luke v. 18–26.
4. The healing of the withered hand—Mark ii. 1–6; Matt. xii. 9–14; Luke vi. 6–11.
5. The stilling of the tempest—Mark iv. 35–41; Matt. viii. 18–27; Luke viii. 22–25.
6. The demoniac of Gadara—Mark v. 1–20; Matt. viii. 28–34; Luke viii. 26–39.
7. The woman with an issue of blood—Mark v. 25–34; Matt. ix. 20–22; Luke viii. 43–48.

* Vide *Introduction* to the work above named, pp. xxvii–xxxviii.

8. The raising of Jairus' daughter—Mark v. 22–24, 35–43; Matt. ix 18, 19, 23–26; Luke viii. 41, 42, 49–56.

9. The feeding of the five thousand—Mark vi. 35–44; Matt. xiv. 15-21; Luke ix. 12–17.

10. The healing of the lunatic boy—Mark ix. 14–29; Matt. xvii. 14-21; Luke ix. 37–43.

11. The healing of the blind man at Jericho—Mark x. 46–52; Matt xx. 29–34; Luke xviii. 35–43.

We get the same result on the hypothesis advocated by Dr. Abbott. The skeleton-Gospel framed by extracting the words common to the three Synoptical Gospels contains accounts more or less brief of all these eleven miracles. The "notes" supposed to have been used by the Evangelists may have contained more miracle-histories; Dr. Abbott thinks they probably did contain those common to Matthew and Mark, and omitted by Luke, the *walking on the sea*, the *cure of the Syrophenician woman's daughter*, the *feeding of the four thousand*, and the *cursing of the fig-tree*.*

Thus far all is plain. But now as to the hypothesis advocated by Dr. Weiss, viz., that the book of *Logia*, compiled according to the testimony of Papias by the apostle Matthew, was the earliest written Gospel, and a common source for all the three Synoptical Evangelists, it is not so clear that it too must have contained miracle-histories. The name raises a presumption to the contrary, for the term *Logia* naturally suggests the inference that the work referred to by Papias was merely a collection of our Lord's *sayings*.† Accordingly the view held by many is that that work could not have been a source for the three Synoptists, at least so far as the deeds of Jesus are concerned, though it may have been, and probably was, the source whence the first and

* *Vide* Article *Gospels*, in Encyclopedia Britannica.

† The words of Papias are: Ματθαῖος μὲν οὖν Ἑβραΐδι διαλέκτῳ τὰ λόγια συνεγράψατο, ἡρμήνευσε δὲ αὐτὰ ὡς ἦν δυνατὸς ἕκαστος.

third Evangelists drew the many words of Jesus which they record in common, and which are not to be found in the second Gospel. But this strict interpretation of the term used by Papias to describe Matthew's work cannot reasonably be insisted on, for the same Father uses the term in reference to the Gospel of Mark also, after having previously more fully described it as a book containing a record both of Christ's words and of His deeds.* The work might appropriately be called a book of *Logia*, if Sayings formed its largest or most prominent feature, though it likewise contained some narratives. But even if we concede that the *Logia* had for its sole aim to collect the words of Jesus, it is hardly possible to conceive of it being entirely lacking in the historical element. A certain amount of history would be necessary to make the sayings intelligible, or at least to bring out their point and beauty. For our Lord's words were not abstract moral sentences, like proverbs, which could be gathered together in a book, like specimens in a museum, without note or comment beyond the briefest label indicating the subject to which they related. Some of them may have been of this description, but many were occasional utterances called forth by special circumstances. In such cases the word and the occasion form an organic whole, and to separate them is to take the life out of both.

It may be taken for granted, then, that the *Logia*, while a collection of sayings, was also, and for the very sake of the sayings, a history. The connected discourses, such as the *Sermon on the Mount*, would have their prefaces, and single sayings would be preserved embedded in their historical matrix. If so, miracle-histories could hardly be wanting, for some of Christ's most characteristic utterances were

---

* For the passage relating to Mark with remarks on it, *vide* Bleek, *Introduction to the New Testament*, i., p. 131.

called forth in connection with miraculous occurrences. Without pretending to exhaustiveness, I give a few samples.

Among the words of Jesus to which a collector, who had at all penetrated into the spirit of His teaching, would be sure to attach importance, are those which indicate the high value He set on *Faith.* Nothing is more characteristic in Christ's doctrine than these utterances, and it would be a very poor collection indeed which was without them. But the recording of these would of itself involve the introduction into the book of several miracle-histories, such as those relating to the *centurion of Capernaum*, the *Syrophenician woman*, the *woman with the bloody issue*, the *lunatic boy at the Mount of Transfiguration*, the *two blind men* spoken of in the ninth chapter of Matthew, and *the stilling of the storm.* The two first mentioned are the most important, and would almost certainly be found in a good collection of *Logia*, not only as indicating the occasions on which two of Christ's most remarkable utterances concerning faith were spoken, but also on account of most significant words then spoken bearing on the moral state of Israel and the relation of the Gospel to the heathen. On the earlier occasion Jesus said, "Verily I have not found so great faith, no, not in Israel," and then went on to predict the exclusion of the chosen race from the kingdom, and the opening of its doors to Gentiles coming seeking admittance from every quarter of the world. That word could not be understood unless it were explained, how the centurion showed the faith so highly extolled, and that would mean relating the whole story of the miracle. On the later occasion Jesus said, "O woman, great is thy faith, be it unto thee even as thou wilt." The very words imply a reference to something asked under peculiar circumstances fitted to provoke strong manifestations of feeling, and granted out of respect to the spirit elicited, and the saying without the story is a lock without a key.

These two stories, therefore, we may be sure were told in the book of *Logia*. Not improbably, also, the pathetic story of the poor woman with the wasting issue, to whom Jesus said in a tone of tender sympathy, "Daughter, be of good comfort; thy faith hath made thee whole." Both for the word and for the deed this narrative deserved a place among the *memorabilia* of the Gospel of Love. The stories of *the lunatic boy* and *the stilling of the storm* might also very appropriately be related under the rubric: *Words concerning faith.* Only the words in these instances were not words in praise of faith manifested, but in blame of faith wanting. To disciples exclaiming in terror, "Lord, save us; we perish," the Master said: "Why are ye fearful, O ye of little faith?" To the same disciples, asking at a later date, "Why could not we cast him out?" the Master said, "Because of your unbelief, for verily I say unto you, if ye have faith as a grain of mustard seed, ye shall say unto this mountain, remove hence to yonder place, and it shall remove, and nothing shall be impossible unto you."

Another group of sayings which must certainly have found a place in any good collection of *Logia*, consists of those in which Jesus indicated His attitude towards the *Sabbath.* These were generally spoken in self-defence against accusations of Sabbath-breaking, and the occasions for the charge in some instances were supplied by acts of healing. Three instances occur in the Synoptical Gospels, viz., the healing of the man with the withered hand, of the woman with a spirit of infirmity, and of the man afflicted with dropsy. The words reported to have been spoken on these occasions are sufficiently remarkable to have insured for themselves a place in a competent collection of *Logia.*

But the utterances on all these occasions seem to have been somewhat similar. In self-defence Jesus said, It is lawful to do well on the Sabbath; or, interrogatively, Is it lawful on the Sabbath days to do good or to do evil; to save life, or to kill? and to convict the fault-finders of hypocrisy, He asked them such home-thrusting questions as these: which of you shall have an ass or an ox fallen into a pit, and will not straightway pull him out on the Sabbath day? doth not each one of you on the Sabbath loose his ox or his ass from the stall, and lead him away to watering? The collector of *Logia*, interested mainly in recording the words of Jesus, may have gathered these all together and attached them to a single narrative, that concerning the healing of the withered hand, found in all three Synoptical Gospels; a suggestion favoured by the fact that in Matthew's version of that incident, we find words combined which in Luke are distributed between that miracle and the cure of the man afflicted with dropsy. But it is not impossible that the book of *Logia* had two narratives of sabbatic miracles, or even three, each with its own peculiar saying attached, and that it was the source whence Luke drew the two narratives not found in the other Synoptics. In that case it is the first evangelist, not the collector, who is responsible for the grouping. Be this as it may, it is almost certain that at least one of the three sabbatic miracles, presumably the healing of the withered hand, had a place in the *Logia*.

The *Logia* would contain, we cannot doubt, the words spoken by Jesus, in self-defence, against the sinister construction put upon His *cures of demoniacs*. These cures formed a very prominent part of His healing ministry, and the apology for them provoked by Pharisaic insinuations is entitled to rank among His most remarkable utterances. There is nothing in the Gospels, in the way of argument, more convincing than the refutation of the charge of casting out devils by the aid of Beelzebub; nothing more solemn or significant than the counter-charge of blasphemy against the Holy Ghost. The record of Christ's sayings on these topics would naturally be prefaced by an instance of the healing acts which gave occasion to them. Possibly the narrative was very brief, giving no details, stating only what was barely sufficient to explain the subject of accusation and defence. Such is the character of the two narratives in Matthew's Gospel, to which we find these attached. In the earlier, it is reported that "they brought to Him a dumb man possessed with a devil. And when the devil was cast out, the dumb spake." Then it is added, that, while the multitude marvelled, saying "it was never so seen in Israel," the Pharisees said: "He casteth out devils through the prince of the devils."* In the later narrative the account is equally meagre, and, on the whole, so similar as to suggest the idea of a duplicate. The sufferer this time is blind, as well as dumb; being healed, he "both spake and saw"; and again the honest crowd express their admiration, saying now, "Is not this the Son of David?"† It is to this miracle the Evangelist attaches Christ's defence, having contented himself in the earlier narrative with simply indicating the Pharisaic accusation. Both these narratives may have been in the *Logia*. They are more likely to have formed the introduction to the debate on exorcism than any other of the same class occurring in the Gospels, such as that of the demoniac in the synagogue of Capernaum, or those included in the Triple Tradition, the interest in all these cases turning on a different hinge.

Besides the foregoing miracle-histories, I merely mention,

* Matt. ix. 32-34.

† Matt. xii. 22-24.

as likely to have a place in the *Logia*, the following: the cure of the *Leper*, in connection with which Jesus spoke an important word, indicating His respect for the Mosaic law* and constituted authorities; the cure of the *Paralytic*, in connection with which He claimed for the Son of Man power to forgive sin;† and the story of the *Stater*, preserved in the first Gospel only, closely connected with the discourse on Humility, and with the dispute of the disciples concerning places of distinction, out of which that discourse took its rise.‡

It thus appears highly probable that the book of *Logia* contained at least these miracle-histories: The *centurion of Capernaum, the Syrophenician Woman*, one of the *Sabbath* miracles, one instance of a *demoniac healed*, the *Leper*, the *Paralytic*, and the *Stater*. Less probable, yet likely, inclusions are, the *woman with the bloody issue*, the *lunatic boy*, and the *stilling of the storm*, and other instances of the Sabbatic and demoniac classes of miracles. The list includes six of the eleven miracles embraced in the Triple Tradition. The *Logia*, while primarily a collection of sayings, was thus, like its companions, the *Urmarkus* of Holtzmann, and the skeleton Gospel of Dr. Abbott, at the same time, a *miracle-gospel*.§

---

* Matt. viii. 4, et parall. † Matt. ix. 6, et parall.

‡ Matth. xvii. 24–27. This section is included by Wendt in his reconstruction of the *Logia*. Vide *Die Lehre Jesu*, Erster Theil, p. 181.

§ For an instructive discussion of the question as to the contents of the *Logia*, *vide* two articles by Weiss in the *Jahrbücher für Deutsche Theologie*, 1864 and 1865, the one entitled "*die Redestücke des Apostolischen Matthäus*," the other "*die Erzählungstücke des Apostolischen Matthäus*." In the latter article the author endeavours to show that the apostolic Matthew must have contained a large number of miraculous narrations, including most of those named above, and others I have not mentioned. His argument has a polemic reference to the view of Holtzmann that the *Logia* was almost exclusively a collection of sayings. The

And now, looking away from details, let us for a moment fix our attention on the general import of the foregoing observations. The literary criticism of the Gospels which in recent years has been growing in popularity, as the negative criticism of Strauss and the historical criticism of Baur have been falling into neglect, is found to differ from the latter not less in tendency than in method. While they were based on and designed to promote scepticism regarding the miraculous element, the new criticism, unbiased by any strong feeling either for or against the miraculous, has shown itself to be in the main conservative. It renders highly probable the existence of at least one written embodiment of the Evangelic tradition, originating in the preaching of the apostles, antecedent to the Canonical Gospels, and makes it almost certain that the primitive Gospel contained a considerable miraculous element. That element thus appears not to have been the product of faith, but an essential part of the original Evangel offered to faith. It has been thought that in the earliest presentation of the Gospel, miracle was not only prominent, but supreme, and that the moral sayings of Jesus to which we now attach the chief importance, were gleanings rather than first-fruits. The aim of the apostles, it is argued, was to show Jesus to the world as the Christ, not as a wise Rabbi, and for that end mighty works were of more value than sage words. On this ground a claim has been advanced for Mark to be reckoned the earliest of the three Synoptical Gospels.* This view must be regarded as one-sided. There is no need thus to oppose words and works, for both must be

---

Logia, as reconstructed by Wendt, also contains a number of miracle-histories.

* So Weizsäcker, vide *Untersuchungen über die Evangelischen Geschichte*, p. 115.

taken into account in forming an idea of the Messianic vocation of Jesus. It was as truly a part of that vocation to proclaim the doctrine of the Messianic Kingdom, setting forth the Fatherhood of God, the brotherhood of men, and the nature of true righteousness, as it was to manifest the advent of the era of grace by miracles of love. An enlightened Evangelist would give both parts of Messiah's work a place in his memoirs as far as his knowledge enabled him. From imperfect information, personal idiosyncrasy, or special needs of the first readers, the record might be defective in one or other respect; but the defect would not be a merit, or supply a ground for a claim to priority. A gospel consisting chiefly of incidents and lacking sayings might, in point of fact, be the earliest, but its one-sided character would be no proof that it was. A similar remark applies to a Gospel of an opposite character. The point to be emphasised is not that preponderance of miracle-histories proves an early date, but that the presence of a miraculous element in a document is no proof of late origin or unapostolic source. As matter of fact, nothing appears to have a better claim to belong to the original apostolic tradition.

Such is the lesson taught us by literary criticism, and we accept it thankfully. But let us remember that there is a higher criticism than any yet named—that, viz., which detects apostolicity by moral tests. The literary monuments of creative epochs have certain well-defined characteristics. There is about them a prophetic breadth, freedom, grandeur, and simplicity, which we look for in vain in other times. Using the term in no merely technical sense, they may be truly said to be *inspired.* The men who are the mouthpiece of such an epoch can not only walk, but fly. Their thoughts have wings of spiritual insight, imagination, and great religious emotions. The apostolic age was one of these inspired epochs. The apostle Paul possessed the Divine gift in highest measure, and his undisputed Epistles exhibit it in all its power and glory. But who can doubt that it was possessed also, if in a lower degree, by the men who had been with Jesus? The companions of the Bridegroom must have entered into the fellowship of His freedom and joy. They could not be for a considerable period in that blessed presence without catching His spirit; all the more that, while they were with Him, the Master made it His chief aim to initiate them into the spontaneity, buoyancy, and liberty of the new era of grace. It is not credible that in this He wholly failed, as the Tübingen theory supposes. The eleven drank of the new wine of the kingdom. They knew that with Christ a new era dawned; and they understood and appreciated its signs. Their sympathy with the new time found expression in their way of speaking concerning their Lord; in the things pertaining to His public ministry that they chiefly retained in their memory, and preferred to relate; and in their manner of relating them. The abiding result is our Gospels. These Gospels throughout, alike in miracle-histories and in discourses, bear the unmistakable stamp of apostolic inspiration, if not of apostolic authorship. It reveals itself to the simplest reader, and it becomes more conspicuous to the scholar whose knowledge enables him to institute contrasts. Every new literary monument of the post-apostolic age but serves to bring into relief the immeasurable superiority of the Gospels in insight into all that relates to the true character of Christianity as the religion of the spirit, and therefore the religion of liberty and joy, and unimpeded fellowship with God. What an astounding contrast in this respect, for example, between the evangelic records of apostolic preaching, and the so-called *Teaching of the Twelve Apostles* recently brought to light! The chief interest of that ancient writing, to my mind, lies just here: not in what it tells us of the beliefs and customs of the early church, but in the difference in spirit between it and the Gospels. This the teaching of the apostles! It is the body of it without the soul, the letter without the spirit, its pure morality but untouched by its evangelic tone, the Gospel conspicuous by its absence, Christianity already reduced to a neo-legalism. Compare the two representations in a few particulars: "*Fast* for those that persecute you,"* says the *Didache*, instead of *pray*, as in the Gospels. It enjoins that before baptism the baptiser and the baptised shall fast for one or two days before, recommending that others who can should keep them company; reducing fasting to an ascetic, compulsory system, contrary to the teaching of Jesus, as recorded in the Gospels.† The *Didache* further directs Christians not to fast in common with the hypocrites, thus explaining the precept, "for they fast on the second day of the week, and on the fifth, but do ye fast during the fourth, and on the preparation day."‡ Jesus in the Gospels gives the same general counsel, but how diverse the reason annexed: "that thou appear not unto men to fast." How puerile the idea that a change of the day can supply a guarantee against hypocrisy; how certainly this stress laid on mere externals will lead to a new development of Pharisaism! Is this what the religious ethics of Jesus have come to so soon—a grotesque, melancholy caricature! In other matters, the descent from the Gospels to the *Didache* is equally glaring. Prayer, like fasting, is methodised, the Christian being directed to repeat the Lord's prayer three times a day.§ The summary of moral duties closes

---

* *Didache*, chap. i.

† *Didache*, chap. vii.

‡ *Didache*, chap. viii.

§ *Didache*, chap. viii.

with this counsel: "If thou art able to bear the whole yoke of the Lord thou shalt be perfect; but if thou art not able, what thou art able that do." * Here is the germ of the Catholic conception of perfection, so contrary to that set forth in the teaching of Christ. The perfection of the *Didache* is quantitative; it is an affair of doing all the Commandments, the higher as well as the lower. The perfection of the Gospels is qualitative; it consists in singleness of mind, without which no duty can be acceptably performed. The *Didache*, like the Gospels, knows of an unpardonable sin; but the unpardonable sin of the *Didache* consists in trying and judging a prophet who speaketh in the spirit;† surely, a sin which might be committed in ignorance, like blasphemy against the Son of Man. So little, indeed, does the *Didache* breathe the spirit of the era of grace, that it hardly seems to be aware that that era has dawned. In the Eucharistic prayers this petition occurs: "Let grace come, and let this world pass away." ‡

It is natural to ask how this low unevangelic tone is to be accounted for. It may be supposed to reveal the bias of a sect, Ebionitic, Judaistic, Montanist. To me it appears simply the index of a too easy descent on the part of the whole church, irrespective of sectarian divisions, from the high level to which for a season the human mind had been raised by the influence of an epoch-making Personality. The Gospels show us that influence at its full tide; in the *Didache* we see it at its ebb. Some would invert the order, and see in the Gospels the advance to a higher view of Christianity from the inadequate conceptions of an earlier period. But this is not the true order. The age of clear

---

* *Didache*, chap. vi.

† *Didache*, chap. xi.

‡ *Didache*, chap. x.

vision and inspiration comes at the beginning, or it does not come at all. That such books as the Gospels ever came into existence is a kind of miracle. The miracle was possible in the creative week of the Christian era, but only then. Gospels appear because a Jesus has lived, and men have been with Him who have understood Him better than the Christian Church has in any later time. The *Didache* is but one of many indications how difficult it has been found by average Christians in ordinary times to remain on the Gospel level. I have characterised it as legal in its religious tone. But what is the whole history of the Church but a long, dreary winter of legalism with bright, calm, halcyon days of restored intuition intervening now and then?

IV.

THE GOSPEL MIRACLES IN RELATION TO THE EVANGELIC RECORDS.

IN the last lecture we were engaged in considering how far the miraculous narrations contained in the Gospels can lay claim to apostolic attestation. In the present lecture we are to consider the position occupied by these narrations in the Evangelic Records. The enquiry, besides gratifying a natural curiosity, will serve the apologetic purpose of enabling us to judge how far the miracle-sections bear the stamp of historicity.

1. We may begin our survey by adverting to a fact too obvious to escape the notice of any attentive reader. The miraculous element in the Gospels is no mere excrescence or external adjunct easily separable from the body of the history, but an essential portion of it, closely woven into the fabric, vitally connected with the organism. Words and works are so united that the one divorced from the other would in many instances become unintelligible. I have virtually anticipated this observation in the preceding lecture in endeavouring to prove that an adequate collection of Christ's sayings must also have been to a considerable extent a collection of acts, and in especial of miracle-acts. Then I used the fact to determine the contents of a document no longer extant. Now I simply note it as an undoubted characteristic of the documents actually in our hands. The remark applies more particularly to the Synoptic Gospels, for though the connection between discourses and miracles in

the fourth Gospel is very apparent, it may plausibly be suggested that it is not a natural objective connection arising out of the events as they actually happened, but one invented by the writer. With regard to the first three Gospels such a suggestion cannot be made with the slightest pretence to plausibility. There the connection between word and deed is evidently not merely in the mind of the writer, but in the actual course of events. The miracles cannot be eliminated from these Gospels without serious mutilation. The first Gospel is perhaps of the three the one with reference to which the process might most hopefully be attempted. Matthew's method is to arrange his materials in masses. He groups a large proportion of Christ's sayings into connected discourses capable of being labelled according to the general tenour of their contents. He follows the same plan to a certain extent with the miracles, giving in chapters nine and ten, at the close of the first great discourse, the *Sermon on the Mount*, a selection of acts showing Jesus to be as great in Power as in Wisdom, forming in all a group of ten miracles, being not less than one-half of all the miracles recorded in his Gospel. Omit these two chapters, and alter the rubric in chapter iv. 23 by striking out the words, "healing all manner of sickness, and all manner of disease among the people," retaining only "teaching in their synagogues, and preaching the Gospel of the kingdom," and you might consider Matthew pretty well expurgated, remaining after all an invaluable record of Christ's public career as the founder of the Christian religion. Yet the work is only half done, and the miracles that remain are very intractable, including among them the healing of the *withered hand*, associated with sabbatic controversies, and the stories of the *Syrophenician woman*, and the *lunatic boy*, connected in different ways with Christ's memorable utterances concerning faith. Moreover the ten miracles so summarily got rid of by the excision of the two miracle-chapters carry along with them much teaching-matter by the loss of which the evangelic record would be greatly impoverished. The discourses of our Lord, as preserved in Matthew, contain many words of priceless worth on many topics of supreme importance. Still, without the utterances of an occasional character, they would be very defective as an account of Christ's teaching. For example, the Sermon on the Mount contains no explicit doctrine of faith, only an exhortation to trust in a heavenly Father, implying that faith is a virtue of cardinal importance in the esteem of the speaker. A similar remark may be made of the other large discourses. We read in them of fidelity to duty amid tribulation, and of humility and forgiving injuries, and patient waiting and watching, but comparatively little of faith. Looking to these greater discourses alone, we should come to the conclusion that in the view of Jesus faith was a thing of subordinate moment. How great a mistake we should thereby commit we learn when we turn our attention to the lesser discourses. These because short are not therefore of less value. To disabuse our minds of the contrary impression, we do well to remember that in all probability the greater number of our Lord's utterances were originally short, pithy sentences, which only gradually grew into larger aggregates in the minds of His disciples through the law of association. In any case it is certain that if some topics naturally lent themselves to extended discourse, others of equal importance would be more appropriately dealt with by brief, pointed remark as occasion prompted. To this class of topics belongs emphatically faith. Christ would best impress on His hearers the importance of this grace by directing their attention to notable instances of it when they occurred, and by pointing out to them the evil consequences resulting from the lack of it either in themselves or in others. Accordingly it was in this way that He gave His disciples their lessons in the doctrine of faith. He taught them to regard it as a great spiritual power by saying to them: see what it can do, what great thoughts it can utter; what difficulties it can surmount; what healing it can bring to body and soul; see also how weak men are without it. Most of these lessons were given in connection with miracles; indeed, we may say all, only some of the miracles were moral ones, such as that wrought on the spirit and conduct of the woman who was a sinner, to whom in presence of unsympathetic Pharisees, incredulous as to moral change, Jesus said: "thy faith hath saved thee, go in peace." Faith and miracle go together, so that to eliminate miracles from the Gospels is simply to eliminate precisely the most characteristic element in Christ's system of doctrine, that by which He was distinguished from the Baptist, whose watchword was not *believe*, but *repent*, and which could not fail to be prominent in the teaching of One who came announcing the advent of the kingdom of grace.

Some of the most precious lessons on faith are associated with the miracles recorded in the eighth and ninth chapters of Matthew's Gospel. Among them is the story of the Centurion of Capernaum, who exhibited a faith unexampled in Israel, and the healing of the palsied man, in connection with which the important truth was taught that faith possesses a vicarious virtue; for it was out of regard to the faith of the friends who bore him to His presence that Jesus cured the sick one in body and in soul. There, also, not to multiply instances, is recorded the stilling of the tempest on the Galilean lake, in connection with which the disciples were betrayed into an unbelieving fear which provoked from their Master the rebuke, "Why are ye fearful, O ye of little faith?" In short, looking to the prominence of faith as a subject of remark in these miracle-histories, we may say that though Matthew in these chapters passes from discourse to deeds, he is still consciously exhibiting Jesus as a teacher. In the Sermon on the Mount he reports Christ's doctrine of *righteousness;* in the miracle section following he reports Christ's doctrine of *faith.*

It is unnecessary to point out in detail how the same intimate connection between miracle-histories and the doctrine of faith reappears in the companion Gospels. I hasten rather to observe that we discover in all three Synoptic Gospels a similar organic connection between miracles and other very important parts of Christ's teaching, among which may be particularly mentioned His doctrine concerning the *Sabbath* and His doctrine concerning the nature of *Pharisaism.* These doctrines were developed largely in an occasional manner, in connection with incidents in the life of Jesus and His disciples. The incidents were in part of a non-miraculous character. Thus a very important contribution to the doctrine of the Sabbath was made in connection with a supposed breach of the Sabbath law committed by the disciples in plucking the ears of corn.* Repeated opportunities for vivid depiction of Pharisaic religion were supplied by censures pronounced on the way of life of the Jesus-circle, in connection with the neglect of fasting and of ceremonial ablutions.† But the most remarkable utterances on both topics were connected with miraculous healings. It was in connection with the healing of the

* Matt. xii. 1; Mark ii. 23; Luke vi. 1.

† Matt. ix. 10; xv. 1: et parall.

withered hand on the Sabbath day, or some similar act, such as the cure of a dropsied man, that the "unforgetable, truly popular" saying, as Strauss very properly calls it, concerning the rescue of an animal fallen into a pit, was uttered. That the saying is a genuine utterance of Jesus no one doubts; and even Strauss admits that from the nature of the case it must have been spoken in connection with a healing act wrought on a Sabbath, though not necessarily a miraculous one.* It was in connection with the cure of a demoniac that Jesus brought His gravest charge against the Pharisees, that, viz., of approaching indefinitely near to the unpardonable sin of blasphemy against the Holy Ghost, by ascribing to Satanic agency what in their inmost hearts they knew to be of God. The whole discourse of Jesus on this occasion, whether in self-defence, or in rebuke of His implacable foes, implies an extensive activity on His part in the cure of demoniacs. A single act of the kind would not have sufficed to provoke the malicious suggestion that He derived His power from an infernal source. Some special act, doubtless, was the occasion of the blasphemy, but many acts were its cause. A department of work, habitual and conspicuous, engendered the mood which, at last at a particular moment, found expression in the daring, injurious, malevolent hypothesis.

The non-miraculous and the miraculous incidents with which these memorable controversies are found associated in the Gospel records must be accepted as alike historical. The former are unmistakably so. Who would ever dream, *e. g.*, of inventing the story about the plucking of the ears of corn? The latter must not be rejected merely because they happen to be miraculous. They must be received

* *Das Leben Jesu*, ii., p. 118.

without hesitation as a part of the history, all the more that they form only a part. Had all the occasions of conflict been miracles we might have suspected invention. As it is, we feel that miracles have a place among the incidents which gave rise to collisions, in the records, because they had a place in the actual history of Jesus.

2. A second fact now falls to be observed, which is the complement of the first. While forming an essential part of the Evangelic history the miraculous element is not unduly prominent. There is little trace in the Gospels of a miracle-mongering spirit, causing the writers to run into extravagance in describing miraculous events, or to multiply the number of miraculous narrations. The style of the miracle-histories, like that of the Gospels throughout, is calm, condensed, sober. There are doubtless perceptible differences. Comparing one Evangelist with another, Matthew's style is the most severely simple, while Mark's runs into pictorial or rhetorical detail in regard both to the circumstances of a miracle, and to the manner in which the miraculous act was performed. But this peculiarity of the second Evangelist appears in the non-miraculous parts of his narrative not less than in the miraculous; in his account of the beheading of the Baptist, or of the encounter between Jesus and the Pharisees in reference to ritual ablutions, as much as in the story of the palsied man, or of the woman with the bloody issue. It is a literary idiosyncrasy, not a sign of a superstitious love of the marvellous. There is indeed another literary phenomenon which may seem to prove that, not Mark alone, but all the Evangelists, recounted the wonderful works of Jesus in a highly emotional state of mind. They all append to their miraculous narrations, at least in many instances, statements concerning the impressions produced on spectators by the events they re-

late. The Synoptists, for the most part, describe the impressions produced on friends, while the author of the fourth Gospel records the impressions produced on foes; the former, as Strauss has remarked, winding up their reports with panegyric, the latter with polemic.* Thus the story of the palsied man, as reported by Matthew, closes with the words: "When the multitudes saw it, they marvelled, and glorified God, which had given such power unto men."† It is not, however, necessary to suppose that these eulogistic conclusions proceed from the heated mood of the writer; they may rather be regarded as originating in a desire to convey a true picture of Jesus as He appeared to His contemporaries. It was quite natural that the eyewitnesses, in relating the deeds of their Master, should also state how these struck beholders, giving special prominence to the favourable impressions made on the general multitude, though by no means glozing over the adverse temper of the Pharisees. Their report of these impressions would form a part of the Evangelic tradition, and so find its way into our Gospels. There is the less reason to suspect the trustworthiness of the panegyric sentences with which miraculous narratives conclude, that the reports of Christ's discourses are occasionally furnished with similar endings.‡

As to the number of the miracles, they amount in all, at most to thirty-five, not more than twenty being found in any one Gospel, and the bulk of miraculous narrative, even in the shortest Gospel, bearing only a moderate proportion to the whole history. In this connection it is important to notice that all the Gospels, and especially the first three, contain very express intimations that the number of mirac

---

* *Leben Jesu*, i., 708. † Matt. ix. 8.

‡ Matt. vii. 28, 29; Mark i. 22.

ulous works wrought was greatly in excess of the number recorded in detail. In all the Synoptists occur frequent paragraphs containing summary general reports of cures wrought in great numbers, similar to those of which their special reports present a few individual samples.* These paragraphs, it is true, may be interpreted in two ways: either as the exaggerations of men who knew little, and eked out scanty special accounts by general statements, or as the historically exact statements of men who knew on good information that much more happened than they actually relate in detail. That the latter is the more correct view may legitimately be inferred from the woe pronounced on the cities of the plain for their unbelief, notwithstanding the mighty works done in them.† That this woe was actually pronounced there is no reason to doubt, and that it was fully deserved may be regarded as equally certain; yet it is remarkable that with regard to two of the three cities named—Chorazin and Bethsaida, scarcely any information as to the works alleged to have been wrought is preserved in the records.‡ Clearly, therefore, many more "mighty works" were done than are individually reported, and it may be assumed that the general fact formed a well authenticated part of the evangelic tradition handed down from the apostles. Besides the general fact the tradition might contain special information as to times and places when and where miraculous cures were wrought in large numbers by Jesus, as, *e. g.*, concerning that memorable Sabbath evening

* Matt. iv. 29; viii. 16; ix. 35; xii. 15; xiv. 14, 36; xv. 30; xix. 2; xxi. 14; Mark i. 32, 39; iii. 10; vi. 55; Luke iv. 40; v. 15, 17; vi. 17; vii. 21; ix. 11; John ii. 23; vi. 2; vii. 31; xii. 37.

† Matt. xi. 20-24.

‡ The cure of a blind man reported in Mark viii. 22-26, occurred at Bethsaida on the *east* side of the Lake.

when at sunset the people of Capernaum brought their sick *en masse* to be healed.* Possibly this was all the Evangelists knew. We are not entitled to assume that they could have given many more individual narrations had they chosen, and that they offer their readers only a few samples of miracle-histories accessible to them in their sources. They probably all knew some more than they relate, but probably also not very many. The selection was not made by them; it existed to their hand in the apostolic tradition. The point to be remarked in reference to the Evangelists is not their moderation in selecting from ample stores of information supposed to be in their possession, but their abstinence from invention, when they knew that so much more had happened than they relate. Those general accounts of wholesale cures, taken along with the comparative paucity of individual accounts, create a strong impression of historical fidelity. Men not severely bent on adhering to fact would have been strongly tempted either to suppress the general reports, or to multiply the individual reports. Because they were honest men they have done neither. They have given us to understand that according to the apostolic tradition the cures wrought by Jesus were numbered not by tens but by hundreds or thousands, and they have been content to report in detail the miraculous acts which for some reason had become current, while the rest were suffered to fall into oblivion. The chief value to us of the general reports lies in the guarantee they supply for the trustworthiness of the special reports. By themselves they are comparatively monotonous and uninteresting, as all generalities are apt to be. But they serve to show

---

* Matt. viii. 16; Mark i. 32; Luke iv. 40.

two things: the boundless sympathy of Jesus, and the perfect sincerity of the Evangelists.*

If now the question be asked how these particular narratives contained in the Gospels came to survive, while so many more marvels faded out of remembrance, the answer is easy. An inspection of the records shows that the survival was due to some circumstances connected with the miracle which made it prominent by comparison with other acts of the same kind. Frequently the individualising element, if we may so call it, was some memorable word spoken on the occasion, whether by Jesus Himself, or by the recipient of benefit, or by spectators friendly or hostile. It is certain that the principle by which fitness to survive was determined cannot have been any supposed superior degree of miraculousness. Thus the cure of Peter's mother-in-law cannot have been deemed a specially great miracle. Evidently it owes its place in the records partly to its early position in the history, but chiefly to the connection of the person cured with a prominent apostle. Again the prominence assigned in the tradition to the raising of the ruler's daughter cannot have proceeded from its being considered a very striking example of the kind of miracle to which it belonged, for the narrative on the first blush at least leaves it open to doubt whether the raised one was really dead. The differentiating principle in that instance was the public position of the father, combined with the impressive contrast between the manner of sympathetic friends and professional mourners and the cheerfulness of Jesus pronouncing the maid to be not dead but only sleeping. It may seem indeed as if the companion-miracle of the healing of the woman with

* Keim thinks these general statements show that the fontal reports (Quell-berichte) of eye and ear witnesses had long since run dry. *Jesu von Nazara*, ii., 129.

the issue owed its preservation in the records to its distinctive miraculousness. As it is reported in Mark, and still more in Luke, it appears to belong to the class denominated by Strauss "involuntary healings," and to bear, as he suggests, an unpleasant resemblance to the ecclesiastical miracles wrought by the relics of saints.* I cannot here go into the question,† but merely remark that conceding all that Strauss alleges, it might have to be admitted that the Evangelic tradition had not kept itself entirely free of a superstitious element which has left its traces in some of the Gospels. But the miracle in question is related by all the three Synoptists, and it is certain that in the features of the story common to all the accounts no superstitious element can be discerned. The salient feature is the faith of the poor sufferer evinced by the thought manifested in act, that barely to touch the garment of Jesus would suffice for her cure. And I may add, it is faith which has immortalised a large proportion of the miracles and secured for them a place in the permanent records of the Gospel History. The infant church by a sure instinct perceived those faith-incidents to be of vital spiritual importance, and listened to them with keen appreciation as they fell from the lips of the apostles. That they marvelled at the miracles as such we need not deny, but they delighted more in the signal displays of faith recounted, and in the generous encomiums of Jesus. Cures at a distance, such as that of the centurion's servant, like cures by mere touch of Christ's garments, such as that of the woman, may have excited special admiration; but in the one case as in the other it was the faith that believed such cures to be possible that awakened the most lively interest. Such I

---

* *Leben Jesu*, ii., 94.

† *Vide* remarks in Lectures V. and VII. on this miracle.

conceive to have been the feeling of the apostolic church: such we plainly perceive to be the spirit pervading the Evangelic narratives.

In these remarks I have tried to explain how certain miraculous acts of Jesus came to be recorded, while many others in themselves not less remarkable were passed over. It remains to add that the attendant circumstances, while accounting for the record, are seldom of such a nature as to excite a suspicion that they not merely preserved but *created* the miracle. The connection between the main incident and its adjuncts, though intimate, is yet accidental. The words spoken suit the occasion, giving to the whole narrative an unmistakable air of reality; yet everything might easily have fallen out otherwise. This observation holds true especially of the Synoptical miracles. In reference to some of the Johannine miracles a different view, as already hinted, can plausibly be suggested. The discourses fit so closely to the miracles that the latter might seem to be fictitious events invented to serve as embodiments of ideas. The miracle says in act what the accompanying discourse says in words. Christ feeds the multitude, and then proceeds to proclaim Himself as the Bread of Life; He opens the eyes of a blind man, and then announces Himself as the Light of the world; He raises Lazarus, and then declares, "I am the Resurrection and the Life." But the first of these instances shows the need for caution in adopting such sceptical hypotheses. The fourth Gospel has the miracle of the Feeding in common with the Synoptists; had it stood alone in John's pages how confidently one might have affirmed it to be nothing but an emblem of the truth proclaimed in the discourse delivered in the synagogue of Capernaum! As the fact stands, there is more room for suspecting invention in connection with the discourse than in connection with the miracle.

3. The phenomena connected with the distribution of the miracles in the Gospels demand attention as suggesting distinctions as to degrees of credibility and importance, and raising questions as to the causes of omission or addition to the common stock, and the sources of incidents possessing only singular attestation. The place of honour in every respect must be assigned to the nucleus of eleven contained in the common tradition of the Synoptists; one of which, the feeding of the five thousand, occurs also in the fourth Gospel. These have been enumerated in last lecture. After these come those narrated in two, which are in all seven, thus distributed:

In Matthew and Mark, *four:*

Jesus walking on the sea. Matt. xiv. 22–33; Mark vi. 45–52; (John vi. 14–21).

The healing of the Canaanite woman's daughter. Matt. xv. 21–28; Mark vii. 24–30.

The feeding of the four thousand. Matt. xv. 32–39; Mark viii. 1–9.

The cursing of the fig-tree. Matt. xxi. 17–22; Mark xi. 12–14, 20–24.

In Matthew and Luke, *two:*

The healing of the Centurion's servant. Matt. viii. 5–13; Luke vii. 1–10.

The healing of the dumb demoniac. Matt. ix. 32, 33; Luke xi. 14.

In Mark and Luke, *one:*

The healing of a demoniac in Capernaum synagogue. Mark i. 23–26; Luke iv. 33–36.

Finally, there are those which are related only in a single Gospel, forming together a large group of seventeen distributed among the four Gospels as follows:

In Matthew, *three:*

The healing of two blind men. Chapter ix. 27–31.

The healing of a demoniac. Chapter xii. 22.

The finding of the stater. Chapter xvii. 24–27.

In Mark, *two:*

The healing of one deaf and dumb. Chapter vii. 31–37.

The opening of the eyes of one blind at Bethsaida. Chapter viii. 22–26.

In Luke, *six:*
- The miraculous draught of fishes. Chapter v. 7-11.
- The raising of the widow's son. Chapter vii. 11-17.
- The cure of the woman with a spirit of infirmity. Chapter xiii. 10-17.
- The cure of the dropsied man. Chapter xiv. 1-6.
- The cleansing of the ten lepers. Chapter xvii. 12-19.
- The healing of Malchus' ear. Chapter xxii. 49-51.

In John, *six:*
- The change of water into wine. Chapter ii. 1-11.
- The healing of the nobleman's son. Chapter iv. 46-54.
- The healing of the impotent man at Bethesda. Chapter v. 1-16.
- The opening of the eyes of one born blind. Chapter ix.
- The raising of Lazarus. Chapter xi. 1-54.
- The second miraculous draught of fishes. Chapter xxi. 1-23.

The first group—the eleven miracles of the *Triple Tradition*—contains samples of the three classes into which the Gospel miracles have been divided: those wrought on *Nature*, those wrought on the *body of man*, and those wrought on his spirit, or on the *spirit world.** To the first class belong the *feeding of the multitude* and the *stilling of the tempest:* to the last the *demoniac of Gadara* and the *lunatic boy.* All the rest exemplify Christ's power to heal the diseases to which the human body is liable, and even to conquer death in which physical diseases terminate. Comparing the list with the works Jesus claimed to have wrought in His message to the Baptist, we find that it contains samples of all the kinds of works there named except one. In the catalogue of miracles reported by the Synoptists "the blind receive their sight, the lame walk, the lepers are cleansed, and the dead are raised up," only the deaf do not hear. On the other hand, cures are wrought of which Jesus in that message made no mention, notably the cure

* For a classification of the Gospel Miracles, *vide* Westcott's *Characteristics of the Gospel Miracles.*

of demoniacs. Comparing the list once more with the miracles less fully attested we find examples of all the sorts contained in the latter. There are nature-miracles generically one with the *water turned into wine*, the *miraculous draught of fishes*, the *finding of the stater*, and the *cursing of the fig-tree.* There are instances of blindness, leprosy, palsy, and demoniacal possession cured answering to those reported by a single evangelist, and there is a raising from the dead which can be put alongside those reported by Luke and John. In short, the miracles of the common Synoptical tradition are *typical;* and thus, besides being themselves well accredited, they serve to accredit all the others. If they are accepted as historical, there is no *a priori* reason for being sceptical as to any of those which rest on the testimony of a single evangelist. It is true that distinctions may be drawn between miracles of the same class in the different lists, as to the degree of miraculousness. Thus it has been pointed out that there is a regular gradation in the three raisings from the dead. The daughter of Jairus is only just dead, if she be dead at all; the son of the widow is being carried out to burial; Lazarus has been dead and buried three days. It has been remarked concerning the whole group of Johannine miracles that they are few but great.* The lame man at Bethesda has been an invalid for thirty-eight years; the blind man was born blind; Lazarus has been so long dead that Martha thinks the process of corruption must have set in. But closely examined these quantitative distinctions amount to little. If the daughter of Jairus was really dead, her recall to life was as much above the course of nature as the resurrection of Lazarus. A man who has been paralysed for a year, and needs to be

---

* Strauss, *Leben Jesu*, ii., 74.

carried about on a stretcher, is as little likely to rise suddenly to his feet and shoulder his bed, as one whose malady has lasted for the best part of a lifetime. Blindness is blindness, whether it be congenital or be the accidental result of an injury to the optic nerve. It is as easy to cure ten lepers as one.

The eleven Synoptical miracles, it thus appears, cover the whole apologetic ground. Of the rest, some may or may not as matter of fact have happened. Defective attestation fairly enough raises that question, for it is legitimate to enquire: if Lazarus was raised from the dead, how came it to pass that so very important and conspicuous an event dropped out of the main current of evangelic tradition? But the eleven typical miracles which that current has brought down to us being accepted as facts, we have no speculative ground for objecting to any miraculous narrative however slenderly attested.

4. But reasons, to which I have not yet alluded, have been alleged for calling in question the historicity of even the best attested miracles. I refer to the phenomena of *discrepant relation.* The miracles of the common tradition are not reported by the Synoptists in precisely the same manner; in some instances the divergencies of the accounts are considerable, and have caused no little trouble to those who have deemed it necessary as matter of faith to bring the Evangelists into perfect accord. We must now, therefore, consider how this topic bears on the historic worth of the miraculous element in the Gospels.

What use Strauss makes of these discrepancies is well known. In the chapter on the Miracles of Jesus he steadily keeps two objects in view: to show, first, generally, that in the miraculous narrations of the Gospels we are not on the firm ground of history, but on the quaking bog of legend and second, specially, that in the variations of the Synoptists there is perceptible a steady progress from the less to the more marvellous, advancing from Matthew, through Luke, to Mark, in whose account the miracle reaches its maximum. Thus, to illustrate the second point by one or two instances, in the story of the Gadarene demoniac, in Matthew's account there are two demoniacs, so that we are not required to think of more than one demon in one man, while in the versions of Luke and Mark there is one demoniac and many demons, involving the specially marvellous phenomenon of multitudinous possession. In describing the demoniac, Matthew contents himself with a single phrase, "exceeding fierce." Luke substitutes for this the more repulsive feature of nakedness, while Mark completes the hideous picture by the accumulation of terrific details. In the description of the behaviour of the demoniac towards Jesus a similar gradation is observable. In Matthew the demoniacs, speaking as the mouthpiece of the demons, deprecate the approach of Jesus as a being whose presence bodes no good to them; in Luke, the unhappy subject of possession crouches at Christ's feet in abject fear; in Mark, seeing Jesus from afar, he runs towards Him and does Him obeisance!* The same growth in the marvellous is alleged to be perceptible in the story of the lunatic boy, in the accounts both of the behaviour of the multitude and of the condition of the sufferer. In Matthew, Jesus simply comes in contact with the multitude in descending from the Mount; in Luke, the multitude meet Him; in Mark, the multitude on seeing Him are greatly amazed, and running towards Him salute Him. Matthew describes the boy as an epileptic who suffers grievously, falling now into the fire, now into the water

* *Leben Jesu*, ii., 24-26.

Luke graphically depicts the action of the spirit on the subject of its evil influence, representing it as tearing him till he foams, bruising him sorely and hardly departing from him. Mark, not content with presenting a still more highly coloured picture, makes Jesus elicit further particulars by interrogating the father, the details combined yielding a most deplorable diagnosis of a disease at once repulsive and incurable. The tendency of the legend as it grows is obvious: to magnify the power of the wonder-working Jesus, the object of popular trust and admiration, the mighty One who could effect cures where others, even disciples, failed, and expel demons even where their grasp of the human subject was most obstinate.* In the story of the palsied man we are asked to see yet another instance showing how the marvellous, like a snowball, grew as it rolled. Matthew simply relates that they brought to Jesus a man sick of the palsy, lying on a bed. Luke tells how the friends who carried the sick man, finding the ordinary entrance blocked by the multitude, made their way to Jesus with their burden through an opening in the roof. Mark finally, not content with this display of zeal, represents the friends not as entering by the roof through an opening already existing, but as expressly uncovering the roof and digging their way through to the presence of Him in whom they placed their hope. The source of these ever-increasing exaggerations is, Strauss thinks, easy to discover. They sprang from a desire to exhibit, in as strong a light as possible, the unbounded extent of popular expectation of help from Jesus. Matthew states that Jesus took notice of "their faith." Luke and Mark seek by their descriptions to explain how the faith manifested itself, saying in effect: they took all this trouble,

---

* *Leben Jesu*, ii., 36.

because they were sure that their labour would not be in vain.*

Now with regard to this alleged growth of the marvellous element in the Synoptical accounts, to speak of that point first, I remark that the plausible and ingenious construction of Strauss tumbles into ruin, if there be any truth in the results arrived at by recent literary criticism in its investigations on the relations of the Synoptical Gospels. The argument of Strauss proceeds on the assumption that these Gospels came into existence in this order: Matthew first, Luke next, and Mark latest. But the whole tendency of recent discussions on the Synoptical problem is to show that Mark's Gospel was the earliest, not the latest, of the three. In this conclusion four such independent and competent investigators as Holtzmann, Weiss, Wendt, and Abbott are agreed, and their agreement is strengthened rather than weakened by the fact that they differ as to the precise relations subsisting between the Synoptists. The respective views of these scholars on that subject it is not necessary to indicate here at length. In last lecture I stated their rival hypotheses as to the primitive gospel in which the apostolic tradition first took written form.† The main diversity of view as to the relations between the three Gospels is that between Holtzmann and Weiss. The former of these scholars, in his work on the Synoptical Gospels previously referred to, maintains that the original Mark supplied the common historical basis for all the three, being most faithfully followed in the order of events by Mark, in some parts closely adhered to also by Matthew and Luke, but occasionally departed from widely through the perturbing influence of another source, the *Logia*, which is conceived to have been

* *Leben Jesu*, ii., 81, 82.

† *Vide* p. 99.

almost exclusively a collection of sayings.* Weiss, on the other hand, contends that the apostolic document compiled by Matthew was a common source for all the Synoptists; that it was a source not only for sayings, but for incidents miraculous or otherwise, and that the canonical Mark was a secondary source for the other two companion Gospels, the writer of the second Gospel deriving his inspiration not only from the common literary source, the original Matthew, but direct from the lips of apostles, and of Peter in particular. It will be seen that on either view the canonical Mark, though not the original Gospel, is the earliest of the three Synoptical Gospels, and that on the view of the more recent investigator the second Gospel, so far from being the latest, was actually in the hands of the writers to whom we owe the first and the third.

Without pronouncing dogmatically in favour of either of these rival theories, I cannot withhold my tribute of respect to the minute and careful researches on which they are based, and I must accept as highly probable the conclusion in which their advocates are at one, the relative priority of Mark. In that case the highly-coloured style of this Gospel in miraculous narrations, as compared with Matthew or even with Luke, assuming it to be a fact, must be otherwise accounted for than it is by Strauss. That the alleged literary characteristic is real, cannot, I think, well be denied. But I am disposed to regard it not as an impersonal feature due to

* In his recently published *Einleitung in das neue Testament* (1885), Holtzmann modifies his views on the Synoptical Problem in some particulars. He admits that the *Logia*, besides sayings, may have contained sketchy narrations in the form of historical frames of inseparable words of Jesus. He is now satisfied that Luke knew the first Gospel as well as the second, and acknowledges that with this admission at least most of the motives for distinguishing an *Urmarkus* from the canonical Mark fall away.

the action of the myth-forming spirit at work in the Christian community, but as a personal quality either of the writer or of the apostle whose oral accounts of evangelic incidents he reports. That a man of Peter's temperament should accumulate graphic details in describing events of which he had been a witness, I think quite natural, and that traces of his emotional style should appear in the pages of one who wrote under his inspiration, if not to his dictation, seems not less likely. That some of these traces, but only some, should be found in Luke, can easily be explained. Luke, according to his own statement, compiled his Gospel from documents, and there is reason to believe that the chief among them were the *Logia* of Matthew, and the Gospel of Mark. His style would naturally be eclectic, reflecting now the influence of one source, now of another, and occasionally borrowing something from both in the same narrative. This is just what we do find. Luke borrows from Mark some of his descriptive touches, but not all; sometimes showing a preference for the simpler style of Matthew, which in turn owes its parsimony in detail to a close adherence to a source in which brief narrations served as introductions to records of Christ's words.

Passing now to the use made by Strauss of discrepancy for the more general purpose of shaking our faith in the historicity of the narratives, there are two ways in which his sceptical tactics may be met. One is by elaborate processes of reconciliation to endeavour to show that the discrepancies in all cases are only apparent. This was the way of the old Harmonists, to whose strenuous efforts to clear the evangelic records of the smallest speck of error all respect is due. But their method is now out of date. Not that we may not still profitably occupy ourselves in bringing Synoptical accounts of the same incidents into agreement, or that this may not be successfully attempted in numerous instances. But for apologetic purposes the method is open to grave objections. It is based on an assumption as to the nature and consequences of inspiration, which is very embarrassing to the apologist. It commits him to a very difficult if not impossible task, that of proving that not a single real discrepancy exists. And the outcome of all his toil is not to convince adversaries, but to leave an impression of special pleading, which makes even believing minds not committed to theories, turn away from voluminous Harmonies of the Gospels with weariness. The other method is to admit that real discrepancies are *a priori* possible, and *a posteriori* probable, and that to all appearance some such do actually occur in the Gospels, and in the miraculous narratives in particular; but while making these admissions, to suggest modes of explaining their occurrence which shall be compatible with the fullest recognition of the historical value of the records on the whole. This method the literary criticism of the Gospels seeks to pursue with fair hopes of success. It suggests as the probable explanation of discrepancies, not vague, floating traditions of evangelic incidents, assuming various forms as they passed from mouth to mouth, but the somewhat uncritical use of written documents by honest but simple men unaccustomed to the art of constructing history as practised by a modern literary expert. The method is new and the solutions are conjectural and tentative, but they point to possibilities if not to certainties. One or two instances will explain the mode of procedure.

One of the most outstanding and best known discrepancies occurs in connection with the story of the demoniac of Gadara. In Matthew's account there are two demoniacs while in Mark's and Luke's there is only one. In a case of this kind the old Harmonistic assumed the accuracy of the account in which a plurality of personages concerned oc-curred, and reduced the divergent narratives into conformity with it on the principle that where two are, there is also one. The new method, on the contrary, assumes that only one demoniac was healed, and proceeds to enquire, how then it comes to pass that in Matthew's version of the story two are spoken of. The suggested solution is that the document on which that version is based contained only a brief account of the incident, making mention of one demoniac, but of a plurality of devils, and that the first evangelist simply inferred a plurality of persons possessed from the plurality of demons possessing. Weiss, who favours this view, uses it as an argument to prove that the *Logia* of Matthew must have contained the narrative of the Gadarene demoniac. The first evangelist, he holds, could not possibly have fallen into the mistake, had he followed his other source, the canonical Mark, where the true state of the case is so clearly brought out, viz., that the one demoniac believed himself to be possessed by a legion of devils. He must, therefore, have found in his other source, the apostolic Matthew, a version of the same story meagre enough in details to leave room for the mistaken inference.*

Another discrepancy of the same kind occurs in the narratives of the healing of a blind man at Jericho, where the first Gospel again introduces two subjects of Christ's curative influence. The Harmonists in this case had a double problem to solve, inasmuch as there is discrepancy, not only as to the number of persons cured, but as to the precise spot where the miracle was wrought—Matthew and Mark placing it at the exit from Jericho, while Luke places it at the entrance. The solution took the form of three miracles

---

*Vide *Jahrbücher für Deutscher Theologie*, 1865, p. 341.

of the same kind, at the same time, about the same neighbourhood, and with very much the same circumstances which seems very much like a *reductio ad absurdum* of this method of dealing with the phenomena of discrepancy. The new method disposes of the difficulties in a very different way. The divergence of Luke from the other Synoptists as to the locality may have arisen from his attending exclusively to the words with which Mark's account opens, "and they came to Jericho"; or it may have been a liberty taken to suit his convenience. He may have placed the opening of the blind man's eyes at the entrance into Jericho, because he had an interesting story to tell concerning Zacchæus the publican which was connected with the exit. The divergence of Matthew from his brother Evangelists as to the number of persons cured Weiss accounts for in this way The story of the miracle at Jericho has got mixed up with the healing of the two blind men reported by Matthew in chapter ix. 27–31. The confusion began with Mark, who borrowed from the latter incident, as reported in the common apostolic source, some of the details to fill up the narrative of blind Bartimæus, such as the title, "Son of David," addressed to Jesus, the question put by Jesus to the blind man to draw out his faith, and the declaration of Jesus, "Thy faith hath made thee whole." Then the author of our first Gospel, coming after Mark, and perceiving that he had made use of the narrative of the apostolic source reported by himself in a previous part of his Gospel, took it to be the same occurrence reported with fuller detail, and introduced at its proper historical place, and so repeated the tale as given by Mark, only putting two blind men in place of one.*

* *Vide* Article in *Jahrbücher*, p. 335, and *Das Leben Jesu*, ii., 427.

The story of the man with a withered hand presents a problem of a somewhat different character. Here Luke follows Mark closely, and both differ from Matthew in two particulars. They represent the Pharisees as watching Jesus to see whether He would heal the sufferer on the Sabbath day, while Matthew makes them ask Him the question: Is it lawful to heal on the Sabbath?—the end in both cases being the same: viz., "that they might accuse Him." On the other hand, instead of the concrete example taken from their own conduct, with which Jesus, in Matthew's version, answers their captious question, Mark and Luke put into the mouth of Jesus, by way of reply to the secret thoughts of the fault-finders, the question which, according to Matthew, they had put to Him. On turning to the narrative of another Sabbath healing, given by Luke in the fourteenth chapter of his Gospel, we find a further complication. There the question concerning the lawfulness of well-doing on the Sabbath recurs, with the slight difference that it is ascribed to Jesus instead of to the Pharisees, and Jesus replies to the question by the same illustration of an animal (ox, ass, or sheep) fallen into a pit which, according to the first Evangelist, He employed in self-defence on the occasion of His healing the withered hand.* Indeed, the two incidents are altogether so like that one is tempted to think it is the same story repeated, with the change of the ailment from a withered limb into dropsy. If that view were adopted, we should have a case somewhat parallel to the substitution in Matt. xii. 22, 23, of a blind and dumb demoniac for the dumb one of chapter ix. 32, 33, assuming that both passages refer to the same event. The discrepancies in the accounts of the residuary miracle would then have to be explained by sup-

* The resemblance is less close when, for the reading in T. R., we substitute that approved by the critics, υἱός instead of ὄνος. *Vide* Lecture V.

posing that Matthew adhered closely to the original narrative of the apostolic source, while Mark reproduces the story in a somewhat free version, and Luke at this point takes Mark as his guide. This theory, however, is open to the two serious objections that it ascribes to Luke a considerable liberty taken with his text, in changing the disease, and a somewhat grave inadvertence in relating, in an earlier part of his work, the healing of the withered hand, following Mark, and then repeating further on the same story, in substance, as taken from the apostolic source, without perceiving the identity of the histories. Accordingly, one is not surprised to find Weiss, who had previously advocated this view* in his *Leben Jesu*, propounding another hypothesis. It is to the effect that Luke took from the apostolic source, without material change, the story of the dropsied man; that Mark was the original authority for the story of the withered hand, in which again Luke faithfully adhered to his source; and that Matthew, in his version, mixed up the two stories.†

This change of opinion puts us on our guard against regarding such solutions as more than conjectures. I do not, therefore, make myself responsible for them. On the contrary, in these, as in many other instances, the critical handling of the Gospels by the author referred to, appears to me too free, and I believe that, without regard to any theoretical claims based on inspiration, a much larger measure of historical accuracy may be ascribed to the Evangelic narratives than he seems prepared to allow. Nevertheless I plead for the legitimacy of such attempts at solving problems connected with discrepancies in parallel accounts, in their own place and for their own purpose. I deprecate hasty

* Vide *Jährbucher* for 1865, p. 339.

† *Das Leben Jesu*, ii., pp. 49–53.

condemnation of them, or indignant interdict against them in the name of dogmatic theories of inspiration, and *a priori* inferences of inerrancy. Let the propounders of such solutions have fair hearing and full opportunity. They do not offer them in an apologetic interest; for the literary critics disclaim apologetic intentions, and claim to be animated solely by scientific love of truth. But their suggestions, nevertheless, are not without apologetic value. It is something to know that if errors in details must be admitted, they had their probable origin in the use of documents unquestionably containing miraculous accounts, and sometimes arose from an Evangelist having before him two independent documents not themselves in conflict. It is something to see how errors may have arisen, and so to find a clue to the historical fact. It may be disappointing to find that the compilers of the Gospels did not possess perfect skill in the use of materials, and that it was possible for them to fall into such mistakes as the critics impute to them. But the historic value of records produced by the most unskilful use of documents is incomparably greater than that belonging to a mass of unaccredited legends. A criticism which, in eliminating some miraculous narratives as duplicates, gives increased certainty as to those which remain, is certainly better than the criticism that throws everything loose, and leaves us in doubt whether there was any residuum of miraculous fact at all.

5. I have now to notice, lastly, what may be called the singularities of the Evangelists in reference to the miraculous element. These may be classed under the two heads of omissions and additions. To the former belong cases in which one of the Synoptic Evangelists omits miracles narrated by the other two. The latter head includes all miracles reported only in one Gospel. The title "omis-

sions" implies that the writer of the Gospel in which an omission occurs was acquainted with the miracle omitted, and might have narrated it had he chosen. If an omission can be accounted for, a miracle reported by only two Synoptists may be virtually as well attested as if it had been given by all the three.

We have to do here mainly with Luke and John. The omissions and additions of the first two Evangelists are comparatively few. Matthew's solitary omission is the healing of the demoniac in the synagogue of Capernaum, and it can without much difficulty be explained. It is quite plain that the first Evangelist desired as speedily as possible to get at the Sermon on the Mount in which the transcendent wisdom of Jesus is revealed. Therefore he passed over several matters narrated by Mark at the beginning of his Gospel, including the miracle in question, and also the healing of Peter's mother-in-law, and the short account of many cures in the evening of the same Sabbath day. In these sections Luke follows Mark closely, and so we may assume would Matthew have done, but for the reason above assigned; for there is good ground to believe that the general plan of the Synoptical sketch of the public ministry of Jesus is to be found in the second Gospel, and that it is adhered to in the first and third except when disturbing influences come in to cause deviation. What then does Matthew do with these omitted sections? Does he go back upon them after the sermon is ended, and take them in, in a subsequent chapter? He does in part, bringing in the cure of Peter's mother-in-law, and the account of the Sabbath-evening cures, in the eighth chapter. But he overlooks the story of the Capernaum demoniac, and why? Apparently because he relates the miracles, like the words, of Jesus in groups, giving samples of the different kinds, and as the group included the story of the Gadarene demoniac the less remarkable Caper naum incident might be dispensed with.

Of the three additions in Matthew the most important is the story of the stater in the fish's mouth. The narrative of the blind and dumb demoniac (chapter xii. 22) is very meagre, and seems to serve merely as a peg whereon to hang the solemn discourse in which Jesus defended Himself against the charge of being in league with Satan. As already hinted, it seems to be a duplicate of the healing of the dumb demoniac recorded in chapter ix. 32, and with equal brevity by Luke, chapter xi. 14. The healing of two blind men in a house* contains, as has been shown in a previous paragraph, features closely resembling those of the story of the blind man at Jericho. On the other hand, the story of the stater is unique. Though reported only by one Evangelist there can be no reasonable doubt as to its historical truth, for the words ascribed to Jesus, in their very originality, bear the unmistakable stamp of genuineness. Whether a miracle was intended, or really happened, is a question on which there may be room for doubt; but it may be accepted as certain that the conversation between Peter and his Master reported in the canonical Matthew found a place in the *Logia* compiled by the apostle of the same name. That the first Evangelist alone has preserved the precious fragment may be due in part to his following more closely the apostolic document than his brother Evangelists, and in part to his better insight into the connection between the conversation on the temple-tax, and the dispute of the disciples on the way to Capernaum concerning places of distinction, and the ensuing discourse on humility and kindred virtues.

---

* Matt. ix. 27–31.

In Mark there are two omissions. He makes no reference to the dumb demoniac, to whose cure Matthew and Luke attach the discourse concerning casting out devils, but reports the discourse without any historical introduction, simply placing the evil thoughts of the Pharisees side by side with the less injurious opinion of the multitude, who merely imagined Jesus was beside himself.* This omission scarce needs explanation. But the other is more surprising. One wonders how any Evangelist acquainted with it could pass over so remarkable an incident as that of the Capernaum centurion. Prudential considerations arising out of a supposed neutrality between Judaists and Paulinists can hardly have influenced one who has preserved the kindred narrative of the Syrophenician woman. Advocates of a Proto-Mark suggest that the miracle has fallen out of the canonical Mark along with the Sermon on the Mount, both being supposed to have found a place in the original source.† But this is only to say that the omission forms part of a larger one still more in need of explanation. Perhaps the best account that can be given of the matter is that the narrative in question did not fall naturally under any of the points of view which guided the Evangelist in compiling his Gospel. The first section of his history has for its obvious aim to show the rapidly growing fame of Jesus at the commencement of His Galilean ministry; in connection with which the healing of the leper might appropriately be related. The next section exhibits the initial phase of the conflict between Jesus and the Pharisees, which the healing of the palsied man and of the man with the withered hand well served to illustrate. The story of the centurion, not coming under either category, was allowed to drop out.

---

* Mark iii. 22.

† So Holtzmann. Vide *Die Synoptischen Evangelien*, p. 78.

Mark's additions are chiefly remarkable as samples of an occasional tendency to give details concerning the miraculous act which invest it with the aspect of a gradual physical process. Baur, bent on proving the dependence of the second Evangelist on the first and third, denies the claim of these two narratives to be regarded as independent contributions to the stock of evangelic history. In the cure of the deaf and dumb man he sees only a specialization of one of the cases reported by Matthew in general terms, and in the cure of the blind man at Bethsaida only a copy of the other miracle with its essential features reproduced. It is only in keeping with this view that he should detect in the means of cure specified in both cases traces of the materialised idea of miracles of a later time, which could no longer be content with the simple wonder-working word, but desired to have the miracle made palpable, by the introduction of middle causes, whereby it became at the same time magical, mysterious, apocryphal.* Unsophisticated readers with no theory to make out, will recognise in the suspected features touches from life, and will not be disposed to grudge Mark these modest additions to the miraculous element.

Three of Luke's four omissions probably had a common cause. The walking on the sea, the Syrophenician woman, and the second feeding form part of one large omission which covers nearly two chapters in each of the first two Gospels, and includes, besides these incidents, the encounter between Jesus and the Pharisees concerning ritual ablutions. If the reason which influenced the Evangelist was the same for all the omitted narratives, it could hardly be either ignorance, indifference, or doubt; for the last mentioned narrative, that relating to ceremonial washings, has

* *Die Kanonischen Evangelien*, pp. 557–8.

a prominent place both in Matthew and in Mark, and is one of the most important and best accredited in the Gospel History. It almost seems as if Luke had been in haste to get to that portion of his materials in which most that is peculiar to his Gospel occurs, and so passed at a bound from the feeding of the five thousand to the confession of Peter at Cæsarea Philippi, giving continuity to the narrative by using the scene at the close of the former event—Jesus alone in the mountains praying—as an introduction to the latter.* Special reasons for some of the omissions may be conjectured. The story of the Syrophenician woman might be distasteful to the Pauline Evangelist, or at least seem to him liable to misconstruction. While really universalistic in tendency, its drift is not apparent on the surface. The word put into the mouth of Jesus restricting His mission to Israel, and the comparison of Gentiles to dogs, lend to Christ's attitude towards the Pagan world an aspect of grudging which might easily be abused by Judaistic partisans. The second feeding might be omitted because deemed superfluous, although in other cases we find Luke reporting two kindred incidents of which his brother Evangelists report only one, the most notable instance being the mission of the seventy added to that of the twelve. In view of the latter fact we are not justified in inferring from the omission that Luke regarded the two feedings as different versions of the same event, for similar reasoning ought to have led him to the conclusion that the two missions were one. In both cases striking resemblances exist which have induced many modern critics to find in the second event only a duplicate of the first, arising out of variations in the narrative.† The question, regarded from a purely crit-

---

* Compare Luke ix. 18 with Matt. xiv. 23, Mark vi. 46.

† Such is the view of Weiss; vide *Das Leben Jesu*, ii., 117, 186.

ical point of view, is a difficult one, on which opinion will probably always be divided, and into which I cannot go here. I must be content to leave it unsettled, so far as the second feeding is concerned, and to recognise it as possible that we have here an instance of a duplicate narrative of one and the same miracle. I merely add the remark that Luke would have been less likely to omit the second feeding had he shared the opinion of some that the recipients of benefit in this instance were *Gentiles.**

The fourth omission might be explained by the jealousy of the Evangelist for the gracious side of Christ's character. In so far as the cursing of the fig-tree was an emblem of judgment impending over the Jewish people, its lesson is anticipated in the parable of the barren fig-tree, in which, however, Jesus, under the guise of the gardener, plays the more congenial part of an intercessor pleading that a year of grace be given to the cumberer of the ground.† It has been suggested that in omissions like those of the cursing of the fig-tree and the story of the Syrophenician woman, having for their aim or effect the removal from the Gospel history of elements which appeared not easily reconcilable with the love of Christ or with the universal destination of Christianity, the Evangelist may not have acted on his individual responsibility, but may simply have followed a "Gentile use" which had gradually sprung up in certain churches and was not created but adopted by him.‡ We need not, however, shrink from the admission that the humane and catholic spirit of Luke guided him in selecting his materials, apart altogether from any supposed Gentile use pre-existing. We

* So Hilary, in Comment. in Matthaeum, cap. xv., and after him Westcott in *Characteristics of the Gospel Miracles*, p. 12.

† Luke xiii. 6.

‡ So Dr. Abbott in article *Gospels*.

can trace its influence not merely in his omissions, but also in his additions to the stock of miraculous narrative.

All these additions bear more or less distinctly impressed on them the stamp of *humanity;* and in one, the cure of the ten lepers, the spirit of universalism finds expression, the point of interest being that one of the ten, and he the thankful one, was a *Samaritan.* The miraculous draught of fishes symbolises the ingathering by Peter and his brother apostles of many saved men into the kingdom of God; the raising of the young man at Nain is an act of kindness to a widowed, childless mother; the cures of the woman bowed down with a spirit of infirmity, and of the dropsied man, are spontaneous deeds of compassion; the healing of Malchus' ear is the reparation by a gentle, forgiving master of the injury done by a rash, headlong disciple.* The fact of their possessing this character is no reason for suspecting these miracles as mere inventions. We may assume that for all his peculiar narratives Luke found vouchers among his sources, and that his function was that of a selecter with a quick eye for whatever was best fitted to exhibit the Christian religion as a religion of grace, and therefore as a religion for the whole world. We are not entitled dogmatically to assert, as a point beyond discussion, that they are all original contributions. The miraculous draught of fishes has affinities with a similar narration in the concluding chapter

* Westcott (*Characteristics of the Gospel Miracles*, p. 63) remarks: "*The healing of Malchus*, which is mentioned by Luke, while the other Evangelists only speak of his wound, seems to lie without the true cycle of the Evangelic miracles. In this Christ is seen to meet and remedy the evils which are wrought among men by the false zeal of His own followers." One is tempted to regard this weakly accredited miracle as an inference, not necessarily first drawn by the Evangelist, from the well-known benevolence of Christ. Christians would be ready to think that of course Jesus must have healed the wounded ear.

of John's Gospel, which have led many to identify the two and to find in Luke's version a transference to the beginning of the history of what really happened at the end. In that case the third Evangelist's account, though the earlier published, would be secondary in relation to the apostolic tradition. The cures of the woman with a spirit of infirmity and of the dropsied man are Sabbatic miracles, having manifest points of contact with the cure of the man with the withered hand. They are probably all three independent incidents; certainly the first named has every appearance of being an original story found by Luke in a source not accessible to the other Synoptists; but that the other two are variants of the same incident may be admitted to be possible.

The possible identity of the miraculous draught of fishes related in John's Gospel, with that recorded by Luke, has already been adverted to. Another of John's miracles has such affinities with one in the Synoptical lists as to suggest the hypothesis of its being a duplicate. It is the cure of the nobleman's son, narrated in the close of the fourth chapter. I do not propose here to discuss the question, or to express any personal opinion on it. I simply defer so far to the opinions of believing critics like Weiss as to recognise the identity of John's nobleman with the Synoptical centurion as possible, while very sensible of the difficulty of reducing the two stories to even radical unity. Deducting these two, and the other two which the fourth Gospel indisputably has in common with the Synoptists—the *feeding of the multitude* and the *walking on the sea*—there remain four which moderate critics, not bent on establishing purely sceptical theories, recognise as genuine, distinctively Johannine miracles, viz.: the *change of water into wine*, the *healing of the impo tent man at Bethesda*, the *opening of the eyes of the blind man*, and the *raising of Lazarus.*

These miracles, and indeed nearly all the miracles recorded in the fourth Gospel, have a markedly different character from the additions of Luke, and, I may say, from the Synoptical miracles generally. The Synoptical miracles are, in the main, miracles of *humanity;* the Johannine miracles are, so to speak, miracles of *state.* They are wrought for the purpose of glorifying the worker. The account of the first miracle has appended to it the reflection: "This beginning of miracles did Jesus in Cana of Galilee, and manifested forth His glory; and His disciples believed on Him,"* and the sentiment recurs as a refrain in the other miraculous narratives. The miracles are, in fact, acts of humanity, but, from the point of view of the narrator, if not of the actor, that seems an accident. It was a deed of compassion to heal the man who had an infirmity of thirty-eight years' duration, but there were many more sick persons at the pool besides him, yet he alone is reported to have been cured, selected apparently to exhibit Jesus conspicuously as a fellow-worker with the Father. In the Synoptical Gospels how often do we read, "and He healed them *all.*"

It cannot be denied that the Synoptical presentation of Christ's miraculous activity appeals to our sympathies more than the Johannine. But the prejudice thence arising against the fourth Gospel may be removed, or mitigated, by the following considerations. The glory which is represented as the aim of the miracles is not of the vulgar, worldly kind. Glorification and humiliation are close of kin, or virtually identical, in John's Gospel. Jesus, on hearing of the sickness of Lazarus, says, "this sickness is not unto

* John ii. 11.

death, but for the glory of God, that the Son of God might be glorified thereby."* But how did the sickness contribute to Christ's glorification? As the exit of the traitor did—† by causing His crucifixion. Then the Evangelist evidently did not make it a part of his plan to give anything like an adequate account of Christ's miraculous ministry. He knew that he gave only a small selection from a large number of miracles; for, in the summary at the close of the twelfth chapter, he makes it a ground of accusation against the Jews that, though Jesus had done *so many* miracles before them, yet they believed not in Him.‡ He took for granted the acquaintance of his readers with the Synoptical tradition, and made his own contributions to the store of Christ's miraculous deeds with a particular purpose in view. Finally, the fourth Evangelist does not give a full account of Christ's motives as a miracle-worker, any more than of His miraculous works. He gives the miracles a special setting for a didactic purpose. Jesus works with a conscious theological aim in his pages, but not necessarily therefore in fact. Result is converted into intention. We can see for ourselves, as the miraculous narrative proceeds, that there was more in Christ's heart than the Evangelist emphasises. Jesus weeps at the grave of Lazarus.§ Love is the motive of the miracle, not merely a desire that the Son of God may be glorified. If we wish to carry away a just impression we must attend, not merely to the preface, but to the body of the story. I do not mean to suggest that the Evangelist invented the prefaces; but I certainly think that, if a free activity of the writer's mind is to be recognised at all in this Gospel, it is in the account of Christ's words rather than in that of His deeds.

---

* John xi. 4. † John xiii. 31. ‡ John xii. 37. § John xi. 35.

The conclusion of our enquiry is that, making due allowance for possible duplicates, there are in the four Gospels some thirty narratives of events ostensibly miraculous. Accepting these accounts as authentic, the question arises, how far are the ostensible miracles real? That is a question on which exegesis may have something to say.

V.

THE GOSPEL MIRACLES IN RELATION TO EXEGESIS—THE HEALING MIRACLES OF THE TRIPLE TRADITION.

It is not proposed to consider in detail all the thirty miracle-narratives with the view of ascertaining in regard to each of them in succession whether it contains a miraculous element. It will suffice to consider the healing miracles of the Triple Tradition as representing the class to which they belong, and the nature-miracles. The former shall form the subject of this lecture, the latter of the next.

The series modestly begins with *the healing of Peter's mother-in-law*,* in which the humanities are more conspicuous than miraculous power. The incident owes its preservation, doubtless, not to its being considered a specially great miracle, but to its being one of the earliest, and to the fact of its having occurred in the home of one of the future apostles, one of the most distinguished of their number.

The disease healed was a fever, a malady to which the dwellers on the shores of the Galilean lake with its hot, damp climate would be specially liable. From the account of Mark, taken from the lips of Peter, it is manifest that the sickness cannot have been of long duration, that indeed it must have come on after the disciple left the house to attend worship in the synagogue. On returning home he brought with him Jesus, his own brother Andrew, and James and John, as guests, expecting to find all well.

* Matt. viii. 14, 15; Mark i. 29–31; Luke iv. 38, 39.

Surprised and disappointed to discover that his relative was laid down on a sick-bed, he reported the unwelcome news to Jesus, partly by way of apology for her inability to serve, partly also, it may be, with expectations of a cure awakened by the remarkable occurrence he had just witnessed in the synagogue, the healing of a demoniac.

The sudden illness might have been nothing more than a feverish attack, and the fact that no effort is made in what may be regarded as the primary narrative to make it appear something more serious, shows how far the writer was from being under the influence of a morbid love of the marvellous. Luke, on the other hand, might plausibly be charged with a tendency to make the most of the miracle. Magnifying phrases certainly do occur in his narrative. The sick one is represented as taken with a "great fever"; Jesus standing over her *rebukes* the fever as He had rebuked the demon in the synagogue, and as on a subsequent occasion He rebuked the wind, as if in presence of a mighty, hostile power. The patient being cured, *immediately* rises up and serves her guests. The expression "great fever" may be either a technical one used by Luke as a physician to indicate that it was a regular serious fever,* not a mere feverish attack, or it may be a merely rhetorical one employed for the same purpose. Taken in the latter sense, it reminds us of a similar expression in the same Evangelist's version of the parable of the mustard seed, in which the mustard plant is represented as becoming "a great tree."† These heightening phrases, however, do not necessarily exaggerate the fact; they may merely indicate a desire to bring out more

* *Vide* Wetstein *in loco,* who quotes Galen and others to show that physicians were wont to distinguish between great fevers and minor fevers.

† Luke xiii. 19, but the reading μέγα is very doubtful.

clearly and fully the actual state of the case as familiarly known in the apostolic church.

Naturalism finds the simple story perfectly credible, and the cure quite natural. This first miracle, says Keim, has a power of conviction like no other. The mitigation of a fever, through a probably unintentional approach, the restoration of clear, bright consciousness by the return of the son-in-law, and yet more by the presence of the honoured guest, through His mild, cheering word, and the sympathetic touch of His hand, assisted by a housewife's sense of honour in reference to the duties of hostess—this is all so plain and humanly natural that we could believe in the recurrence of such an event now.* It may be so, but all this implies that the fever was slight, or that after the excitement of the day was over it returned and ran its course. In that case it is difficult to understand how it ever came to be talked about even in credulous Galilee, or found a place in the evangelic records; especially difficult to comprehend how it could make so profound an impression as to cause the assembling of a great multitude on the evening of the same day bringing their sick to be healed.†

The miracle wrought in the house of Simon has this peculiarity, that the disease cured, however severe, was temporary, whereas the objects of Christ's healing ministry were usually persons suffering under chronic maladies. It has been thought necessary to find a reason for this exception, and it has been suggested that Jesus took advantage of such opportunity as offered to supply to a nascent group of dis-

---

* Vide *Jesu von Nazara*, ii., 220.

† Keim regards the healing of the demoniac in the synagogue as unhistorical, and therefore is obliged to ascribe the excitement in Capernaum not to it, but to what happened in Peter's home.

ciples a sign that the kingdom of heaven was at hand.* Less formal or far-fetched is the idea of Schleiermacher, that as the matron of the house had been disabled for service, Jesus freed her from sickness that she might be able to attend to her duties.† Most felicitous is the hint of Calvin, who calls the miracle "*domesticum et interius gratiae suae specimen.*" ‡ It was a domestic miracle, which restored sunshine to a home that had been suddenly darkened by the shadow of disease, wrought by one whose vocation it was to bring peace and health wherever he sojourned, and who could not without incongruity remain under the same roof with grief or trouble.

In the story of the *Leper*,§ which comes next in the series, we are brought more unmistakably into the presence of the miraculous. The sudden cure of a case of leprosy is not so easily explained away as the cure of a feverish attack, or even of a "great fever." The deadly malady was deeply rooted in the flesh, which it consumed piecemeal, and was not to be charmed away by psychical influences: by the sympathy of the benevolent, or by faith and hope somehow awakened in the breast of the sufferer. The only alternatives open to naturalism, therefore, are: either with Strauss to deny the historicity of the narrative and resolve it into a myth, or to fall back on the exegetical device of Paulus, and to find in the occurrence not a cure, but merely a judgment of Jesus on the case of a leper already convalescent to the effect that he was clean. Keim oscillates between these alternatives, candidly owning that, failing both, the admission of a miracle cannot easily be avoided. In support of the mythical hypothesis stress is laid on the exaggerative elements in

* Steinmeyer, *The Miracles of our Lord*, 53.

† *Das Leben Jesu*, p. 220. ‡ *Comment. in quatuor Evangelistas.*

§ Matt. viii. 1–4; Mark i. 40–45; Luke v. 12–16.

the accounts—Matthew's environing crowd of witnesses Mark's sensational report of the great impression made by the cure; Luke's description of the person healed as a man *full of leprosy;* on the symbolic significance of leprosy as an emblem of sin, and on the prominence which the cure of his disease has in the Old Testament, especially in the histories of Moses and Elisha. Yet withal it is felt to be impossible to treat the incident as purely unhistorical, in view particularly of the threefold tradition, and the injunction of Jesus to the leper to go and show himself to the priest, which bears a stamp of reality not to be gainsaid. Therefore recourse finally is had to the other alternative—not healed, but only pronounced clean. That is to say, we are to understand that Jesus did nothing more than the priest did when a convalescent leper presented himself for inspection. If it is asked why the man should seek this small boon, the reply is, to save the trouble and expense of going to Jerusalem. If it is further asked, why seek such a boon from Jesus? the answer is, because He was a Rabbi, not to say the Christ; and already the scribes had encroached on the prerogatives of the priest, and taken upon them to pronounce lepers clean. A third query naturally suggests itself: if this was what Jesus did, why insist on the leper going to the priest to have done a second time what had been done already? The answer is, because while willing to comfort the sufferer, depressed in spirit by a long illness, by an assuring word, and a sympathetic touch, Jesus desired to keep His own place, and to give the priests theirs. But, once more it may be asked, how account for the sensation produced by the event if this was all that happened? All the answer that is forthcoming is that the people were struck with admiration at the heroic philanthropy and resolution of Jesus.*

* *Jesu von Nazara*, ii., 172–5.

This rationalistic view of the narrative, as presented by Paulus, was so severely handled by Strauss in his first *Leben Jesu* that one cannot help thinking that nothing but desperation could have induced such a writer as Keim to revive it. The criticism of the author of the mythical theory is at once acute and forcible. Its gist is as follows: If the reply of Jesus to the request of the leper, "I will, be thou clean," merely meant, "I declare thee clean," how superfluous the added words of the Evangelist Matthew, *καὶ εὐθέως ἐκαθερίσθη ἀυτοῦ ἡ λέπρα*,* which in that case would mean "his leprosy was declared clean." Further, on this view we must conceive the words *θέλω, καθαρίσθητι* as separated in utterance by an interval of time, during which Jesus examined the symptoms to see whether He could pronounce the leper technically clean. First He says, "I am willing if I can," then proceeds to ascertain the state of the case; then, after the lapse perhaps of some minutes, pronounces the opinion, "you are clean." How utterly contrary this division of the two words into as many sentences to the impression produced by them as they stand in the pages of all the three Evangelists. Then to what end remove miracle from this narrative so long as you have a claim to the performance of similar miracles put into the mouth of Jesus elsewhere, as in the message to the Baptist where we read, "the lepers are cleansed." †

These observations, based on the simplest and probably the primary version of the story, that of the first Gospel, leave hardly any room for doubt that, in the sense of the Evangelist, what is reported is a cure, not a medical opinion. That the other Evangelists thus understood the matter is conceded, and is indeed self-evident from the manner in

---

* Matt. viii. 3.

† *Leben Jesu*, ii., 47.

which they describe the result. Matthew's word ἐκαθερίσθη is ambiguous, and might mean not only "was cleansed" in the sense of healed, but "was pronounced clean." But Luke, as if with express design to eliminate the ambiguity, avoids the word and says, "immediately his leprosy departed from him." Mark, retaining the word, associates with it Luke's expression, and says, "his leprosy departed from him, and he was cleansed," not thereby stating two different facts, but simply stating the same fact in two different ways, so supplying an instance of the duality characteristic of his literary style.

It confirms us in the conviction that the narrative before us is the account of a veritable cure when we find, as we do, that only on that view do all its details become invested with a worthy, serious meaning. How deeply significant do the "if thou wilt" of the leper, and the "I will" of Jesus, preserved in all the versions, become when we understand that a cure was asked and granted! The man had learnt enough of Christ's power to believe that He could, but he had not yet learnt enough of His love to be sure that He would. He feared that He might shrink from him in involuntary disgust. The solemn, deliberate "I will" of Jesus was meant to assure him on that score. Already by a touch He has given the most convincing demonstration of a sympathy victorious over loathing, and now He adds the corresponding word expressive at once of sympathy and of power. On the rationalistic hypothesis the leper's doubt would have reference to Christ's willingness to usurp a function properly belonging to the priests. Courage, not love, would be the thing in question.

The injunction laid upon the leper becomes intelligible on the hypothesis that a miraculous cure was wrought on him. "See thou tell no man, but go show thyself to the priest." Why this interdict of speech if all that happened was that the leper was declared clean? Was Jesus afraid to let it be known that He had taken it upon Him to pronounce such an opinion? Then it would appear that the leper after all was justified in doubting his courage. How unlike Jesus this unheroic timidity. He was never afraid to let all men know that He had done whatever He deemed it right to do. But assume that the true state of the case was that Jesus wrought a cure, and left it to the priest to declare the patient cured, and all becomes clear, natural, and Christlike. Two things had to be done to make the benefit complete. The disease had to be healed, whereby the sufferer would be delivered from the physical evil; and it had to be authoritatively declared healed, whereby the sufferer would be delivered from the social disabilities imposed by the law upon lepers. Jesus conferred one half of the blessing, and He sent the leper to the priest to receive from him the other half. He did this, not in ostentation or by way of precaution, not to parade His power before the sacerdotal officials, or to prevent misconstruction, but chiefly, if not exclusively, out of regard to the man's good, that he might be restored not only to health but to society. Hence also the injunction of silence. From the narratives of Mark and Luke it might be inferred that the motive was to prevent unhealthy excitement among the people by the report of the miracle. But that at most was only a secondary aim. The primary end concerned the man healed. Jesus wished to prevent him from contenting himself with half the benefit, rejoicing in restored health and telling everybody he met about it, and neglecting the steps necessary to get himself universally recognised as healed. Apparently this was just what he did: making a great talk about his cure, and doing nothing more. The temptation to this course was great. How difficult for one who had long suffered under a horrible disease to keep silence about his deliverance. Then it would seem that custom had to a certain extent broken down the law which excluded lepers from the society of their fellow-men. One evidence of this is supplied in the fact that a leper could come into the presence of Jesus, in the midst of a multitude, as Matthew relates, or in a city, according to Luke, or even in a house or synagogue, as Mark's narrative seems to imply.* The cause of this laxity may have been knowledge of the fact, now generally recognised by physicians, that leprosy, though loathsome to sight, was not contagious. Be this as it may, in any case there was great danger of the healed man thinking that if he was well it did not much matter what either priest or people thought. In view of this we comprehend the sternness with which Jesus delivered His injunction, a feature which we owe to Mark, who at this point doubtless had his information from Peter, an eyewitness, who remembered well the remarkable behaviour of his Master on the occasion. "Putting on a threatening appearance," so the report runs, "He straightway drove him forth, and saith to him, See thou say nothing to any man." The first impression made by this part of Mark's narrative is that it is overdone. Why such passionate anxiety to prevent the noising abroad of a miracle wrought in view of many spectators, which therefore really could not be hid? Take it, however, as having reference principally to the leper himself and all becomes plain. With as much sternness as He can command thrown into his manner, Jesus says in effect: You are healed, but remember you

---

* This has been inferred from the word ἐξέβαλεν, v. 43. But the inference is not inevitable, as the same word is used by Mark in his account of our Lord's temptation. τό πνεῦμα αὐτὸν ἐκβάλλει εἰς τὴν ἔρημον; i. 12.

are still socially a leper; leave this place where legally you have no right to be, and do not go forth to tell everybody about your cure, but go straight to the priest, and get him to declare it for a testimony to the whole nation. It is the sternness of love bent on insuring that the benefit conferred shall be the greatest possible. Much more Christlike this sternness than the unheroic prudence which would conceal a usurpation of priestly functions.*

It is wholly unnecessary to prove at length that the great sensation produced, according to the second and third Evangelists, by the occurrence, is better accounted for by a miraculous cure than by the skilful discovery and generous proclamation of convalescence. On all grounds, therefore, we seem shut up to the conclusion that the story of the leper is the record of an act of healing not explicable by natural causes, and constituting a true miracle, well entitled to the place of honour at the head of the wonderful works by which the first Evangelist exhibits Jesus as mighty in deed, having previously exhibited Him as the Great Teacher. It is possible that another motive may have had an influence in securing for it the distinguished position, viz.: a desire to make prominent Christ's respect, in practice as in theory, for the Mosaic law, as shown in the direction to the leper to show himself to the priest. But we cannot err in ascribing to the writer of the first Gospel, also, the tact to discern that he

---

* *Vide* Weiss, *Das Leben Jesu*, i., 534; also, *Das Matthäus-evangelium*, and *das Marcus-evangelium*, in loc. Weiss thinks the ἐξέβαλο in Mark v. 43, implies that the leper was not yet cured, and that the thrusting him out had reference to the danger of infection. He supposes, that as in the case of the ten lepers, the disease left him as he was on the way to the priest. *Das Marcus-evang.*, p. 73. On this view Mark is inconsistent with himself, as in verse 42 he follows Matthew in representing the cure as immediate.

could not better commence his catalogue of wonders than by putting in the forefront the cure of a case of leprosy.*

In the story of *the Paralytic*† the refuge of naturalism from miracle lies, not in exegetical subtlety, but in *moral therapeutics.* In diseases of this type there may be a much closer connection between physical and mental states, and the bodily ailment may be more or less amenable to treatment through spiritual channels. That such a connection actually existed in the case of the palsied man seems to be implied in the fact that Jesus began His curative treatment by speaking to the sufferer about the forgiveness of sin. It is certainly remarkable that, in this instance, the first word uttered should be: "Courage, child, thy sins are forgiven thee." One might rather have expected such an opening in connection with the cure of such a disease as leprosy, which was the very chosen emblem of sin. The reason, doubtless, is to be sought in the sufferer's state of mind. It was, we may assume, apparent to the discerning, sympathetic eye of Jesus that the man regarded his bodily ailment as the result and penalty of his misconduct, and that his sense of guilt was a greater burden to his spirit than the loss of his physical powers. In that case, the proclamation of pardon was an appropriate prelude to a cure, as a prepara-

* The healing of the ten lepers (Luke xvii. 12-19) raises no new questions. The lepers there stand at a respectful distance (πόρρωθεν) and call for help. Jesus simply tells them to go and show themselves to the priests, and, as they go, they are healed. One, finding himself healed, returns to give thanks, so acknowledging Jesus as the source of cure. The interest here is chiefly ethical: companionship is established between men of hostile nationalities by a disease which excludes them from all other fellowship; the one who returns to give thanks is a Samaritan, nearer the kingdom than his Jewish fellow-sufferers, a fact carefully noted by the Pauline Evangelist, who makes Jesus also acknowledge and reward it, in words which sound like a Pauline formula: Thy faith hath saved thee.

† Matt. ix. 1-8; Mark ii. 1-2; Luke v. 17-26.

tion for the reception of the physical benefit. But naturalism regards it not merely as the prelude, but as the cure itself. The cheering word of Jesus it conceives as removing the weight from the sick man's spirit, which acted as a paralysing influence on his bodily frame, and sending an electric stream of fresh energy through his whole nervous system. To make this view more easily credible the disease is supposed to have been more imaginary than real—the helplessness of a hypochondriac, who thought he was unable to move his limbs, but who, on being delivered from the depressing sense of guilt, soon discovered that he was labouring under a delusion;* or the ailment is conceived to have been recent, slight, and temporary, curable by time or baths, and also by sudden shocks of emotion, or by calling into play the latent will-force.†

A very different idea of the malady is suggested by the accounts supplied by Mark and Luke of the efforts made by friends to bring the sick man into the presence of Jesus. These efforts suggest the idea of urgent need, and not improbably indicate previous unsuccessful attempts to introduce the sufferer to the notice of the great Healer. But these graphic details as to the manner in which the bearers of the paralytic gained access to Jesus, in spite of the crowd, are regarded with suspicion as a legendary invention designed to illustrate the boundless confidence of the populace in the curative powers of Jesus, or to show in other words how well the faith of the friends deserved the notice which according to the first Evangelist Jesus took of it. But such suspicion is purely gratuitous. The truth doubtless is that these interesting particulars concerning the ascent on the roof of the house in which Jesus was, and the letting of the

---

* So Paulus.

† So Keim.

sick man down through an opening into the chamber below were taken by Mark from the lips of Peter, an eye-witness, and borrowed from him with slight alterations by the third Evangelist. It is surely no fault that, besides being graphic, they do throw light on the words in Matthew's narrative, "Jesus seeing their faith," which as they stand in his text require explanation, nothing being stated to show in what respect the faith of the parties referred to was noticeable. The additions of the second and third Evangelists may not have been introduced for this express purpose, but they certainly do serve the purpose. What they show directly indeed is rather the zeal of the friends than their faith,* but such zeal would not have been forthcoming unless it had been supported by a firm conviction that their labour would not be in vain, that Jesus would be found both able and willing to heal.

The inference drawn from the energetic conduct of the friends as to the condition of the sufferer, is borne out by significant touches in the narratives which together convey a picture of pitiful helplessness. "Borne of four," "their faith," "child,"—how much is implied in these expressions! As to the second, the faith alluded to is that of the four men, the paralytic not being included, though the contrary for theological rather than exegetical reasons, is often assumed. This restriction is justified by the fact that the faith was manifested through the exertions made to gain access to Jesus, in connection with which the paralytic was altogether passive, as also by the repetition of the term "paralytic" after it had been used immediately before: "Jesus seeing their faith says to the paralytic."† Taking

* So Weiss.

† Matt. ix. 2; Mark ii. 4, 5; Weiss, *Das Matthäus-evangelium*, refers to this point is proof that αὐτῶν refers to the four men only.

this expression thus interpreted along with the other two, there rises before our view the image of a miserable object unable at once to walk and to believe, impotent alike in body and in soul; needing on the material side of his being to be borne on a couch by four strong men, and on the spiritual side to be carried in the arms of their vicarious faith, a veritable child, as Jesus pathetically called him.*

Hostile critics present in the crowd contributed their part to the proof that the cure of this poor sufferer was no commonplace occurrence, both by being witnesses of an act whose significance they would have denied if they could, and by supplying Jesus with an occasion for indicating the measure of its significance. The scribes took exception to the assurance given of the forgiveness of sins. It is an invasion of the divine prerogative they thought, and said by frowning looks if not by articulate words. There was no just occasion for censure, even on their own view that God alone could authoritatively pardon; for what Jesus had said did not necessarily amount to more than a declaration that there was no reason for despair in past sins, however heinous, such as any man may make to a fellow-man, who heartily believes in the grace of the Father in heaven. It was the utterance of human sympathy by the brotherly Son of Man, rather than a judicial sentence of absolution solemnly delivered by Messiah. But Jesus took the opportunity afforded by Pharisaic censure to claim a right which at first He did not exercise; saying, in effect, Not only do I possess the power, shared by all men of loving hearts, of awakening in the breasts of the sinful hope towards God by declaring unto them the forgiveness of sins, but I the Son of Man

* Luke instead of τέκνον has the colder term ἄνθρωπε, curiously avoiding a word which might have been supposed to have special attractions for his genial humanistic spirit.

claim authority to pronounce in God's name that the sins of this man are actually forgiven. And in proof that He is no blasphemer, arrogating to Himself this authority, He proceeds forthwith to execute the physical cure, offering the δύναμις brought into play as the evidence of the εξουσία. In irony he asks which is the *easier*, to say, thy sins are forgiven, or to say, Arise, and walk. One who can afford to ask such a question must have great confidence in his power both to say and to do.

Whether Jesus had the right to forgive sin was a question that might be endlessly debated, but whether or not He had the power to heal could be decided on the spot. The words were spoken; what followed? The paralytic arose before all, lifted up the pallet on which he had been carried, and walked away home. The man was manifestly healed, whether miraculously or otherwise. That the cure was miraculous, as Jesus indirectly claimed, is borne out both by the silence of the scribes, and by the admiration of the multitude who pronounced what they had witnessed extraordinary and unparalleled. The terms in which the Evangelists report the comments of the spectators vary, but the import in all three cases is the same. They had never seen the like before—a man disabled, as they knew this man to be, suddenly rising to his feet completely restored.

The healing of the *withered hand*,* being a Sabbatic miracle, the attention of the Evangelists is concentrated on the controversial accompaniments, and no pains are taken so to describe the condition of the diseased member as to exclude minor forms of ailment, and make the cure appear beyond doubt supernatural. No magnifying phrases occur in any of the accounts, not even in that of Luke, who characterised

---

* Matt. xii. 9–14; Mark iii. 1–6; Luke vi. 6–11.

the illness of Peter's mother-in-law as a great fever, and represented the leper as full of leprosy, and who as a physician could easily have described the malady in terms showing it to be of a serious character—an atrophy or wasting, incurable by natural means. His solitary addition is that the hand which was withered was the *right* hand,* which was probably an inference from the expression used by Mark, "having *the* hand withered," † the article naturally suggesting the *working* hand, the disablement of which involved the greatest loss. The only thing approaching to heightening phraseology is to be found in Matthew, whose descriptions are usually very sober in tone, and meagre in detail. He states that the hand was restored "whole as the other,"‡ implying, not merely recovery of power of movement, but complete removal of morbid symptoms. The sudden restoration of an atrophied member to a normal state of health would, as even Keim admits, be nothing short of a miracle.§

This lack of definite information respecting the nature of the disease and the extent of the cure is easily accounted for. The offence of Sabbatic healings did not lie in their being miracles, but simply in their being cures. Legal rigorists interdicted healing on the Sabbath day, however insignificant the amount of work involved; and some even went the length of pronouncing it unlawful to comfort the sick. It would thus have been quite beside the purpose of the narrative, which was to exhibit Christ in collision with

* Ver. 6.

† Ver. 1. The *one* sheep in the apologetic example, Matt. ver. 11, may represent the right hand, as the one valuable instrument of work.

‡ Ver. 13.

§ He compares it to the multiplying of a few loaves into food for thousands. *Jesu von Nazara*, ii., 465.

the scribes in reference to Sabbath observance, to have emphasised the miraculousness of the cure. It would have been to give the place of prominence to an irrelevant accident. Yet, however irrelevant, this course would have been followed if the Evangelists had been infected with a morbid passion for the marvellous; and the fact that they have made no effort to signalise the extraordinary character of the cure, while tending to make the presence of a miraculous element in this story less obtrusive, gives increased value to their testimony when, as in the case last considered, they do make the miraculous aspect prominent.

The vagueness of the Evangelists is the opportunity of rationalistic critics, who throw out a variety of suggestions, all tending to minimise the disease and bring the cure, whether partial or complete, within the sphere of natural agencies. The hand is supposed to have been affected with inflammation, rheumatism, or a sprain; all ailments producing stiffness in the member, but not so that it could not be moved by an effort of will.*

The best evidence that the case was of a more serious character is the displeasure with which the Pharisees witnessed the cure. In this instance no admiring comments are put into the mouth of the people, though, according to all the accounts, the incident happened in the synagogue, the Evangelists, as already said, having no desire to bring the miraculous element into the foreground. But the effect of the healing act on the minds of Christ's persistent antagonists is carefully recorded, not to prove the miracle, but to explain the growth of a hostility that was to have a tragic end. The men with whom Jesus had quite recently been in conflict over a supposed breach of the Sabbath law

* *Vide* Keim, *Jesu von Nazara,* ii., 465.

by His disciples were witnesses of this new offence; for it was in the synagogue which they frequented and in which they bore rule that it occurred.* They were irritated by the double transgression, and their rage is very credible, though it may seem exaggerated. "This fellow Jesus and his companions breaking the Sabbath again, and within so short a time of the last offence, when they rubbed the ears of corn, and so were guilty of a kind of threshing!" No wonder the zealots for the traditions were angry. But they would have been less angry if there had been no miracle. Their plotting against the life of the Sabbath-breaker was an involuntary confession that he had made himself notable as a worker of wonders. They would rather have been able to say, He achieved nothing worth mentioning, than that He broke the Sabbath by healing the withered hand. And they might have said that had the facts been as rationalistic interpreters fondly imagine. Then they could have made light of the whole matter and said, There was really no cure: He merely said, Stand forth; then afterwards, Stretch forth thy hand, which as it chanced the man was able to do. The whole performance was an impudent bravado in a spirit of defiance. That this line was not adopted was, doubtless, due to the fact that the hand was known by all present to be in such a state that it could not be stretched out, making the inference inevitable that in some way or other the power to use it was communicated by Jesus.†

---

* *εἰς τὴν συναγωγὴν αὐτῶν.* Matt. xii. 9.

† The other two Sabbatic cures recorded by Luke (xiii. 10–17; xiv. 1–6) are also very briefly described. The first of the two cases was one of chronic muscular contraction of eighteen years' standing. Luke represents the woman as having "a spirit of infirmity," causing her body to wear a fixed stooping posture. The expression suggests the idea of possession, though probably it ought not to be too strictly taken. (*Vide*

We come now to the narratives relating to *Demoniacs* The cure of persons described as δαιμονιζόμενοι occupied a very prominent place in Christ's healing ministry. In summary accounts of that ministry, as in the instructions to the twelve in connection with the Galilean mission, the expulsion of demons is mentioned as a separate department. The number of single narrations of cures belonging to this class is another index of prominence. Besides the three principal, typical, cases of the Capernaum and Gadara

---

remarks on demoniacal possession.) Luke appears to adapt his language to that of Jesus when He spoke of the woman as bound by Satan. This statement in turn is not to be interpreted prosaically. The phrase "whom Satan hath bound" is wittily employed to bring the case of the woman into analogy with that of the ox or ass. Christ's defence is very spirited. "You unloose an ox or ass bound to the stall, that you may lead him to the watering. *A fortiori*, I may heal this poor woman. For she, too, is bound by Satan, and bound for eighteen years, not for a few hours, and she is a human being, a daughter of Abraham, not a mere brute beast." Satan is referred to in general terms as the head of the kingdom of evil, physical as well as moral, and no inference may be drawn (Weiss and Trench) as to the woman's past habits and character. The sudden release of the sufferer from her chronic infirmity was certainly a marvel, if not a very outstanding miracle. The other case was a dropsy. Much depends on whether it affected the internal organs or merely the external parts. In the former case attempts at naturalistic explanation would be desperate. No descriptive details are given as to the disease. The case is described by the single word ὑδρωπικὸς. The apologetic illustration is adapted to the nature of the malady, an ox (or a son) fallen into a well, in danger of life, also, through water. The rule in the Talmud regarding such a case was that if the animal was in danger of its life it might be lifted out, not otherwise. The practice in our Lord's time may have been less strict. Or, perhaps, we should assume that Jesus had in view such a case. If that be so, then we may reason back from the danger of the animal, to the dangerous character of the disease. The ox is in danger of being drowned, and the man is in danger of being drowned also by the water gathering about his vitals. The proof of the miracle thus would lie in the line of defence as implying an illness of the most serious nature. The reading ὑιος (ver. 5), though the best attested and generally adopted by critics, certainly seems unsuitable to the connection.

demoniacs, and the epileptic or lunatic boy at the hill of transfiguration, there are those of the dumb, and blind and dumb, demoniacs briefly reported by Matthew, and that of the daughter of the Syrophenician woman; to which may be added as a somewhat doubtful case the woman bowed down with a spirit of infirmity, making in all seven.

In this class of cases there is a plethora of the supernatural. A miraculous element appears not only in the cure but in the disease; the superabundance of miracle presenting a *σκάνδαλον* to unbelief, and even to faith. Yet unbelief finds in the fact not only a stumbling-block but a consolation. The supernatural character of the disease offers a way of escape from miracle alike in the disease and in the cure. Possession from the naturalistic point of view was of course not an objective reality, but a hallucination. The physical and mental ailments under which demoniacs appear usually to have suffered are to be regarded as the effects of that delusion, and may therefore readily be conceived to have been amenable to the curative influence of moral therapeutics. A demoniac was not a seriously diseased person, but simply a man whose self-consciousness was fettered by morbid moods, melancholies, and the superstitions of the time. It is no great marvel that he should have been restored to himself by contact with such a healthy nature as that of Jesus, with its holy repose and its commanding presence and will.*

This view, according to which the fancy of possession was the primary fact in the demoniac state, and the psychical or physical ailment, whether madness or epilepsy, secondary and subordinate, is very convenient for naturalistic interpreters, as making the cure easy at once to be wrought

* So in effect Keim, *Jesu von Nazara*, ii., 199.

and to be believed. But it is not in accordance with fact. Much nearer the truth than this theory of recent rationalism is the older idea of such writers as Lardner and Farmer, according to which the radical fact in the case of demoniacs was some form of mental or nervous disease, and demoniacal possession merely a current theory as to its cause.* Whatever more ailed the demoniac, this at least is certain to begin with, that he was afflicted with real disease of the brain and nervous system, sometimes to a distressing extent. This is the sure datum from which we must start in all our attempts at diagnosis of this most mysterious and perplexing malady. This position is to be firmly maintained, not only as against those who, like Keim, make a superstitious opinion about demons entering into men the generating stuff of the disease, but also as against those who, taking a more serious view of the demoniac state, find the radical fact and the generating cause of all other symptoms in moral depravity. This view, advocated by Olshausen, and more recently by Weiss, not less than the other, is without foundation in the evangelic records. The demoniac of the Gospels is not one in whom "the sinful condition has reached a climax, where the man no more has sin, but sin has him; where he is helplessly and willessly given over to the enslaving power of sin." † This concep-

---

* For Lardner's views vide *The case of the Demoniacs mentioned in the New Testament;* Works, vol. I. Farmer expressed similar views in *An Essay on the Demoniacs of the New Testament.*

† Weiss, *Das Leben Jesu*, i., 452. Olshausen distinguishes between the demoniac and the wicked man who has given himself wholly to evil by representing him as one in whom there is a resistance to evil, an inner conflict. This inner conflict, however, does not, in his view, of itself make a man a demoniac. The demoniac state is further differentiated by disease of the nervous system caused by sensual indulgence. Trench follows Olshausen closely. On Olshausen's theory, *vide* Strauss, *Leben Jesu*, vol. ii, 14–18.

tion cannot be carried through without gratuitous assumption, and even arbitrary criticism of the texts. It is, for example, utterly irreconcilable with the narrative of the *epileptic boy*,* which represents him as having been a sufferer in the manner described from childhood; that is at an age at which he could not have been addicted to sinful indulgences. Weiss, perceiving this, maintains that this was not a case of demoniacal possession, but simply of epilepsy, also called lunacy because the periodic attacks more or less coincided with the changes of the moon. In justification of this position he adverts to the fact that in Matthew's version no mention is made of possession till the close; and even then the allusion comes in in such a way as to suggest that at this point the first Evangelist leaves the guidance of the apostolic document he has hitherto followed, and suddenly and awkwardly adapts his manner of expression to the representation of the case given by Mark, who undoubtedly conceived it as an instance of possession, and framed his narrative throughout in accordance with this view, Luke herein following his example.† But this criticism does not avail to set aside Mark's view as unauthentic, but we may assume that his representation rests on the testimony of Peter; so that even if it be admitted that the original apostolic source, Matthew's *Logia*, followed in the main by the canonical Matthew, made no mention of possession, it would simply be a case of one apostolic authority contradicting another. And in any case, even admitting that in representing the lunatic boy as possessed the Evangelists merely expressed their own opinion, we must take that opinion into account in forming a judgment as to

* Matt. xvii. 14–21; Mark ix. 14–29; Luke ix. 37–49.

† Matt. xvii. 18, "And Jesus rebuked *him* and the *demon* went out of him," instead of "rebuked the *demon and he*," etc.

what passed for possession in the apostolic age. The fact that all three agree in the representation conclusively proves that the epileptic youth would have been popularly regarded as a demoniac. His case, therefore, must be taken into account as a relevant fact in framing a theory as to the nature of possession.*

The main support of the theory that the predisposing cause of possession and the source of all other accompanying evils was moral depravity, is the speech of Christ in self-defence against the charge of casting out demons by the aid of Beelzebub. "If Satan cast out Satan," He said on that occasion, "he is divided against himself," † by implication representing His work in curing demoniacs as a casting out of Satan, and just on that account, not Satanic in inspiration, but wrought rather by the Spirit of God. But if the expulsion of demons was an expulsion of Satan, it is a natural inference that the demoniacs were, like Judas and the Pharisees, though perhaps in a different way, children of the devil. But it must be remembered that the kingdom of Satan is very comprehensive. It is the kingdom of evil; not merely of moral evil, but of physical evil viewed as the direct effect, or as the symbol of moral, or as in sympathy and affinity with it. Satan must be conceived not less comprehensively. The Satan idea has not only an ethical side, of which we are accustomed to think too exclusively, but also a physical. He is not only the father of those who sin, but he is the tyrant of those who suffer, especially those

* *Vide* Weiss, *Leben Jesu*, ii., 318–20; also his Works on *Matthew* and *Mark* in loc. His view that lunacy was not included under demoniacal possession may seem justified by Matt. iv. 24, when the σεληνιαζόμενοι are mentioned as a separate class after δαιμονιζόμενοι. It only shows, however, that there was a certain want of strictness in the use of terms in speaking of such diseases.

† Matt. xii. 26.

who suffer from diseases which touch the mind, and so disable from entering into the kingdom in a way which ordinary physical maladies do not. There is reason to believe that our Lord, in His apologetic speech concerning the casting out of demons, had the physical aspect of the Satanic idea chiefly in view,* and that He had no intention of classing the poor demoniacs with the men who had surrendered themselves to the power of the wicked one. If He had been asked where such men were to be found, He would have pointed, not to the demoniacs, but to the very persons against whose calumnies He was defending Himself, whom He regarded as coming indefinitely near to the unpardonable sin of speaking evil of the good, knowing it to be good.

Not moral depravity, then, though doubtless in many instances that feature was not wanting, and not the mere morbid superstitious fancy of possession was the fundamental fact in the state of the demoniac. The most *certain*, and in that respect the primary datum, was a real physical or mental disease. In every case of which we have details there was a disease, either madness, or epilepsy, or dumbness, or dumbness accompanied with blindness, or chronic muscular contraction. These diseases were as real as are the mental and nervous maladies with which our experience makes us familiar; and they must not be explained away because one happens to think that the notion of possession was a delusion. To those who are inclined to follow this course these questions may be put: were there no insane persons in Judæa in our Lord's day? were none of them cured by Him? and where is the record of them? That there were many such sufferers cannot be doubted; that many of them experienced the benefit of Christ's healing power may also be taken for

* This is the view taken by Beyschlag, vide *Das Leben Jesu*, vol. i. p. 294.

granted; and that the cure of maladies, so fitted to call forth sympathy, would be wholly overlooked in the records is not credible. But there is no account of any such cures, unless we find it in the narratives of the demoniacs.

Regarding it then as a settled point that possession was always connected with some form of real disease, the question arises, what was possession itself? Was it an additional symptom, the differentiating feature of the demoniac state, or was it merely an inference from the other symptoms and their supposed cause? Practically the question resolves itself into this, was possession an objective reality, or was it only a current belief, a theory for explaining certain morbid symptoms which are now accounted for otherwise? It is a difficult and delicate question on which there is much division of opinion, not merely as between deniers and affirmers of the supernatural, but even among those who sincerely believe in miracles in general, and in the miracles of Christ in particular. The general question of the supernatural is not involved, nor is doubt or denial of the special form of the supernatural presented in possession based on *a priori* grounds in all instances, some being content to let the whole question rest on the facts as reported in the Gospels. To pronounce dogmatically that possession is impossible would, indeed, be presumptuous; for we know too little about the world of spirit, and the connection of spirit with matter, to be able to say what is possible. That there should be one spirit or soul virtually united to a bodily organism, and acting on it through the brain and nervous system, is the great mystery. To the Materialist it appears a mystery too great for credence; and probably no one who believes in a separate essence called a soul, the substratum of the phenomena of thought and feeling, would be inclined to pronounce it impossible that a second soul might occupy and use or abuse the same corporeal organisation, oppressing the legitimate tenant, interrupting normal functions, and producing a variety of morbid actions.

When appeal is made from speculation to the Evangelic reports the evidence seems somewhat indecisive. In favour of the reality of possession, in the sense just explained, is the behaviour ascribed in some instances to the demoniacs themselves, who are represented as speaking in the name of another who has them in his power, yet not so entirely as to involve the complete loss of self-consciousness; the very duality of consciousness manifested by the sufferer, speaking now in his own name and now as the mouthpiece of the demon, seeming to supply convincing proof of the presence in the same man of two wills. But other facts might not without show of reason be adduced to justify hesitation in accepting this view. One is that no distinction seems to be recognised in the Gospels between ordinary insanity and epilepsy and the demoniac state. There are no separate accounts of cures of persons suffering from these diseases. In ailments of another class a distinction is made. Thus some demoniacs are represented as blind and dumb, but all blind or dumb persons are not represented as demoniacs. In view of this distinction the absence of distinction in the other cases becomes the more significant. One is tempted to infer that the notion of possession was but the device of an unscientific age to account for the *appearance* of an oppressed will or personality exhibited in mental disease, and in epileptic attacks in a marked degree, and in a less obtrusive manner in other ailments.* A difficulty might be found

* Thus Weizsäcker says: The unity of the diseases (associated with demoniacal possession) is only that of a general popular idea which embraced in it all that gave the impression of an oppressed personality, therefore not only insanity and mental diseases in general, but also nervous disorders, and derangement of the organs by which spiritual intercourse is carried on. *Untersuchungen*, p. 375.

in applying this hypothesis to the case of a blind or dumb demoniac, but the theorist would probably surmount it by assuming that in such a case the loss of vision or hearing was not due to disease in the organ, or to any accidental injury it had sustained, but to an interior psychical cause destroying the mental faculty of perception, and revealing its presence to the beholder in the aspect of the afflicted person. The greatest difficulty would be experienced in attempting to bring into conformity with the hypothesis the case of the woman bowed down with infirmity, in which the symptoms of a subjected will are very obscure. If there was a foreign will at work in that instance it showed itself, not by using the body as its instrument in morbid action, but by preventing the will of the individual from using the body in normal healthy activity—*i. e.*, as a spirit of infirmity, not of demoniac strength, as in the Gadarene and the epileptic boy. In the case of the infirm woman we seem to be on the debatable borderland between ordinary diseases and the peculiar class denominated demoniacal, and it does not seem easy to find a reason for relegating it to that category which would not apply to the case of the paralytic.

Another fact which the advocates of what may be called the modern view of possession might naturally regard as on their side is the close correspondence of the form which possession assumed in any given case to the characteristics of the accompanying disease. In the case of the Gadarene demoniac, where the disease is raving madness manifesting itself in ungovernable violence and preternatural strength, possession assumes the form of *plurality*. The man calls himself *Legion*, thinking of himself as the habitation of a host of demons whose united power makes them irresistible as a legion of Roman soldiers. " We are many," he is repre sented in Mark's account as saying, speaking in the name of the demons, and the third Evangelist endorses the statement by adopting it as his own explanation of the title.* The notion of one person being possessed by a multitude of spirits appears so strange that one eagerly seeks escape from it in the conjecture that it was merely an inference from and a vivid concrete expression of the superhuman force exerted by the demoniac in bursting the chains and rubbing to pieces the fetters with which they essayed to bind him. In the case of the epileptic youth, on the other hand, who was subject to recurrent attacks of his malady, possession is represented as *intermittent.* The spirit seizes him when an attack comes on, and leaves him when it passes off.† The way of the spirit seems to be inferred simply from the characteristic phenomena of the disease.

The foregoing remarks are not offered as an argument on either side of the question as to the reality of possession. Their aim and effect is rather to exhibit the subject as one beset with difficulty on which it is excusable to be in suspense. Such is the state of mind in which many find themselves in reference to it, and I am content to adapt my argument to that attitude. For the purpose of these lectures it is not necessary to decide the question, the only matter of vital importance to the enquiry to which they are devoted being the substantial historicity of the relative Gospel narratives, which, as will appear, remains intact whatever view may be adopted on the present topic. It may indeed not unnaturally be feared lest uncertainty as to this should make everything uncertain; not only the truth of the records, but the inspiration of the Evangelists, and even the claim of Jesus to be an infallible and trustworthy guide. There can be no

* Mark v. 9; Luke viii. 30. † Luke ix. 39.

doubt that an impression that the character of Christ is in some way involved more than anything else leads devout minds to regard the reality of demoniacal possession as a matter not open to dispute. How far that impression is well founded is a question on which I would rather not enter. I will merely remark that if it were indeed so that the veracity of Christ, or His competency to guide men infallibly in moral and religious truth, would be compromised if the reality of possession were denied, no believing man would hesitate to accept it as if it were an article of faith. Some, however, who are by no means disposed to assert either that possession is impossible, or that it did not really exist in Judæa in our Lord's day, have earnestly maintained that the state of the case is not so; contending that even if Jesus knew possession to be merely a current and unfounded opinion as to the cause of certain diseases, He was not required either by the law of veracity or by His vocation to proclaim the fact either to the sufferers, or to the disciples, or to any person whatsoever. If, says one well-known writer, "if possession was mania, the real ground of the popular error was an erroneous opinion as to the cause of a natural disorder. The popular belief, in fact, ascribed it to supernatural instead of natural causes. So far, but no farther, it touched religious questions. To correct the error involved not merely the teaching of religious truth, but in this particular case the enunciation of sounder principles of mental philosophy. I think that I may fearlessly affirm that the teaching of scientific truth, either mental or material, did not come within the scope of our Lord's divine mission." * It is assumed in this statement that Jesus did

* Prebendary Row, *The Supernatural in the New Testament*, p. 259. Four chapters of this work are devoted to the subject of possession. They contain a careful and dispassionate discussion of the question in all its bear-

not Himself share the popular belief. To many it has appeared very difficult to reconcile this assumption with the words of Jesus bearing on the subject as reported in the Gospels, and hence the alternative question is raised, can ignorance on such a matter be imputed to Him without compromising His infallibility? On this point the view of Weiss is worthy of notice. Regarding possession as essentially a moral phenomenon, he holds that Christ's infallibility is not compatible with His being in ignorance as to its nature; but he admits that if the matter in question were merely a problem in psychology or psychiatry, ignorance might be ascribed to Him without prejudice to His infallibility, which relates only to moral and religious truth.* Be this as it may, one thing is certain: we cannot conceive Jesus as having any part in the superstitious notions of demons entertained by such a writer as Josephus, who regarded them as the spirits of deceased wicked men entering into the living and taking delight in working all sorts of mischief, and apparently had faith in the power of charms or of smelling herbs held to the nose to expel them or draw them out from the bodies they inhabited.† As He transformed current ideas of the Messiah and the Kingdom

---

ings. The author's position is this: That we are not entitled to assert that possession was impossible; that the data in the Gospels being scanty, it is not easy to decide the question of fact; that even if we regard possession as only a current theory to explain insanity and kindred diseases, the essential facts remain unaffected, and the historical truth of the narratives untouched; that the inspiration of the Evangelists, being granted to enable them to give a true account of Christ's teaching and life, is not compromised by representing them as sharing a popular error in psychology or medicine, and that Christ's mission did not require Him to correct such errors.

* *Leben Jesu*, i., 452.

† Vide *De Bel. Jud.*, vii., 25. 3, *Antiq.*, viii., 2, 5. The passages are quoted and commented on by Lardner. Works, vol. i., p. 507.

of God, so we should expect to find Him transforming at least, if not discarding, the idea of possession. He certainly reformed the practice of exorcism, for He cast out demons by a word, without the aid of spells or smells; insomuch that the people marvelled at the contrast between His way of working and that common among exorcists, and said: 'What new doctrine is this? for with authority commandeth He even the unclean spirits and they do obey Him." * In a similar manner we should expect to find Him purifying the conception of possession; and in point of fact He did this in His apologetic discourse on the cure of demoniacs, by placing possession under a universal and ethical point of view, representing it as a manifestation of the power of Satan, the great antagonist of the kingdom of God.†

Turning now to the question how far the truth of the narratives relating to demoniacs depends on the objective reality of possession, it may safely be affirmed that all the main features of these remain unaffected, whatever view is adopted on that subject. Grant that the idea of possession was simply a current theory to account for certain morbid symptoms whose true causes were then unknown; grant that the theory as held not only by Jesus, but by pagans at the commencement of the Christian era, was merely a survival of the rude ideas concerning ghosts entertained by primitive men.‡ Still, substantial historicity, if not absolute inerrancy, can be claimed for the relative evangelic accounts. The facts are, of course, stated in terms of the theory, but they are not created by or for the theory. So far is this from being the case, that in some instances, notably in the case of the epileptic youth, the facts faithfully

* Mark i. 27. † So Weizsäcker, *Untersuchungen*, p. 376.

‡ Such is the view of Mr. Herbert Spencer, vide *Principles of Sociology*, p. 242.

described in accordance with the known symptoms of the physical malady determine the form of the theoretic element.

The truth of the position laid down may be tested by applying it to three of the most outstanding features of the narratives; the demoniac speaking in the name of the demons, the recognition of Jesus as the Christ, and the destruction of the herd of swine. Can these features not be retained if the reality of possession is given up; must they in that case be regarded simply as inventions of the Evangelists? It may suit sceptical writers like Strauss to take up this ground, but such wholesale unsettlement of the history on account of one debatable point is not justifiable. There is no difficulty in conceiving of the insane man in the synagogue of Capernaum, or the madman of Gadara, thinking of himself as possessed by an evil spirit, and speaking as its mouthpiece, when a universal belief in the reality of such possession prevailed. This belief, shared by the sufferer before disease overtook him, might readily assume the morbid form of a fixed idea that he himself was so possessed, and become one of the most outstanding marks of mental aberration. Analogous facts are presented in confessions made by reputed witches on trial, of compacts between them and Satan. That the current opinions of an age may be reflected in the diseased fancies of the insane, is shown by the fact stated by Minucius Felix, that persons on whom exorcists practised their healing art, speaking in the name of the possessing demon confessed themselves to be Jupiter, Saturn, and Serapis, these gods being then regarded by Christians as real beings, demons, though now they are accounted purely imaginary.*

---

* This fact is referred to by Beyschlag, *Das Leben Jesu*, p. 293. The

The recognition of Jesus as Messiah may seem to present a more difficult problem. Such recognition is represented as a frequent occurrence in connection with the cure of demoniacs,* and it appears in the narratives relating to the demoniacs of Capernaum synagogue and of Gadara. In both cases it seems difficult to account for the recognition as an utterance of the possessed echoing popular ideas; in the one case because it occurred at a very early period, in the other because it happened in a part of the country previously, so far as we know, unvisited by Jesus, and where He was probably little known. This feature accordingly Strauss regards as unhistorical, tracing its introduction into the evangelic tradition to a desire to bring honour to Jesus through the involuntary testimony of the demons to His Messiahship. As praise was prepared for Him out of the mouths of children, when the mature refused to acknowledge Him, as even the stones were ready to cry out in case human beings should be silent, so it was thought meet that, failing recognition from the Jewish people whom He had come to save, it should be forthcoming from demons; whose testimony, because they had nothing to expect from Him but destruction, was impartial, and because of their higher spiritual nature, trustworthy.† But curiously enough the same tradition which is supposed to have set such value on demoniac testimony contains an express statement that Jesus refused to receive it. There is no reason to call in

---

words of Minucius Felix are these: Haec omnia sciunt pleriqui, pars vestrum, ipsos dæmonas de semitipsis confiteri quoties a nobis tormentis verborum, et orationis incendiis de corporibus exigentur. Ipse Saturnus, et Serapis, et Jupiter, et quidquid dæmonum colitis, victi dolore, quod sunt, eloquuntur. *Octavius*, p. 77. Ed. Foulis. The confession is supposed to be made by the demons, and it is argued that they would not make such a confession to their own shame if they could help it.

* Mark i. 34; Luke iv. 41. † *Leben Jesu*, ii., 22.

question the reality of the testimony, supposing it to proceed not from the demons, but from those who were believed to be possessed by them. Even at the early period at which the incident in the synagogue of Capernaum occurred, such a recognition as is ascribed to the demoniac might readily take place. The Messianic hope was immanent in the hearts of the Jewish people, ever ready to break forth into expression, and it was quite to be expected that, when the Messiah came, among the first to recognize Him should be those diseased in their minds, especially those whose thoughts moved within the religious sphere.* Insanity is much nearer the kingdom of God than worldly-mindedness. There was, doubtless, something in the whole aspect and manner of Jesus which was fitted to produce almost instantaneously a deep spiritual impression to which children, simple, ingenuous souls like the Galilean fishermen, sinful, yet honest-hearted men like those who met at Matthew's feast, readily surrendered themselves. Men with shattered reason also felt the spell, while the wise and the strong-minded too often used their intellect, under the bias of passion or prejudice, to resist the force of truth. In this way we may account for the prompt recognition of Jesus by the Gadarene demoniac. All that is necessary to explain it is the Messianic hope prevalent in Gadara as elsewhere, and the sight of Jesus acting on an impressionable spirit. The view of the Blessed One acting on the remnant of reason drew the poor sufferer to His presence in instinctive trust and expectation of benefit. The same view acting on the dark element produced repulsion and fear. Hence the self-contradictory attitude, as of one saying, It is the Christ; He is come to save me; He is come to destroy me. Such a wit

* So Weizsäcker, *Untersuchungen*, p. 378.

ness Jesus could not accept. The testimony He desiderated, the testimony that was of value was not that of a demoniac but of a demoniac healed and in his right mind.

That part of the history of the Gadarene incident which relates to the swine, necessarily undergoes some modification if the objective reality of possession be given up. In that case the destruction of the herd cannot be regarded as the effect of the demons leaving the man and entering into them. But the event itself may remain, though it is an event unexplained. Strauss treats the whole incident as mythical, the outgrowth of popular opinions concerning demons and their habits, and the methods employed by exorcists in their expulsion. Demons craved embodiment; unclean themselves, they preferred unclean abodes; therefore, if they must leave the man they would gladly go into the swine; the drowning of the swine served the purpose of a proof that the demons had really been cast out of the man; it was a test analogous to that of the upsetting of the basin of water in the story of Eliazar, the exorcist, told by Josephus.* The author of *Philochristus* resolves the story into a myth or figure petrified into fact, in another way, viz., by supposing that it took its origin in a morbid notion of the maniac that he was possessed by a whole legion of swine, which, in telling the story afterwards, he represented as going out of him and rushing down into the sea.† The theory of Strauss is discredited by the fact that in the Gospels the way of dealing with demoniacs ascribed to Jesus has nothing in common with the arts of exorcists; and as for the other hypothesis, it is a pure conjecture, which has nc point of support in the narrative. There is no reason tc

* *Das Leben Jesu*, ii., 34–6.

† *Philochristus*, p. 133. Vide, also, *Onesimus*, book iii., § 6.

doubt that there was a herd of swine in the neighbourhood, and that at the time the demoniac was restored to reason they were drowned in the Galilean lake. Of course, if the explanation of the occurrence given in the evangelic tradition be set aside, it remains unexplained and unconnected with the main event, and appears as a mere accidental coincidence. But it may easily have been connected therewith in another way, *e.g.*, by the demoniac rushing upon the herd and producing a panic in it. No mention, indeed, is made of this circumstance, but it is intrinsically probable, and it is not the only omission. Thus, Matthew does not even state that the man was cured; that is left to be inferred from the fact that the devil went out of him into the swine. Then, while the man, after his cure, is represented by both Mark and Luke as clothed, it is not explained by either whence the clothing was procured. The chief difficulty in connection with this view is that Jesus is represented as granting permission to the demons to enter into the swine, a circum stance which has created much perplexity to interpreters on moral grounds, as involving Him in responsibility for the destruction of property, not to speak of the questionable position in which He seems to be placed, as negotiating with the demons. Weiss meets the difficulty by denying that Jesus gave such permission, resting his denial on the fact that in the narrative of the first Evangelist, which he thinks gives the tradition in its purest form, as recorded in the apostolic document, Jesus is represented as replying to the request of the demons with the single word "Depart" (ὑπάγετε),* which does not in itself express permission,

* *Das Leben Jesu*, ii., 40; *Das Matthäus-evang.*, p. 240; *Das Marcus-evang.*, p. 177. Weiss, while believing in the reality of possession after a fashion, for the demons, in his view, as in Olshausen's, appear to be impersonal, mere personifications of Satanic influence, never

though it might not unnaturally be interpreted as implying it, as it has been by the other Evangelists. Unless we are prepared to take our stand upon the absolute inerrancy of the records, this suggestion seems worthy of serious consideration. If it be adopted we are free to conceive the course of events as follows: The man, acting as the mouthpiece of the demons, asks permission for them to go into the swine. Jesus disdaining to make terms with unclean spirits, and taking no notice of the request, utters the stern order, Depart. The demoniac thereupon rushed on the swine with fury, now playing the part of *agent* for the demons, as before he had played the part of *spokesman.**

The history then remaining intact in its main features, whatever view is taken as to the nature of possession, the question finally comes up: to what extent can a miraculous element be recognised in these demoniac-narratives? It can be very briefly answered. We have seen that whatever more ailed the demoniacs they certainly were afflicted with real and often serious mental and nervous diseases, such as madness or epilepsy. In the two cases of this class of cures reported in the Triple Tradition, the physical ailment was of an aggravated character. The Gadarene demoniac was a raving, dangerous madman; the lunatic boy had been subject to violent epileptic attacks from childhood. The sudden and complete cure of such diseases rises above the level of nature as conspicuously as the cure of the leper. How thankful should we be if it were in the power of physicians to restore at once to mental health the

---

theless holds that the swine were driven into the sea by the demoniac in the last paroxysm of his disease.

* Beyschlag (*Leben Jesu*, 294) takes this view: "As formerly (he remarks) the man in his madness devoted himself to the demons he felt within him, as organ of speech, so now as organ of action."

multitudes of poor mortals who pine in our lunatic asylums. Strauss lays down two canons with regard to this class of cures: The more the evil lay simply in a distemper of the spirit on which Jesus could work directly through His word, or in a slight disorder of the nervous system on which it was possible to work beneficially through the mind, the easier could Jesus put an end to such conditions by a word (λόγῳ, Matthew viii. 16), and immediately (*παραχρῆμα*, Luke xiii. 13); the more, on the other hand, the evil was established as a bodily disease, the more difficult is it to conceive a purely psychological and immediate cure. The second canon is, that to work effectively in a spiritual way the whole bearing of Jesus as a prophet must co-operate: hence His power so to work would be greatest in times and places where He had longest and most exercised His prophetic office.* By these canons of moral therapeutics the two cases of the Triple Tradition are inexplicable. They are either miracles, or they did not happen as reported. The only way of escape is to deny the completeness and permanency of the cure. If this can be done with plausibility in the case of the lunatic boy, whose disease was in its nature intermittent, it cannot reasonably be attempted in the case of the Gadarene demoniac. There were lulls in the tempest of his disease, doubtless, but never till he came into contact with Jesus had he been seen sitting calmly, decently attired, and in his right mind—sane as any man in all the country. His paroxysms of violence may have been followed by periods of exhaustion, when he could be clothed and manacled and in appearance tamed, but it would not be difficult to see that the demon only slumbered. To all it was manifest that it was otherwise with him now: to Jesus, who con

* *Leben Jesu*, ii., 43.

sidered him capable of going home to his friends to tell them of his restoration; to the inhabitants of Gadara, who marvelled at his tale, because it was evidently true.*

On arriving at the western shore of the lake from the excursion to Gadara, Jesus found new work awaiting Him, new forms of human suffering demanding His attention The records of the *healing of the woman with a bloody issue*, and of *the raising of the daughter of Jairus*,† tell the story of fresh manifestations of healing power which were closely associated in the apostolic tradition with the restoration of the Gadarene demoniac. The former of these two events was a mere incident occurring on the way to the house of the ruler to rescue his daughter from the gates of death, which would not have found a place in the Evangelic history if the person benefited could have helped it. She

---

* In the case of the Capernaum demoniac (Mark i. 21–28; Luke iv. 31–37), as the first occurrence of the kind, the attention both of the spectators and of the reporters was naturally chiefly fixed on the method of cure, by a word, without use of the arts of exorcists, the new doctrine as to power (*διδαχὴ καινὴ κατ' ἐξουσίαν*). There are no particulars as to the physical ailment of the demoniac, and the whole narrative is rather colourless. On this ground Keim thinks this is not a real occurrence, but simply a *That-programme*, like the change of water into wine in John ii. and the preaching-programme in Nazareth, in Luke iv. 16–30, with features borrowed from the Gadarene demoniac, especially the deprecatory speech of the demons (*Jesu von Nazara*, ii., 165–203). Weiss, regarding the story as historical, yet admits that the words put into the mouth of the demoniacs are borrowed from the Gadara-case. The plural "us" he thinks unsuitable where was only one, and Jesus had done nothing to call forth such a speech. It is, he thinks, a representative story in which Mark reproduces the features with which Peter was wont to describe such cases: *Leben Jesu*, i., 448. Most commentators explain the plural by saying that the one demon speaks in name of all. The phrases *φωνῇ μεγάλῃ, ῥίψαν, μηδὲν βλάψαν αὐτόν* (Luke iv. 33, 35), Holtzmann regards as indicating a wish to heighten the miracle. Weizsäcker regards this as a real occurrence and as the source of the great gathering in the evening.

† Matt. ix. 18–26; Mark v. 21–43; Luke viii. 40–56.

meant to steal a cure, and if Jesus had been like ordinary men He might have passed on, taking no heed of her attempt. The interest of the story lies just in that attempt of the sufferer, and its frustration by Jesus, and the motives of the two actors. In comparison with the human interest the miraculous element, though present, falls into the background.

Jostled by the crowd accompanying Him to the house of Jairus, Jesus becomes aware that some one is touching Him, not with an involuntary pressure, but with nervous finger and conscious aim. Quick to apprehend the presence of need He divines what it means: it is another victim of the world's woe drawing near for help. He desires to see and know the unknown sufferer. We need not assume that the case in all its details was known to Jesus from the first, and that He had in His mind a cut-and-dry plan for dealing with it. We should take the story as it stands, and impute no more initial knowledge to Jesus than is claimed for Him by the Evangelists.

The sick one hidden in the crowd, being detected, tells a tale which fully explains her desire for concealment. She suffers from a female ailment which she is ashamed to divulge. It is a hidden ailment which must be made known by the sufferer, not one which, like leprosy, palsy, or insanity, reveals itself; yet an ailment which a woman would rather silently bear than confess. How can she speak of it in a crowd, or even to Jesus alone, supposing she had the chance? And yet her need of His help is great, as appears from the accounts of all three Evangelists, and especially those of Mark and Luke. Her illness has lasted for twelve years, during which time she has sought the aid of all available medical skill to no purpose. Her means wasted she remains a confirmed invalid, weak, worn, heartless; no hope for her anywhere unless it be in the Man of whose deeds of power and mercy she has heard. In Him she *has* hope. She even ventures to hope that a cure may be wrought by the bare touch of anything connected with Him, were it but the hem of His garment, and without His knowledge. Such accordingly is her plan, the mixed product of shame, desperation, faith, and superstition.

It succeeded so far as the cure was concerned. The effect of the touch was instantaneous; she felt in her body that she was healed of the plague. Had she obtained the benefit as she intended, without her benefactor being aware, she would have returned home rejoicing in the recovery of health, acquainted with the virtue residing, as it appeared, in Christ's *garments*, unacquainted with Christ Himself, and without that experience of His sympathetic interest which could turn a physical into a spiritual blessing. But this was happily prevented by the sudden question of Jesus, who touched me? calling forth in a grateful heart a generous impulse to self-revelation in spite of womanly shame. Her confession had its reward in a reply in which delicacy, benevolence, and respect were blended. Jesus accosted her as "daughter," as if she were a child who could have no experience of the disease wherewith she was afflicted, spoke approvingly of her faith notwithstanding its crudeness, and confirmed the cure which she had furtively procured by her stealthy touch.

For everything in this pathetic story, for the particulars relating to her ailment, and for the fact of her cure, the woman herself must have been the voucher. Mark speaks of her as telling Jesus *all the truth*. We may assume that the expression covers not merely what Luke mentions—why she touched Jesus, viz., to obtain a cure of some unacknowledged disease, and that she had got relief, but all the details as to the nature of the disease and her past efforts for the recovery of health, as reported most fully by Mark. It is not necessary to impute to the Evangelist a desire to magnify the miracle, as the motive inducing him to report these details, taken, we may assume, from the mouth of Peter. They really add little fitted to serve that purpose to the one fact mentioned by all three Evangelists, that the illness had lasted for twelve years. It is observable that Mark, in speaking of the cure, uses language which implies permanence. "The fountain of her blood was dried up," he says, Luke's phrase being "her issue of blood staunched." * Whether the statement rests on special information does not appear.

Naturalistic theologians have no hesitation in accepting this narrative as it stands in Matthew's Gospel as a substantially true history. They regard the case narrated as a veritable instance of a faith-cure, and deem it quite within the limits of natural possibility that a strong hope might have a beneficent effect on the physical malady at least for a time.† In the narratives of Mark and Luke the result seems to be represented not merely as a faith-cure, but as an involuntary cure drawn by the touch of faith from the person of Jesus, without the co-operation of His will; just such a cure as the woman had hoped to steal. Such a healing virtue, immanent in Christ's body and acting spontaneously, is a stumbling-block, not only to naturalism, which sees in it the product of a miracle-mongering spirit that has left its traces in the Evangelic records, but also to faith which deems it indispensable to the ethical significance of the miracle that Christ's will should be at least a concurrent

* *ἐξηράνθη ἡ πηγὴ τοῦ αἵματος αὐτῆς* Mark v. 29; *ἔστη ἡ ῥύσις τοῦ αἵματος αὐτῆς* Luke viii. 44, obviously a weaker phrase.

† So Keim, *Jesu von Nazara*, ii., 467.

factor. Whether the second and third Evangelists really did share the woman's crude ideas is a question on which opinion differs, as also how on their representation the miracle is to be conceived. It has been suggested that the cure must be divided into two stages, a temporary amelioration brought about simply by faith in relation to which Jesus was passive, and a permanent, complete cure wrought by an act of Christ's will after becoming acquainted with the sufferer and her history.* But this view cannot be adopted if we are to interpret strictly the statement of Mark, that the fountain of blood was dried up immediately after Christ's garments had been touched. Further remarks on this topic are reserved for another place.†

The raising of the daughter of Jairus, while with its companion miracles belonging to a class distinct from the miracles of healing, may legitimately be brought under this category, because it was in the form of a request for the healing of a sick one that the case was brought under the notice of Jesus. So we learn from Mark and Luke, who both by different phrases put into the mouth of the father describe the sufferer as dying.‡ Matthew, looking to the form which the case ultimately assumed, and concerned here, as always, only about the essential fact, and above all the word spoken by Jesus, omits this circumstance, and makes the request of the father one for the revival of a child just dead; a request which it probably would not have entered into his mind to address to Christ, however great the trust he placed in His miraculous power.§ The

* So Steinmeyer, *The Miracles of our Lord*, p. 61, Clark's Translation.

† *Vide* Lecture VII.

‡ ἐσχάτως ἔχει, Mark v. 23; ἀπέθνησκεν, Luke viii. 42.

§ "Matthew" may have found the story in the *Logia*. Mark, having his information direct from Peter, besides stating exactly how it stood with point open to question in this case is whether it was ever at the last anything more than a case of sickness healed. Doubt finds its fulcrum in the words of Jesus, "The child is not dead, but sleepeth." On the ground of this saying it is even confidently affirmed by many that the fact of the child being still alive when Jesus came to the house must be held to be beyond dispute, unless we are prepared to call in question His word. Yet this inference is really not justifiable. Jesus cannot have meant to pronounce on the question whether death was real or apparent, seeing that when He spoke the words He had not yet entered into the chamber where the child lay; unless, indeed, we are to suppose that He spoke from a knowledge independent of observation, which would be to substitute a miracle of knowledge for a miracle of power to recall from the state of death. In the circumstances the statement must be taken to mean, dead or not, the state is transient, the child will revive as from a sleep. It has been supposed that Jesus employed ambiguous language, because He did not wish to be regarded as a raiser of the dead, and therefore desired the multitude gathered around the house to remain under the impression that it was not a case of real death. Hence, also, is explained the exclusion of the crowd from the sick chamber and the admission only of the parents and the three favoured disciples. None might be allowed to see the dead one brought back to life save those who might be trusted to keep the secret.* It certainly accords with this view that a strict prohibition was

the sick one, supplies additional particulars: her age, twelve years; the name of her father, Jairus; and his rank, a ruler in the synagogue. Luke follows Mark and adds that the daughter was an only child, which may be an inference from Mark's θυγάτριον expressive of tenderness *Vide* Weiss.

* Weiss, *Das Leben Jesu*, i., 549; *Das Marcus-evangelium*, in loc.

imposed on the witnesses not to divulge what had happened. But apart from the morality of such an attempt by mystifying language to keep the public in the dark, it may be regarded as improbable simply on the ground of futility. The assembled mourners and curious spectators were so convinced in their own minds that death had taken place, that when the child revived they would much more readily infer that a miracle had been wrought by the man whom they had been accustomed to see doing wonders, than that they had been mistaken in their first opinion. There is, however, more force in the remark that the injunction to keep silence implies that the event which had taken place was a raising from the dead, and that it would have been nothing short of idle and false mystification to have said so solemnly to the parents and the disciples, "do not tell," if all that had happened was a return to consciousness of a sickly maiden that had fallen into a swoon. Why make so great a mystery of a thing so simple and natural, which might happen of its own accord without the exertion of any miraculous influence?*

But may the apparent death not after all have been but a swoon? As such, naturalistic critics will persist in regarding it, and of course the possibility of a temporary faint simulating death cannot be denied. Nevertheless, if our judgment is to be determined by the narrative and not by *a priori* reasoning, this hypothesis must be pronounced highly improbable. Two circumstances are of importance in this connection: the gradual approach of the state of apparent death, and the unhesitating confidence with which all who had an opportunity of observing pronounced it a case of real death. The father described his daughter as

---

* *Vide* Weiss, *Das Leben Jesu*, i., 551.

dying, suggesting the case of one gradually sinking, according to all usual appearances, under some mortal disease. Subsequently the sick one is reported to be actually dead, and so assured are the family of the fact that the customary arrangements are made for having the sad event duly lamented by sympathetic neighbours or hired mourners.* It is not to be supposed that this assurance was without ground. Doubtless the difference between a swoon and a sickness ending in death was familiar to the bereaved and their friends not less than to rationalistic commentators. If they laughed when Jesus declared that the maid was only sleeping, it was because according to all experience there was no room for entertaining so hopeful a view. Their laughter was rude and irreverent, but from their point of view quite natural, and not without its apologetic value. Sceptical laughter more than once performed an apologetic function in the history of revelation. Sarah laughed when it was announced to her that she should have a child. That laughter meant that she was far past the time of child-bearing, and is a sure sign that the birth of Isaac was a miraculous event. The exiles of Babylon laughed when they heard the news of their recall. The laughter meant that grief was calm and hope dead within them, and justified the prophetic representation of the restoration as a new species of Providential miracle. Even so the mourners at the house of Jairus laughed bitterly at the suggestion of Jesus because, knowing the nature of the illness and having received from the family the announcement of its fatal termination, they could have no reasonable doubt that to speak of sleep was but to mock grief. That laughter is our best evidence that the deed of Jesus was nothing short of a raising from the dead.

* Matthew speaks of τοὺς αὐλητὰς.

It remains to add that the third Evangelist leaves us in no doubt how he understood the event. After the words addressed by Jesus to the deceased, "Child, arise," He introduces into his narrative the statement, "and her spirit came again,"* with manifest intention to describe the case as that of a dead person come to life. This may be regarded as a reliable indication of the construction put upon this evangelic incident in the apostolic church.†

The cure of *the blind man at Jericho* ‡ is the solitary rep-

---

* καὶ ἐπέστρεψεν τὸ πνεῦμα αὐτῆς, viii. 54.

† The three raisings from the dead recorded in the Gospels provoke questions not easy to answer. A benefit to friends, was the restoration to life a benefit to the dead? How adjust such restoration to the supposed finality of the state after death? How are we to conceive of the consciousness of a dead one brought back to life? As to the first question an apology seems to be made for the act in each case. Jairus' daughter was an only child. The young man of Nain was the son of a widow. Lazarus was the head of a much-beloved family broken-hearted for his loss. They are viewed as exceptional cases. The third difficulty Weiss disposes of by supposing that the entrance into the new form of life of departed souls had not yet taken place, the soul had not wakened out of the death slumber into the consciousness of the Beyond. This seems like denying that death had really taken place, but Weiss defends himself against the charge by saying that return from apparent death takes place in a natural way, while in the three Gospel cases it came about not by natural means, but by the immediate agency of God. *Leben Jesu*, i., 555–6. Trench speaks of the last echoes of life ringing in the body after death, for a while, and of the body as full of the reminiscences of life. It is difficult to attach any definite meaning to such words. Beyschlag, speaking of the raising of Lazarus, remarks that the ἤδη ὄζει of Martha cannot have been intended by the writer to exaggerate the miracle by making it consist in restoring life to an already putrefying corpse. One bent on magnifying the miracle would have represented the interval that had elapsed since death not as four days, but rather as four years or centuries, and would not have put the ἤδη ὄζει in the form of a mere inference, a mistaken one as the author thinks. *Leben Jesu*, i., 300. That may be so, but it is difficult to think of a body out of which life has fled four days, as still having within it "echoes of life,' as if the soul had not yet quite left it.

‡ Matt. xx. 29–34; Mark x. 46–52; Luke xviii. 35–43.

resentative in the Triple Tradition of those miraculous works of Jesus which had for their result restoration of lost power to organs of sensation, more particularly to the organs of hearing and vision. Of this class of miracles five are recorded in the Gospels; the one before us, the similar one briefly narrated in the ninth chapter of Matthew, two peculiar to Mark—one a case of blindness, the other a case of deafness accompanied by dumbness—and the healing of the man blind from birth reported in the ninth chapter of the fourth Gospel. No effort is made by the Synoptical Evangelists to make the typical case appear as miraculous as possible. Their chief interest as narrators lies in another direction, viz., to exhibit the blind man as contributing his quota to the homage paid to Jesus on His final journey to Jerusalem, by giving to Him the Messianic title "Son of David." The Evangelists, in common with the apostolic church, recognised it as a significant fact, that while the Christ received only indignity at the hands of the rulers and leaders of Israel, His claims were acknowledged by blind men calling to Him for help, and by children crying Hosanna in His honour.

While no attempt is made to emphasize the blindness that the miracle might appear the greater, it is sufficiently apparent from the narratives that the lack of vision was real and complete. All the accounts imply that the man was dependent on his ears for his knowledge that something unusual was taking place. This comes out most clearly in Luke's version, where it is said that "hearing the multitude pass by he asked what it meant." In introducing this clause Luke does not add to the fact to magnify the miracle, but merely with superior literary skill tells a self-consistent tale, and states explicitly what his brother Evangelists mean when they speak of the man as "hearing that it is Jesus the Nazarene," or that "Jesus passes by." A similar remark applies to the statement occurring further on in Luke's narrative that Jesus commanded the man to be *brought* to him, which removes a vagueness traceable in the companion accounts at this point.

Total blindness is implied in Mark's description of the man as "Bartimæus, the son of Timæus the blind beggar." People would not call a man "the blind beggar," or blind Bartimæus, who was simply suffering from an affection of the eyes, impairing but not destroying vision.

The earnestness with which the man called after Jesus, provoking the rebuke of the crowd, and only stimulated thereby to call morc loudly, revealed the serious character of his disease. It was the behaviour of one who felt that now he had a chance of being delivered from a great affliction It may be added that that behaviour, while showing that the sufferer was stricken with physical blindness, also indicated that he possessed clear spiritual vision, and had faith as well as need to be healed. He saw Jesus with the eye of his mind as the Christ. He had heard of His sayings and deeds, though he had seen nothing, and reflecting on all that had come to his ears, he had arrived at the conclusion that this was the promised King and Saviour of Israel. Hence for the neutral name "Jesus the Nazarene," used by the crowd, he substituted "Jesus, son of David." Hence, also, the energy with which he cried, "have mercy upon me." It was the cry not of despair, but of firm faith and high hope, revealed in word and tone and even in gesture, as when he cast away his garment, leapt up, and came into the presence of Jesus in answer to His invitation.

With such significant indications of the inner state, it could hardly be necessary that Jesus should enquire, What will thou that I should do unto thee? Manifestly the blind beggar wanted not an alms but restoration of sight. An alms he could get from any one; it was something more precious he expected from the Son of David.

What he expected he obtained. Jesus said, Go, or See, thy faith hath saved thee. According to Matthew's version He touched the visionless eyes. Perhaps the statement means nothing more than that Jesus granted the boon craved. The touch was in no case a means of cure, but only a symbolic or sacramental sign to aid faith, and such aid in the present case was not needed. If only a word was spoken, without any accompanying act, as seems to be implied in the accounts of Mark and Luke, the present cure stands in striking contrast to the two cures belonging to the same category peculiar to the second Gospel. In the case of the deaf and dumb man,* Jesus put His fingers into his ears, and touched his tongue with saliva, and looked up to heaven, and sighed, and then only spoke the word Ephphatha. In the case of the blind man of Bethsaida,† He spit on his eyes, and put His hands upon him, and asked him if he saw aught. On learning that vision was as yet imperfect, He put His hands upon his eyes, and the cure was complete. From the careful manner in which these details are given, it has been inferred that the second Evangelist regarded the acts as means of cure, and imagined that the healing virtue lay in the spittle and the touch. But if he had entertained that opinion he would have introduced such acts into all cases of the kind. The story of Bartimæus suffices to show that he had no theory on the subject, and simply reported according to the facts. The practice of Jesus seems to have varied, and His action to have been adapted in each case to the mental state of the person healed. One He healed by a

* Mark vii. 31–35.

† Mark viii. 22–26.

word, another by word and deed combined. He restored vision to the blind man of Jericho in presence of the crowd. The deaf and blind men, of whom Mark tells, He took aside from their fellows and healed them where there were none to witness. In the case reported by the fourth Evangelist, the action ascribed to Jesus seems fitted rather to increase than to cure blindness. The anointing of the blind man's eyes with clay appears to have been an acted parable symbolising the effect of Pharisaic teaching; the sending of the sufferer to the pool of Siloam, an emblem of the counteracting influence of the Christ. Jesus said in effect: the function of the blind guides of Israel is to aggravate the natural spiritual blindness of men. My function is to wash away artificial obstructions to vision, and to restore lost power to the organ of sight. To assign such symbolical significance to the accompaniments of the miracle may be, in appearance, to undermine its historicity; but there remains in the story an amount of solid realism which guarantees its credibility as an authentic reminiscence of the Jerusalem ministry.

VI.

THE GOSPEL MIRACLES IN RELATION TO EXEGESIS—THE NATURE-MIRACLES.

OF all the miraculous acts of Christ those in which the subject of action was inanimate nature have ever been most exposed to sceptical assaults. The reasons of this are not difficult to discover. These events, or the chief of them, such as the feeding of the multitude, the change of water into wine, and the walking on the water, if miraculous at all, are so in a very high degree. They stand in no analogy with the acts of ordinary men. In the case of the healing miracles, or many of them, it is otherwise. It is possible to recognise a certain resemblance between them and curative acts wrought by some men on others, which, however remarkable or unusual, are not commonly regarded as supernatural. In virtue of this resemblance Christ's healing works, though miraculous in degree, may be deemed natural in kind; and if our bias is strongly naturalistic we may easily convince ourselves that even in degree the miraculous element may be reduced to very moderate dimensions. Thus Schleiermacher, whose tendency was to reduce the quantum of miracle in the life of Jesus to a minimum, accepted the healing miracles as manifestations of an enhanced power over disease due to the specific dignity of Christ, similar in kind to that exercised by superior persons on the bodies of their fellow-men.* Then, secondly, the

* *Das Leben Jesu*, p. 218. Schleiermacher admits that this view applies only to some of Christ's healing acts. Certain of them, such as the healings at a distance, he regards as passing over into the category of nature-miracles.

motive or purpose of these nature-miracles is not always very apparent. In the case of the healing miracles a thoroughly satisfactory motive lies on the surface. Without knowing all the ends served by them in connection with the mission of Christ, or the Christian revelation, we see at once that they were works of benevolence in full harmony with the gracious spirit of Jesus, and altogether worthy of one whose vocation it was to be the Saviour of mankind. In the case of the nature-miracles, on the other hand, it is sometimes difficult to discover what end was served, or to see how the apparent end can be reconciled with the known character of the actor. The miraculous production of wine at Cana, or of bread in the desert, does not appear to have been called for by any urgent need of the guests; the walking on the water was not demanded, so far as one can gather from the surface of the record, by any danger to which the disciples were exposed; the cursing of the fig-tree seems out of keeping with the calm, genial temper of Jesus; and the finding of the stater in the fish's mouth seems a departure from the general principle on which He acted, not to use His miraculous power for His own behoof. It might thus plausibly be affirmed, with reference to some if not all of these nature-miracles, that they are merely show-miracles,* serving no other purpose than to evince the divine, supernatural power of Jesus. If this were really the fact, the prejudice against this class of miracles would be shared by many who do not stumble at the miraculous as such, and one would feel strongly inclined to sympathise with the sentiment frankly expressed by Schleiermacher that the entire elimination of nature-miracles from the Gospels would be a welcome result of criticism and exegesis.†

* In German phrase, *Ostentationswunder*.

† *Das Leben Jesu* p. 239.

For, without anticipating the question as to the use or function of miracles, which will come up for discussion at a future stage, the general statement may here be made that every miraculous act of Christ must be conceived of as congruous to His Messianic vocation, and serviceable to the interests of the divine kingdom. None of the miracles, of whatever class, can be regarded as mere displays of power; they must all be viewed as arising naturally out of their occasions, and serving a useful purpose in connection with Christ's work as the Herald and Founder of the kingdom of heaven. Any reputed miracle which did not satisfy this requirement would be justly liable to suspicion.

At present, however, we have to deal, not with the problems of motive and function, but simply with the exegetical question, how far the narratives as they stand shut us up to put a miraculous construction on the so-called nature-miracles. It is a question to be considered without prejudice or foregone conclusion; for while it is a matter of faith that we should recognise the presence of a miraculous element in the Evangelic history as a whole, it is not a matter of faith, but simply a question of fact and of exegesis, whether a miracle must be recognised in any particular event. Orthodox commentators have thought it possible to resolve the standing still of the sun recorded in the book of Joshua, into a poetical apostrophe. In like manner we must entertain it as a possibility, at least, that exegesis may reduce one or more Gospel miracles to natural events.

We may conveniently begin our consideration of this group of miracles by taking up first the two which find a place in the Triple Tradition—the *stilling of the storm* and the *feeding of the multitude*.

The former of these occurrences * commends itself to

* Matt. viii. 23–27; Mark iv. 35–41; Luke viii. 22–25.

every candid reader as an authentic reminiscence of disciple days. One cannot be surprised at the preservation in the apostolic tradition of an incident in which the bearing of Jesus appeared in such a heroic light, in contrast to the panic-stricken behaviour of companions whose previous occupation might have been expected to make them superior to their Master, in the one respect at least of coolness and self-possession amid the perils of the deep. Nor need we doubt that the details of the story are all substantially historical: that there was a storm such as were common on the lake, involving apparent danger; that the disciples were afraid of the ship sinking, and in their fear awakened Jesus as He lay calmly sleeping in the hinder part of the ship; that He chid them for their lack of faith, then rebuked the winds and the waves; and that soon after the wind ceased and there was perfect calm. Some, indeed, find in the Evangelic narratives only a slender basis of fact overlaid, past recognition, with ideal elements borrowed from the Psalter.* Others, less sweeping in their scepticism, confine their doubts to the address of Jesus to the winds and waves. This Schleiermacher regards as suspicious, whether viewed as spoken to the elements, or as really intended for the ear of the disciples. On the former view the words, he thinks, are meaningless, as rebukes and commands have no existence for inanimate objects like the sea or the storm; on the latter view they wear an aspect of ostentation as designed to point out that the resulting calm is the effect of the speaker's will.† Weiss concurs in these objections, though admitting that stress cannot be laid on the argument

---

* So Keim after Strauss. Vide *Jesu von Nazara*, ii., 482. That there is a fact-basis Keim infers from the circumstance that not the deliverance but the *Majestätsbeweiss* is emphasized.

† *Das Leben Jesu*, p. 234.

from the appearance of ostentation, as Jesus might not think it worth while to avoid that, out of regard to the educational effect on the minds of His disciples. His main objection is that the whole description of Christ's attitude towards the storm is dominated by the idea of the state of exaltation. Jesus in the boat on the Sea of Galilee is not Jesus as He was on earth, but Jesus seated at the right hand of God and invested with divine power and glory. It is a majestic picture which takes a strong hold of our religious imagination, and keeps its hold in spite of criticism; nevertheless, it is, thinks our author, totally out of accord with the state of humiliation. He who promised to the disciples that they should see the angels of God descend upon Him to communicate to Him divine miraculous power, who declared to the Pharisees that He cast out devils by the Spirit of God, who at the grave of Lazarus testified that God had raised the dead in answer to His prayer, cannot in the days of His flesh have commanded the elements with divine omnipotence as is represented in the narrative before us. The inference is that the rebuke of the winds, and the command to the sea, Peace, be still, must be set down to the invention of the Evangelist.*

This is criticism based on a dogmatic theory as to the relation in which Jesus stood to the power by which His miracles were wrought. The theory is that Jesus did not perform miracles by a power resident in Himself and at the disposal of His own will like any natural faculty, but simply drew by faith or prayer on the power of God His Father, who was ever ready to lend Him all needful support in connection with His Messianic mission. This theory will be noticed in another place.† It may be admitted here that it

---

* ***Das Leben Jesu,*** ii., pp. 35, 36.

† *Vide* Lecture VII.

is not without apparent support in some texts, and therefore is entitled to respectful consideration. But it must not be regarded as established because it fits in to a certain number of the passages which bear on the question, and then employed as a test of the historicity of other statements which do not seem to harmonise with it. Our theory must be adjusted to all the texts as they stand, instead of the texts being manipulated to square with our theory. But even if the hypothesis in question were accepted, it would not follow that we must reject the address to the storm as a mythical product of faith in the exalted Christ. The address is compatible with either way of conceiving of the miracle; it is indeed compatible with any construction of the resulting calm, whether with Paulus we view it as a natural event, or with Weiss as a Providential deliverance brought about by the miraculous power of God, or as a miracle accomplished by Jesus Himself according to the common opinion. It expresses in dramatic form suited to an emotional state of mind confidence as to the issue; confidence either that the storm will soon cease of itself, or confidence in the Divine protection, or confidence in the speaker's own power. No inference, therefore, can be drawn from the words, either as to the reality, or as to the precise character of the miracle. There is thus no motive for suspecting the genuineness of the utterance put into the mouth of Jesus in the narrative of the second Evangelist (*σιώπα, πεφίμωσο*), which certainly bears a stamp of originality, and looks like an authentic reminiscence of one who was present on the memorable occasion. The objection that the words are meaningless as addressed to the winds is prosaic. In any case Jesus could not so speak as if the words were to be literally heard and obeyed by the storm. The spoken word could only be the symbol of a power lying behind. As such it was a perfectly natural utterance. The true view to take of the apostrophe to the storm is to conceive of it, not as spoken, with express intent to influence either the winds or the disciples, still less as addressed to Satan, the prince of the power of the air,* but as the spontaneous expression of victorious faith and heroic self-possession.

But now to come to the main point. Jesus spake and the storm ceased. What was the connection between the word and the event? Was it a happy coincidence, or a proof of the sagacity of Jesus in foreseeing that the tempest would soon be past, or was it a miracle wrought either by Divine Providence or by Christ's will? There can be no doubt, according to the narratives, what view was taken by the disciples. They said in astonishment, "the wind and the sea obey Him." † A very natural inference, it may be said, if the calm happened to ensue immediately after Jesus had by some form of language manifested a majestic tranquillity of spirit, especially if He made use of the precise words reported; yet the inference, after all, was probably a mistake, and the event only a lucky accident.‡ At most it might be only a result in itself probable, and as such foreseen and confidently predicted by Jesus. In that case His word of command, Peace, be still, would mean: it is a violent storm, but it will soon exhaust itself; § and His rebuke of the disciples for want of faith would be a rebuke for thinking that there was any need of waking Him, as if He had said, where is your faith, there is really no danger? ‖ The nature of the case lends to these naturalistic sugges-

* So Trench after Maldonatus. † Matt. viii. 27, et parall.

‡ So substantially Beyschlag, *Das Leben Jesu*, i., p. 306.

§ So Paulus. ‖ So Schleiermacher, *Leben Jesu*, p. 234.

tions a certain measure of plausibility. The sudden cure of a chronic and serious disease like leprosy or palsy is out of the range of ordinary experience; but the sudden cessation of a storm on a mountain lake, sudden in its rise and of tropical violence while it lasts, is not improbable. The calm might come just after the last and most alarming paroxysm. But other things have to be taken into account before arriving at a final decision. First, as to the rebuke for lack of faith: that could hardly mean there is no danger, for the very reference to faith implies danger. Had there been no danger, then the appropriate reproach had been, where is your weather-skill; do you not know how it is wont to be with these lake-storms, or have you forgotten how many you have come through unscathed? Then the very fact that these experienced fishermen feared is significant. It shows the storm to have been one of exceptional violence. Then finally the construction put by them on the result points it out as something out of the common course which their experience could not lead them to anticipate. We seem, therefore, to be shut up to the conclusion that a marvel of some kind happened either through the will of Jesus, or through the special providence of God. Which of these alternatives is to be adopted is a question of subordinate moment. In favour of the latter is the fact that in chiding His disciples for their lack of faith Jesus spoke of faith absolutely. If He had been about to work a miracle, the reproachful question would more appropriately have taken the form, where is your faith *in me?* The faith desiderated seems to be the faith which He Himself possessed in perfection—confidence in God that He would not suffer those whose lives were of such value to the kingdom to perish in the storm.*

* So Weiss, *Das Leben Jesu*, ii., 36.

We come now to the greater miracle of the *feeding of the multitude,** "the greatest and best attested of all the nature-miracles," † which nevertheless must ever be a stumbling-block to all in whom there is the least taint of the leaven of naturalism. Specially instructive is the treatment which this Gospel incident receives at the hands of Schleiermacher, whose weight as a theologian and position in regard to the miraculous, midway between faith and scepticism, entitle him to more serious attention than we are inclined to accord to the views of Paulus and Strauss, the extreme representatives of anti-miraculous exegesis. Schleiermacher objects to the supernatural view of the occurrence on three grounds: First, the feeding viewed as a miracle was aimless—there was no urgent need for a miraculous interposition; second, the transaction is inconceivable—we cannot tell not merely how it happened, but what happened, we can form no idea of what a spectator might have witnessed; third, it does not appear to have been regarded as a miracle by Jesus Himself.‡ The first objection must be sustained so far as is involved in the admission that the supreme motive of the miracle cannot be found in the necessities of the people.§ The second objection Schleiermacher explains by remarking that in other cases we can distinctly conceive what occurred and could have been seen, though we cannot understand how it was brought about. The fig-tree is green to-day; to-morrow, after being cursed, it is withered. But what did the apostles do and see when they divided the five loaves and two fishes among the thousands? If the pieces mul

* Matt. xiv. 13–21; Mark vi. 30–34; Luke ix. 10–17; John vi. 1–14.

† Keim, *Jesu von Nazara,* ii., 490.

‡ Vide *Das Leben Jesu,* pp. 213, 229, 234.

§ On this *vide* next Lecture.

tiplied in their hands they must have seen it, and might have been expected to report it, yet in the Gospels we find nothing of the kind. Or if the morsels given to individual groups increased in the hands of the recipients that also must have been seen, but neither is there any trace of this in the narratives.* Now, it is quite certain that we cannot gather from the records at what point the multiplication of the food material took place; whether in the hands of Jesus, new loaves starting into being as the previous supply was exhausted; or in the hands of the apostles; or in the hands of the eaters. But supposing one or other of these things to have happened, and to have been witnessed by the apostles, they may not have deemed it necessary in relating the incident to go into such details; in which case these would not find their way into the evangelic tradition. The silence of the narratives justifies the inference that the apostles *did* not tell what they saw; but it does not prove that they *could* not have told what took place.

The third of the objections above enumerated is based on words reported by the fourth Evangelist to have been spoken by Christ shortly after the feeding in the synagogue of Capernaum: "Ye seek me not because ye saw miracles, but because ye did eat of the loaves and were filled." † Recognising the fourth Gospel as the authentic work of the apostle John, Schleiermacher was in a strait betwixt his belief in the historicity of its narratives and his aversion to the miraculous. In the case of the miracle at Cana he contented himself with the observation that though the transaction stood in no analogy with any ordinary human actions it was in keeping with the social spirit of Jesus and had a

* *Leben Jesu*, p. 229. Similarly Weiss, *Leben Jesu*, ii., 194.

† John vi. 26.

satisfactory motive;* and he disposed of the raising of Lazarus by saying that it was not a work of Jesus, but of God in answer to His prayer.† In the case before us he sought escape from miracle altogether by emphasizing the use of the plural, *σημεῖα*, in the above quotation. His argument is that had the singular been used (Ye seek me not because ye saw a miracle), it would have involved the tacit admission that the feeding was a miracle, and that the employment of the plural, on the other hand, has the effect of excluding that transaction from the class of miraculous events.‡ Unfortunately for the argument the Evangelist himself in the same chapter calls the event a *σημεῖον*, which may be held as an evidence that he at least did not understand the words he ascribes to Christ as denying its claim to this character. Schleiermacher does not overlook this fact, but points to it as an indication of helplessness on the part of the Evangelist, urgently demanding some critical hypothesis for its solution.

The distinguished theologian referred to did not himself offer any hypothesis, but left it as a problem for the future. Since his time many have handled the theme, and among others two of the most recent writers on the life of our Lord, Weiss and Beyschlag, who concur in a view which now calls for consideration. That view is that the feeding, if miraculous at all, was a Providential, not a creative miracle. That God could have provided for the wants of the multitude by a creative act is not declared impossible,§ but it is held that there is no clear ground in the records

* *Leben Jesu*, p. 235. † Ib., p. 233.

‡ *Leben Jesu*, p. 234. Beyschlag, without adopting Schleiermacher's argument, concurs in thinking that the words of Christ by implication assert the non-miraculous character of the feeding. *Leben Jesu*, p. 311

§ Not at least by Weiss.

for believing that such an act took place, and that they leave it open to suppose that the needful provision was made in some other way. The essential facts of the story are simply that Jesus, having resolved to feed the multitude, and knowing only of a few loaves and fishes available for the purpose, nevertheless proceeded to carry out His intention, and that the thousands present actually received enough to satisfy hunger, and there was still something over. We are to conceive of Jesus beginning the distribution in ignorance whence the adequate supply was to come, but in full confidence that it would be forthcoming somehow, through the providence of His Father. By what means it was divinely ordered that His expectation was fulfilled the records do not inform us; they are as silent on this point as on the supposed miracle of creation. But we can conjecture. We may imagine that His influence on the spirits of men moved such as had provisions with them to put them at His disposal, and it is credible that in the vast crowd, embracing many who were on the way to the passover feast, not a few were in this position, and that the stores of food in their possession were actually enough to make one meal for all.*

This hypothesis is really a revival of the views of Paulus, with the exception that Jesus is supposed to have begun the distribution in entire ignorance whence the supply was to come, and believing that His Father would provide, even if it should be by a creative miracle. But the suspicious company in which we find the hypothesis is no reason why we should refuse to look at it on its merits. Whether true or false it is in itself perfectly legitimate. We are not required by any consideration to find in any particular

* Weiss, *Das Leben Jesu*, ii., 196. Beyschlag, *Das Leben Jesu*, p. 310.

Gospel incident a stupendous miracle if the texts themselves do not bear witness to it. Whether the multitude were fed by a miracle of creation, or in some other less extraordinary way, is simply a question of fact and of exegesis. And with reference to the hypothesis now under consideration it may be admitted to be intrinsically probable that there was a much larger store of provisions in the crowd than was at first known to the disciples and their Master.* It may also be admitted that even a providential miracle in the circumstances would not be without its tribute of glory to God and to Jesus. But there are considerations which make one pause before adopting this view of the event. First of all, the people seem to have regarded the occurrence as a veritable miracle. But how could they do so if they knew that the food had really been supplied by themselves? That the event should have appeared in a miraculous light to Jesus Himself is less surprising. He was in the position of Abraham when called to sacrifice his son Isaac. The patriarch had then to solve the problem of reconciling his confidence in the divine promise of a seed with the death of the heir through whom alone, so far as could be seen, the promise could be fulfilled. The triumph of his faith was that he accounted that God was able to raise Isaac up even from the dead; and from thence he really received him in a figure. To Abraham's faith before the event Isaac appeared slain and then raised to life. Even so the faith of Jesus accredited His Father with the will and the power to feed the multitude by an act of creation, and for that faith the feeding was an act of creation, although it might be nothing more than an act of special

* From John's account it might be inferred that the five loaves and two fishes were obtained by purchase from a lad who was there selling bread, and had yet so much remaining. So Weiss, *Leben*, ii., 190.

providence similar to that by which a ram was substituted for the destined victim of Abraham's devotion. The disciples do not seem to have shared their Master's mental attitude, or to have had any insight into His thoughts. The one fact clear to them was the total insufficiency of the apparent supply of food for the demands of the hour. As they moved about among the people, arranged in parties of fifty or a hundred, they would of course discover that the actual supply was greater than they had at first imagined, and one fails to see why they should have put a miraculous construction on the transaction, which, nevertheless, we must assume them to have done, as the only explanation of the place which it obtained in the Evangelic tradition as one of the most outstanding memorabilia of the life of Jesus. But least of all intelligible is a miraculous construction on the part of the multitude. And yet such a construction is the only rational explanation of the enthusiasm whose outcome was the determination to make Jesus a king. Of this enthusiasm express mention is made only in the fourth Gospel,* but it is evident from the Synoptical narratives that something of the kind had taken place; for what else is the meaning of the significant fact mentioned by Matthew and Mark that Jesus had to compel His disciples to take ship and sail over to the opposite side?†

The narrative of *the second feeding*‡ has an important bearing on the nature of the transaction reported to have occurred a second time. It has already been acknowledged§ that, from a merely critical point of view, the question whether the second feeding was a distinct event, or only a duplicate and variation of the first, is beset with difficulty. In favour of the former alternative is the simple fact that in

* John vi. 14.
† Matt. xiv. 22; Mark vi. 45.
‡ Matt. xv. 32–38; Mark viii. 1–9.
§ *Vide* Lecture IV., p. 147

records whose substantial historicity is indubitable two feedings are reported. Several differences in detail point in the same direction. The occasion or motive of the second transaction is distinct from that of the first. Jesus is moved to compassion by the destitution of a multitude which has been with Him in a place distant from supplies for the space of three days. In this case the initiative proceeds from Him, not as in the other, from the disciples. Then the numbers of the people, of the available loaves, and of the basketfuls of fragments left over, vary in the two cases. The names for the baskets differ in the two stories, a minute yet curious circumstance.* But on the other hand the general resemblance of the two occurrences is unmistakable, and there are various general considerations which strongly tempt one to see in the second feeding only a duplicate of the first, which has found a place in the records owing to variations in the manner of relating one and the same event in the sources whence the Evangelists obtained their information. The locality of the two feedings seems to be much the same.† Then it does seem surprising that the disciples, after seeing how the multitude had been fed on a former occasion, should have been again perplexed by the lack of supplies, especially as the earlier occurrence was of quite recent date. Another surprise is that a need for such a transaction should have arisen again so soon; that is to say, that Jesus should again have gathered around Him a great crowd

* *κοφίνους* in the first feeding, *σπυρίδας* in the second.

† On the northeastern shore of the Sea of Galilee, near Bethsaida. But it has been maintained that Matthew places the second feeding on the western side. Weiss, who takes this view, thinks that the first Evangelist changed the locality because he thought it unlikely that two events so similar should have happened in the same place. *Leben Jesu*, ii., 187, note. Matthew represents Jesus just before the second feeding as engaged in healing on the mountain, *τὸ ὄρος*, by the Sea of Galilee.

full of the enthusiasm of discipleship, after the wholesale desertion which took place shortly after the first feeding in consequence of His refusal to be made a king, and the disenchanting effect of His discourse in the synagogue of Capernaum as reported by the fourth Evangelist.* Once more it is observable that the second feeding did not lead to a renewal of the attempt to put the crown of a people's sovereign on the benefactor's head, which nevertheless it might have been expected to do. These considerations point to a difficulty in fitting the second feeding into a historical view of the course of events which have led some writers on the life of Jesus, not sceptical in their general attitude, without hesitation to deny that it ever had any existence except in the pages of Matthew and Mark.†

Personally I am not inclined to dogmatise on this question of historical criticism. I rather desire to point out a difference between the two feedings of greater importance than any yet named. It is that if the first feeding might conceivably have been merely a providential miracle, the second could not have been of that character. The situation is so described as to exclude the possibility of such a construction of the event. The people have been three days away from their homes, and have nothing to eat, and

* John vi. 66.

† So Weiss. Weiss explains the presence of this second feeding in the first and second Gospels thus: Mark found a narrative of the feeding in the apostolic document (λογία). He also heard the story from the lips of Peter, varying from the written account in several particulars. The variations led him to think there had been two occurrences of the kind, and accordingly he gave the Petrine version as a second feeding. The author of the canonical Matthew, writing after Mark, and having his Gospel in his hands, adopted the second feeding from it, while taking the first feeding from the λογία. This theory traces the mistake to the uncritical use of sources, and leaves the historicity of the event, split into two thereby, untouched.

Jesus proposes to provide food for them, lest if dismissed unfed, they should faint by the way. This fact doubtless exercises a biassing influence on the view taken of the critical question by those who are unwilling to recognise in the feeding a creative miracle. But a creative miracle is not got rid of by denying the reality of the second feeding. For the narrative of it at least remains, and if in that narrative we are to find merely a version of the story previously told, it follows that those who are responsible for that version must have conceived the first feeding as a creative miracle. If the variation proceeded from Peter, it shows us how one of the eye-witnesses viewed the transaction, viz., not as an unlocking of the stores actually present among the people fed, but as a miraculous provision of food for a vast multitude for the most part destitute of supplies. The significance of the situation in the case of the second feeding cannot be escaped except by supposing that the setting of the story is an invention of the Evangelist, to make it wear less of the appearance of being a mere repetition of a tale already told.*

* This seems to be the view of Weiss, who remarks that Mark fails to assign any clear motive for the second feeding, and thinks the motive actually assigned improbable. *Leben Jesu*, ii., 187, note.

It is no part of my plan to discuss theories of these nature-miracles based on a denial of the historicity of the narratives. I may, however, just allude to the metaphorical theory of Dr. Abbott, which finds in some or all of these miracles metaphors turned into prose. The feeding of the multitude thus resolves itself into a literal prosaic embodiment of the idea, Christ by His teaching the bread of life. Regarding the two feedings as two versions of the same legend, Dr. Abbott finds in the narrative of the second evidence that the tradition originally connected the incident with our Lord's passion. He founds on the expression ἤδη ἡμέραι τρεῖς προσμένουσιν μοι (Mark viii. 3; Matt. xv. 32), which he renders "three days still remain to me." The original tradition he takes to have been "Jesus called his disciples, and said to them, I have compassion on the multitude, because three days still remain to me before the Passover (when He was to be offered up for men), and they have no bread; then

The incident of the *walking on the sea* * stands in close connection with the memorable transaction on the eastern shore of the lake, which has just been under consideration After feeding the multitude, Jesus directed the disciples to take ship and make for the opposite shore, leaving Him behind. It was on this voyage that the peculiar experience befel them which is now to occupy our attention. There can be no reasonable doubt in this case as to what the Evangelists mean to relate. The clever device of the older rationalism for getting rid of the miracle, that, viz., of assigning to the Greek preposition ἐπὶ the sense of *above* instead of *upon* is now entirely out of date, and it is admitted by recent interpreters of all schools that in the story as it stands in all three Gospels, Jesus is represented as appearing to the disciples walking over the sea in the neighbourhood of their vessel. Certainty on this point, however, has not sufficed to prevent or allay doubt as to the reality of the miracle even in believing minds. These doubts rest on various grounds. In the first place, the miracle has appeared to many to be without an aim. In the narrative of this second sea-anecdote, no mention is made of any imminent danger similar to that which had alarmed the disciples on the earlier occasion. And even if there was danger implied though not expressed, what need, it has been asked, for a miraculous journey over the sea to come to their relief; why not still the storm at a distance by prayer, or by the exercise of personal power?

He bestowed the bread upon his apostles. Afterwards the apostles in turn bestowed it upon the multitude." The bread Christ meant was truth. Vide *Through Nature to Christ*, p. 452. The construction ἡμέραι τρεῖς, corrected into ἡμερας in T. R. is peculiar (on this *vide* Winer, Part iii., sec. 62, note 3, who regards it as a parenthesis), but there can be no doubt that the meaning is "the people have remained with me three days."

* Matt. xiv. 22–33; Mark vi 45–52; John vi. 15–21.

Then, secondly, stress has been laid on the fact that the incident occurred in the darkness of night, or in the dim uncertain light of early morning, when it could not clearly be seen what happened. Lastly, advantage has been taken of certain elements in the account given in the fourth Gospel, to which special importance must be attached if that Gospel emanated from the apostle John, an eye-witness. These are that whereas in the first and second Gospels Jesus is represented as entering into the ship, in the fourth it is simply said that the disciples "were willing to receive Him into the ship"; and the statement that "immediately the ship was at the land, whither they went."* The one raises a doubt whether Jesus really did enter the ship, the other states a fact which appears to render such a procedure wholly unnecessary, and even to suggest an entirely different view of the whole circumstances of the case. If the disciples reached the shore immediately after seeing their Master they must have been nearer the land than they had imagined. If so, is not all occasion or need for a hasty journey over the sea for their relief done away with, and are we not left free to suppose that the simple facts of the case were that, just when they had got quite close to the shore they saw Jesus walking past them, not on the sea but on the land, having got thus far on the way from the scene of the feeding round the northern end of the lake towards Bethsaida, the appointed rendezvous? †

But how then, one naturally enquires, is the origin of the story, as told in the Gospels, to be accounted for? If the facts were so simple, whence this miraculous construction of them? Two answers have lately been given to the question. One traces the wondrous tale to mistaken im

* John vi. 21.

† Beyschlag, after Bleek, *Das Leben Jesu*, p. 307.

pressions of the disciples at the time. In order to rejoin His disciples, Jesus had to go round the lake during the night. Before they expect Him they see Him in the grey morning twilight, appearing in the midst of the waves breaking on the shore, without being aware how near they are to the strand. Prone to believe in the miraculous, excited by the darkness and the storm, and ever on the outlook for the extraordinary in their Master's conduct, they say to themselves, He has come to us over the waves, and cling to this romantic belief even after they have set foot on the shore, and found Him standing there. The other view makes the story as it stands in the Evangelic tradition the product of reflection in after days, when Jesus had been glorified, and experiences of disciple-days in His company began to be transfigured in the believing imagination of the apostles. At first they did not imagine that Jesus had come to them walking on the waters. They understood that He had come round the end of the lake on the land. But one thing impressed them greatly: the coincidence between their Master's appearing in view and their speedy arrival at their destination. It seemed to them more than a coincidence. It was a special Providence; there was a causal connection between the two facts: it was because of the appearing of Jesus that they had at once got to land. Out of this first impression and inference sprang later the idea that Jesus had come to their aid across the sea, as set forth in all the Gospel narratives; whence finally flowed the representation in the secondary form of the tradition, as given in Matthew and Mark, that Jesus actually entered the ship, and that thereon the wind ceased.*

The grounds of doubt are so far from being frivolous that

---

* So Weiss, *Das Leben Jesu*, ii., 208.

one cannot be surprised at attempts being made to eliminate this nature-miracle even by men not occupying the position of theoretic naturalism, and judging of the Gospel narratives simply from the view-point of substantial historicity. Of the two solutions above indicated the former is to be preferred, as at once the less artificial and involving the least sacrifice of the historical trustworthiness of the Evangelic tradition. It finds therein the record of an honest impression made upon eye-witnesses at the time, not the later invention of a devout imagination. It assigns to the walking on the water subjective if not objective truth, as so appearing at the moment to the eyes of the disciples. Not less than the other, however, it assumes that the Synoptical accounts depart from the original fact in representing Jesus as entering into the ship, and that all the accounts are mistaken as to the nature of the main incident. Must we then acknowledge the force of the objections, and in defiance of the Evangelists acquiesce in the verdict that no such thing as a walking on the water ever took place in the life of Jesus? Before doing so it will be necessary to be quite sure that we have taken into account all the elements of the story, and put a right construction on them. First, as bearing on the question of motive, the superstitious terror of the disciples is significant. Was not that terror which mistook Jesus for a spirit, an index of a mental excitement, caused by danger, which would have had no existence on a calm night? The statement made both in Matthew and in Mark that when Jesus entered the ship the wind ceased points in the same direction. The interest of the divine kingdom seems to have been exposed to a twofold peril at that crisis; on one hand through a false enthusiasm among the people, and on the other through a storm on the lake threatening the lives of the few faithful though as yet unenlightened followers of the Christ. Jesus having first dealt with the one peril on the land, proceeded next to deal with the other on the deep. That no other way of dealing with it than the one spoken of in the records was possible cannot be alleged, and why precisely that method was adopted it may be difficult to explain. That it sins against the law of parsimony in miracle may be plausibly asserted. But it certainly cannot be regarded as evidence that Jesus really did not cross the sea for the purpose of cheering and saving His disciples amid danger, that He wished to pass their storm-tossed vessel by on one side. That may simply have been a manœuvre delicately adapted to a state of mind easily scared by the too sudden appearance of an unexpected friend. Then as for the text in the fourth Gospel from which it has been inferred that when Jesus appeared to the disciples they were close to the shore, is it quite certain that the interpretation of it on which the inference is based is correct? The Evangelist says, Therefore were they willing to receive Him into the ship, and straightway the ship was at the land. The "therefore" contrasts the present willingness with the past fear. They were willing now to receive one whose appearance in the neighbourhood of the ship had scared them before, having become aware who it was. That the will was followed by the deed is implied by the καὶ at the commencement of the second clause of the verse. Had the intention been to say, they were willing to receive Him, but it was unnecessary, for immediately the ship was at the land, the proper conjunction to use would have been ἀλλὰ or δὲ not καὶ. The fact that it is not used may be held to counterbalance the employment of the imperfect ἤθελον instead of ἠθέλησαν, which seems to imply an unfinished action. The εὐθέως, "straightway," it is not necessary to take strictly. It may simply contrast the short time taken to accomplish the remainder of the voyage compared to the tediousness of the first part when the disciples toiled in rowing against wind and waves.* The estimate of the distance reached when Jesus appeared, given by the fourth Evangelist, does not of itself prove that they were still a good way from the western shore. If it was correct they were not then much more than half way across, for the lake was above forty furlongs broad.† But they might have been mistaken, and have made greater speed than they imagined, or the wind might have driven them out of their course towards a nearer point of land. Yet on the whole it is not probable that experienced sailors, who had made the same voyage in all sorts of weather, were so completely out in their reckoning as to think they were only half way across, when they were within a few yards of land.

The two remaining incidents of the lake, the *great draught of fishes* ‡ and the *stater in the fish's mouth*,§ may here conveniently be considered.

The former of these need not detain us long. The interest in this case centres not in the miraculous element, but in the two questions, Is the incident historical, and is it in its true place in the Evangelic history? The circum

---

* Godet, *in loc.*, thinks that the arrival was instantaneous and by miracle. The ἤθελον he takes to mean, they had barely time to take Him in when the ship was at the land. He is of opinion that a continuation of the voyage by the laborious process of rowing with Jesus seated in the boat would be out of keeping with the regal magnificence of the walking on the waters. But surely this is to introduce a theatrical element into the incident. A miraculous propulsion of the boat at lightning speed would be a miracle of mere ostentation.

† Matt. and Mark represent the disciples as being ἐν μέσῳ τῆς θαλάσσης when the evening came in. If the fourth watch found them still not much more than half way, the storm must have been violent enough.

‡ Luke v. 1–11; cf. John xxi. 4–9. § Matt. xvii. 24–27.

stances that the narrative is found only in one of the Synoptical Gospels, and that not, as we might have expected, the one containing the Petrine tradition; that an incident is recorded in the appendix to the fourth Gospel so similar as to suggest the hypothesis of a duplicate; and that an emblematic significance is assigned to the occurrence in the words reported to have been spoken by Jesus, lend plausibility to the notion that here we have to do not with an actual event, but simply with a symbolic story invented to embody the promise made to Peter by his Master that he should become a fisher of men.* Of those who are prepared to recognise in the incident something more than a metaphor transformed into a fact, some have doubted whether it is in its true place in Luke's Gospel, and ought not rather to be assigned to the post-resurrection period, as in the fourth Gospel. In this connection stress is laid on the exclamation of Peter on seeing the great draught of fish, Depart from me, for I am a sinful man, O Lord; which, as connected with the period of the first call to discipleship, seem to lack point and appropriateness, but gain deep meaning when conceived of as spoken by Peter when his humiliating denial of his Lord was fresh in his recollection.† But one has no great difficulty in imagining such an excitable, impressionable man as Peter uttering the words at any time, without any special occasion for calling his sin to mind, viewing them simply as an expression of reverence. Strauss characterizes Peter's fear as superstitious, and not at all new-testament like.‡ Granted, but what then? Was it to be expected that the disciples at the time of their first call should be men of the new testament in their thoughts and feelings? On the con

* Mark i. 17. † Weiss, *Das Leben Jesu*, i., 430.

‡ Strauss, *Das Leben Jesu*, i., 562.

trary, was it not the very aim of their vocation that they might be associated with Christ, and in His company gradually imbibe the spirit of the new Christian era, the era of the better hope, when we no longer stand afar off in fear, but draw nigh to God in filial trust? Peter's exclamation, as reported by Luke, is in keeping with the initial period of discipleship, and just on that account it supplies no ground for transferring the incident to the later period when discipleship was about to pass into apostleship. At that late time Peter might have more reason than ever before for calling himself a sinful man, but his sense of unworthiness was not so likely then to express itself in the form of a, Depart from me.

Looking at the incident in connection with its probable aim, it seems equally appropriate at the beginning and at the end of the history. Christ's purpose probably was to inspire Peter with enthusiasm for his spiritual vocation. There was a need for this at both periods, and in view of this fact it becomes credible that the narratives of Luke and John are not variations of the same history, but records of distinct events. The earlier event served the purpose of winning Peter to the life of discipleship, the later of inspiring him with devotion to the heroic career of the apostolate.*

As for the nature of the action recorded, it has been variously conceived as a miracle of power controlling the movements of the fish and directing them into a particular course,† or of supernatural knowledge of the place where the fish were to be found at a certain moment, or of pro-

---

* Schleiermacher says this miracle promoted increase of gain, or diminution of need and care, and was therefore unsatisfactory in motive *Leben Jesu*, p. 213. In reality it put an end to Peter's earthly calling.

† So Trench. Godet, and many others.

phetic clairvoyance in the exercise of a faculty natural to man, but possessed by Jesus in a preternatural degree,* or so far as Jesus was concerned a mere act of trust in a special Providence of God making itself subservient to His designs.† It is not necessary, and the narrative does not enable us, to decide peremptorily between these various views. We are not even absolutely shut up to the belief that there was a miracle in the case in any form or degree. It is not an impossible supposition that the knowledge possessed by Jesus was such as might be obtained by observation. Traces of such a great shoal of fish might be visible on the surface to any one who happened to be looking in the proper direction. A well-known writer remarks: "The density of the shoals of fish in the Sea of Galilee can scarcely be conceived by those who have not witnessed them. Frequently these shoals cover an acre or more of the surface, and the fish, as they slowly move along in masses, are so crowded, with their back fins just appearing on the level of the water, that their appearance at a little distance is that of a violent shower of rain pattering on the surface." ‡ But, while this description clearly proves the possibility of becoming aware of the presence of a shoal by observation, the supposition that our Lord acquired the knowledge which enabled Him to give directions to the fishermen, in this way, is rendered very improbable by the fact that the draught of fish appeared to Peter marvellous not only in itself, but in connection with the agency of Jesus; for that he recognised Jesus as somehow the cause of the extraordinary and utterly unlooked for success is manifest in his words. Yet it is noticeable that the nar

* So Beyschlag, *Leben Jesu*, i., 304.

† So Weiss, *Leben Jesu*, i., 430.

‡ Tristram, *Natural History of the Bible*, p. 285.

rative does not lay stress on that agency in explaining the emotions of Peter and his companions, but simply on the quantity of fish taken. "Astonishment," we read, "took possession of him and all that were with him at the draught of the fishes which they had taken."* And it may be admitted that the purpose of the transaction did not absolutely demand a miracle. Christ's aim was not merely to attach the disciples to Himself, but to fire them with zeal for their new vocation. For that end, what was wanted was not a mere miracle as displaying supernatural power or knowledge, but an experience in connection with their old vocation which, whether brought about miraculously or otherwise, should take possession of their imagination as an emblem of the great future which lay before them in their new career as apostles, or fishers of men. The phenomenal draught of fish, however brought about, fulfilled this purpose better than a small take could have done, even though the fish had been expressly created before the eyes of the disciples. Such a miracle would have filled them with astonishment at the worker, but it would not have awakened in their breasts wondering thoughts and high hopes in reference to the work and progress of the Divine Kingdom.

The story of the *stater in the fish's mouth* offers no handle to the patrons of the metaphorical theory, which resolves certain of the Gospel miracles into figures transformed into facts. The point open to question in this case is whether there was a fact and not merely a word without any deed, or at least any closely corresponding. Whether any action followed, and of what precise nature it was, is left to be inferred for the record is silent. The word ascribed to Jesus is

---

* Luke v. 9.

beyond all doubt authentic, bearing as it does that unmistakable stamp of originality which characterizes so many of His sayings. That it is found in Matthew only is no just ground for calling its authenticity in question. The first Gospel either is, or is based on, the collection of *Logia* ascribed to the apostle Matthew by Papias; and if remarkable words such as those occasioned by the demand of the Temple-tax were to have a place in the Evangelic records, it is there we should expect to find them. Their absence from the second and third Gospels is to be accounted for probably by the consideration that their record of Christ's utterances at this period bears marks of condensation. The first Evangelist showed good judgment in preserving this conversation between Peter and his Master in reference to the tribute-money, instead of leaving it out, as if of minor importance in comparison with the discourse on ambition recorded by all the Synoptists. He doubtless perceived that it contributed to the same end, the chastisement of that evil spirit which had led the disciples on the way home to Capernaum to dispute which of them should be greatest in the kingdom of heaven. It is when viewed in this connection that the whole incident becomes luminous, and that the words of Jesus appear full of instruction. With the design of teaching the foremost disciple a lesson of humility and self-effacement Jesus directed his attention very pointedly to three things, saying in effect: I might if I choose stand on my dignity and with a show of reason refuse payment; nevertheless I am willing to pay; and my reason for consenting, mark it well, is to avoid giving offence, in a spirit of meekness.

What we are concerned with here is the manner in which payment was made, and the connection between it and the direction given by Jesus to Peter. The great body of believing interpreters in all ages have taken that direction in its literal and plain sense as it stands in the Gospel, and assumed that it was acted upon and literally fulfilled, Peter going to the lake and catching a fish with a coin in its mouth or stomach sufficient to pay the tribute for himself and his Master; and so have found in the incident a miracle of power or of knowledge, consisting in providing that such a fish should be present where Peter cast his line, or in knowing that it should be there ready to be caught. Such a miracle on its physical side may appear grotesque, but on the ethical side it presents an impressive contrast between the intrinsic dignity of Jesus and the indignity of His earthly state. A royal Person appears therein impoverished and degraded, yet in the very act which reveals the meanness of His condition asserting His royalty. Nor can any fault be found with the miracle on the score of motive. It was not wrought for gain, or for the purpose of personal advantage. It is no exception to the rule that Christ made no use of His miraculous powers for His own behoof. Neither is it a valid objection to this miracle that it was not urgently needed for the ostensible purpose of paying the tribute, inasmuch as in Capernaum one so well known could have had no difficulty in obtaining the needed sum from friends. This is doubtless true, but it does not prove the miracle to be superfluous. For the end in view was not mere payment, but in the act of paying to teach a lesson which could not be so impressively taught by a common mode of discharging the debt, as by a parabolic action of a supernatural character.

There does not appear, therefore, to be any reason why this particular miracle, viewed abstractly, should be a stumbling-block to any to whom the miraculous in general is not an offence. Nevertheless dissents have been entered to the traditional interpretation by theologians entitled to a respectful hearing. No one has ventured to follow Paulus in his attempt to unite faith in the accuracy of the record with a naturalistic view of the transaction by taking the verb *εὑρήσεις* as meaning not "find" but "obtain," and construing the direction to Peter as having for its import, Go fish in the lake, and selling what you catch, procure the needful sum of money. That the verb can bear the meaning "procure" is not questioned, but it has been generally acknowledged that as it stands in Matthew's text it can only be rendered "find," as in the authorised version. Most of those who doubt the reality of the miracle regard the form in which Christ's direction to Peter appears in the Evangelic tradition as based on some misconception of His words. Thus Weiss thinks that the original state of the case was that Jesus sent Peter to fish that he might raise the money in the usual way of his ordinary calling, adding for his encouragement that God could easily bless his efforts, so that what was needed might be forthcoming; which pious reflection, it is supposed, was transformed in the oral tradition into a promise that God would bestow success through a special miracle.* Beyschlag conjectures that Jesus sent Peter to catch one fish of value sufficient to yield in sale the required sum, and that through misunderstanding of the ambiguous word *εὑρίσκειν*, supposed to have been employed, the impression had arisen that He had told the disciple to catch a fish with a coin in its mouth.† Ewald, on the other hand, regards the words recorded in the Gospel as a substantially correct reproduction of what Jesus said, but from the fact that it is not stated that such a fish was found, and that the tribute was paid in the manner described, he infers that the words were not meant to be taken prosaically

* *Das Leben Jesu*, ii., 147.

† *Das Leben Jesu*, 304.

as a business direction, but were a spirited proverbial utterance based on known though rare examples of money found in fishes.* Farrar, without suggesting any solution, confesses himself perplexed in these terms: "The peculiarities both of the miracle itself and of the manner in which it is narrated, leave in my mind a doubt as to whether, in this instance, some essential particular may not have been either omitted or left unexplained." † Such doubts, on such grounds, may be expected to reappear in exegetical literature. This very peculiar nature-miracle cannot be regarded as an absolute certainty, but at most as a probability.

The change of water into wine, at the marriage feast in Cana, the earliest of the nature-miracles, and the beginning of all Gospel miracles, is in some respects the most perplexing. Symbolically interpreted, as proclaiming by a parabolic deed the genius of the Christian era, and its superiority to the legal era now passing away, or as exhibiting the free, humane, genial spirit of Jesus in contrast to the austere spirit of the Baptist, the story is most welcome to the believing mind, and has been the fruitful theme of many edifying homilies. But faith rises from the letter into the pure, serene region of mystic contemplation through a thorny thicket of difficulties on which sceptical critics delight to expatiate. Unless prophecy be the chief or sole end of the miracle, it appears to have no aim. A hint of such may indeed be found at the close, where it is stated that by this first sign Jesus "manifested forth His glory." If the glory meant be that of the Divine Logos demonstrated by the exercise of creative power, then does not the transaction become a solitary example of a show-miracle, *Ostentationswunder*, wrought merely for an evidential pur-

---

* *Geschichte Christus*, 467. † *The Life of Christ*, ii., 46.

pose? If, on the other hand, the glory referred to be something more special, the glory, viz., of Christ, as the Inbringer of the new era in which the water of Judaism is replaced by the rich, nourishing wine of grace, why is there no hint of the import of the parabolic action in a Gospel so prolific in discourse illustrative of the spiritual significance of Christ's works; why does the narrative not wind up with edifying comments similar to those contained in chapter iv. on the worship of the Father, or in chapter vi. on the Bread of Life? Or are we to find a clue to the immediate design of the miracle in the word of Mary to her Son, "they have no wine," and say that the motive was to furnish a fresh supply for the entertainment of the guests? But to what end add more when men have already had enough, if they have not indeed drunk to excess, as seems to be hinted in the speech put into the mouth of the ruler of the feast? Above all, why add so much more; six waterpots full, each vessel containing two or three firkins apiece, or some twenty gallons, the whole amounting to about one hundred and twenty gallons? To these puzzling questions relating to the subject of motive have to be added others relating to the mutual behaviour of Mary and Jesus. The mother has recourse to her Son, as if confident in His power to extricate them out of their convivial embarrassments. The Son first repels His mother's advances with at least a show of harshness, then immediately proceeds to comply with her wishes, the hour which a moment ago was not come being now come. Whence the mother's confidence? Has she seen her Son work miracles already—if not, how should she expect a miracle now, or does she not expect a miracle, but look for belief by natural means? And how is Christ's strange and apparently inconsistent behaviour to be accounted for?

It may not be possible to answer all these questions satis

factorily, but the difficulties they present have their consolations for the apologist. They help to show that we are dealing with history and not with mere fiction; that we have here to do with something more than a mere *That-programme*, in which the doctrine is everything and the deed nothing but a framework.* A fictitious history with a doctrinal tendency would have contained some words indicating the key to its interpretation. A writer inventing a story for a didactic purpose would have avoided introducing into his narrative features likely to prove a stumbling-block, such as the jest about the worse wine given when men have well drunk, and the abrupt reply of Jesus to Mary. The best explanation of the introduction of these particulars is just that they actually happened.

Assuming then that we have before us a history and not a fiction, there can be little doubt what the writer means to relate. He tells the wondrous story of a large quantity of water changed into wine by the miraculous power of Jesus. This is the beginning of miracles he would record, not any abated form of the marvel such as water made to taste as wine by the enchantment of Christ's spiritual discourse,† or by the exercise of some magnetic influence throwing the guests into a state of hypnotism.‡ He represents the ruler of the feast as tasting water that had become wine,§ as in a subsequent allusion to Cana he speaks of it as the place where Jesus made the water wine.‖ This settled and it being assumed that the report proceeds from John an apostle and eye-witness, it might be supposed that there was no alternative left but to accept the miracle however

* So Keim, *Jesu von Nazara*, ii., 503.

† So Ewald, *Christus*, p. 328. ‡ So Beyschlag, *Leben Jesu*, p. 308.

§ v. 9. τό ὕδωρ οἶνον γεγενημένον.

‖ Cap. iv. 46. ὅπου ἐποίησεν ὕδωρ οἶνον.

hard to conceive in itself, and notwithstanding all its accom panying difficulties; unless we are prepared to fall back on the solution of the older rationalism, which in this instance appears at its worst, and to think of the transaction as a natural event mistaken for a supernatural by a disciple who ike the other guests had "well drunk."* But a recent writer on the Life of Jesus, believing in the authenticity of the fourth Gospel, and believing that in the narrative before us the author offers to his readers a creative miracle in which the glory of Christ as the divine Logos was shown forth, has found it possible to strike out for himself a new path. It is to discover in the record not the literally exact account of the event as it happened, but the transfigured view of it entertained by the aged apostle regarding all the details of the earthly life of Jesus in the light of the idea of that life as a whole as the self-manifestation of the Logos.† That is to say, the writer referred to deals with the Johannine account of the miracle at Cana, somewhat as we have already found him dealing with the Synoptical narrative of the stilling of the storm, which he regards as having undergone modification under the influence of the apostolic conception of the exalted Christ. Three questions occur to one in reference to this hypothesis. If this is the view to be taken, what was the original fact-basis of the transformed idealised

* The view of Paulus is to this effect: Jesus wished to make a present of wine, got, of course, in a natural way, to the newly married couple, and to do it in a jocular manner suitable to the festive occasion, making believe it was water changed into wine, which a company that had ndulged freely might easily be persuaded of. Jesus allowed them to think so not to spoil the jest. John is supposed to have been in the secret. Another writer quoted by Strauss (*Leben Jesu*, ii. 218), thinks John was more or less intoxicated and shared the delusion of the guests. The "glory" shown forth by the transaction was the glory of a geniality remote from the sternness expected of the Messiah.

† Weiss, *Das Leben Jesu*, i., 363.

story; are there any elements in the narrative to justify such a view; and is it credible that an eye-witness would take such liberties with facts, and what are the consequences of such a supposition?

As to the first of these questions, the fact-basis we are given to understand was a Providential miracle. Jesus, in unconditional trust in God, and in reponse to His mother's appeal, had promised help. On turning to the circle of His attendants, in the hope that through some of them, say Nathanael, who had connections with Cana, the needful supply of wine might be forthcoming, He found that there was no resource in that quarter. At length in a way humanly unforeseen, though naturally brought about, the means presented themselves for meeting the difficulty which had arisen. Whether Jesus gave orders to fill the water-pots with water, as represented, is not said; if He did, then He must have entered on the business, as in the case of the feeding, believing that God would send help from above, even if it should be by a creative miracle. But as it turned out that was unnecessary; wine was provided in some natural way, yet in a way so remarkable as to produce on the minds of the disciples the impression of a true miracle.*

But if there was a miracle in the case, why not a miracle of creation? Is there anything in the narrative to justify us in declining to accept its own representation of the occurrence? Besides the isolated character of a creative miracle which is an argument not taken out of, but brought to, the record, the one thing alleged is the disproportionateness of the effect said to have been produced by the miracle to the greatness of the cause. The sole result specified is the

* *Leben Jesu*, i., 364.

strengthening of the faith of the disciples. Surely, it is argued, if a miracle of creation had taken place, it ought to have made an impression worthy of commemoration in a wider circle, even among the whole assembled guests, if not among the whole population of Cana. Does not the fact that no mention is made of such a wide-spread impression point to a transaction occurring within the inner circle of the disciples, and appreciable by them alone in its mysterious character?* This is an argument *e silentio*, which can scarcely be recognised as legitimate, seeing the narrative, while saying nothing as to the effect of the miracle on the outside circle, clearly implies their knowledge of it. It is stated parenthetically that the servants who drew the water knew whence the wine came, whose excellence surprised the governor of the feast, and it may be taken for granted that what they knew would very soon become known to all, and the story pass round the astonished company, We poured in water and we drew out wine.

But assuming that the miracle was originally providential, how did it ultimately become transformed in the thoughts even of eye-witnesses into a miracle of creation? The answer is, the details of the transaction faded away from recollection, and only the impression of a wonderful event remained, and in the light thrown on disciple-experiences by the bright image of Christ's whole earthly life, this event, extraordinary at the first, naturally assumed a yet higher character.† In other words, distance lent enchantment to the view. It is a plausible theory, but not satisfactory. In the first place, the narrative bears no trace of forgetfulness of detail, but on the contrary exhibits distinct evidence of vivid recollection. The writer remembers what passed be-

* *Leben Jesu*, i., 364. † Ib., 364–5.

tween Mary and Jesus, all about the water-pots, their number and capacity, and the filling of them to the brim, and the humorous observation of the master of the feast on tasting the newly-made wine. The transformation of the miracle into a creative one on the part of an eye-witness possessing so good a memory, can hardly have been involuntary or spontaneous. And if the transformation was conscious and intentional, does it not tend seriously to shake our confidence in the Evangelist as a witness to the words and deeds of Jesus? If, for the glory of the *Logos*, he could convert a miracle of Providence into the far more imposing miracle of creation, how can we be sure that he would not convert a purely natural event into a miracle, or that he would report Christ's words faithfully any more than His deeds, or that even the doctrine of the Divine *Logos* is anything more than a Johannine creation? And if John cannot be regarded as a true and faithful witness as to the things of Christ, what do we gain by establishing the authenticity of his Gospel? What is the great difference between a life-history transformed beyond recognition in the mind of an apostle, and the same history idealised under the influence of theological tendency by an unknown writer of the second century? The authenticity of the fourth Gospel being assumed, two alternatives lie before us: either on the authority of an eye-witness to accept the miracle as reported, or to admit that the testimony even of an apostle is no sure guide to the truth concerning the deeds and words of Jesus.*

---

* Weiss complains that some of his critics confound his view with that of Paulus. It differs from the latter in the worthier account it gives of the attitude of Jesus, and in assuming that there was a miracle *of Providence* at least. It agrees with it in regarding the supply of wine as brought about by natural though unexpected means. Weiss' theory is a cross between Paulus and Baur.

The last of the nature-miracles, *the cursing of the fig-tree*,* forms a strange, startling contrast to the first. In this Jesus appears in genial aspect, sympathising with the festive mood of the occasion, and using His miraculous power in a most generous way to bestow a marriage present on the newly-wedded; in that His manner is severe, His temper appears morose, and His action the opposite of benevolent. Just in this contrast lies one of the chief difficulties connected with this weird story of the last days. The loving-hearted man who began His career by changing water into wine to promote good cheer among a wedding party, ends by cursing a fig-tree on which He seeks but finds not figs to satisfy His own hunger. What can it mean? Has His temper become so corroded by the bitter experiences of the past three years that He can be irritated against an object without sense, and that even when the tree which provokes His resentment is not in fault, as a tree can be by not bearing fruit in its season?

Of course this is impossible. No right-minded man can believe that Jesus used His miraculous power to take revenge on a tree which had disappointed His expectations. If the last nature-miracle be historical, the key to its interpretation must be found in the same direction as in the case of the first, viz., in assigning to it a symbolical character. The apparently irrational procedure must be viewed in connection with the prophetic function of Christ, and regarded as a prophecy in action. We must conceive the leafy but fruitless tree as representing to the Prophet's eye the people of Israel offering to its Messiah an enthusiastic homage which cannot be counted on, and the curse pronounced on the barren tree as a foreshadowing of that people's coming

* Matt. xxi. 18–22; Mark xi. 12–14; 20–25.

doom. A symbolic act of the kind recorded is intrinsically probable. The hopelessly bad spiritual condition of Israel and her approaching judgment were constantly present to Christ's mind, and formed the frequent subject of His discourse, during the passion week. The parables of the two sons, the vinedressers, and the marriage feast, spoken in the temple in these last days, all bear more or less directly on the theme. Jesus was in such a mood, He was so filled with the prophetic spirit, that one can hardly imagine Him seeing the unusual phenomenon of a fig-tree covered with leaves, yet having no fruit, without the resemblance it bore to Israel suggesting itself to His thoughts. And it was natural that He should speak as He felt. The miraculous consequence may astonish us as it seems to have astonished the disciples, but that Jesus in presence of that symbolic tree of evil omen should have uttered some such words as the Evangelists put into His mouth, can seem unlikely to no one who adequately conceives the tragic situation and its attendant emotions.*

The one serious objection to the symbolic interpretation is the lack of foundation for it in the records. This is the more noticeable that the occurrence was not unaccompanied with a moral. The disciples having expressed their surprise at the speedy withering of the tree, Jesus, we are told, went on to speak of the power of faith to do even greater things, as if the mere miracle, and not its spiritual significance, were the point of importance. Had it only been recorded that He made the reflection: so shall it be unto this generation! In both the narratives hunger is represented as the means of bringing the fig-tree under the notice of Jesus. Hunger at such a time, shortly after leaving a

* Weizsäcker, *Untersuchungen*, p. 548, thinks the word of cursing historical, and the miracle a legendary outgrowth.

friendly home in Bethany, may appear improbable, but the more pertinent remark is that it seems irrelevant to the prophetic purpose. Without being hungry Jesus might have noticed the tree, and used it as an emblem. Must we then conclude either that the symbolic interpretation is a mistake, and that the transaction really was of the character it bears on the surface, the cursing of the tree being an end in itself and not a means to an end, or that the Evangelists reflect a tradition which had failed to catch its true meaning? Were one shut up to a choice between these two alternatives one could not hesitate to adopt the latter as the less evil. Better sacrifice the insight or accuracy of the reporters than impugn the moral character of Jesus.

If the narratives disappoint us by their silence as to the prophetic import of the miracle, they may be thought to compensate for the loss by throwing light on the manner of its happening. In discoursing on the power of faith in connection with the blasting of the tree, Jesus may be held to imply that it was by faith—the faith of God, as it is called in Mark—that He Himself had brought about the result. In that case the order of events may be conceived of thus: Jesus speaks the prophetic word, No man eat fruit of thee hereafter for ever, and passes on. God sets His seal to the prophecy, and smites the tree with the hand of death, a sign to all who see it of the doom which ere long a punitive providence shall inflict on His faithless elect people.*

The fact that Luke omits this incident, and in its stead records a parable of kindred import peculiar to his Gospel, offers a tempting opportunity to the advocates of the metaphorical theory. The view they favour is that the story told by Matthew and Mark is simply Luke's parable of the

* So Weiss, *Das Leben Jesu*, ii., 444.

barren fig-tree * turned into a miracle-history. It will be observed that this view implies that the miracle was at first conceived as symbolical in import. The course run was this: first there was a prophetic parable, then the parable was transformed into a prophetic miracle, then the miracle lost its original significance, and degenerated into an event whose motive and meaning were misunderstood as recorded in the first two Gospels. What might happen to an invented history might happen also to a real history, and the story as it stands in the Evangelic records may quite well be the narrative of an actual occurrence whose import, if not misapprehended, is at least inadequately exhibited by the reporters.

It has been remarked that Luke's parable is more faithful to the spirit of Jesus than the miracle recorded by his brother Evangelists. It *appears* so, and the appearance may have had some weight with Luke as a reason for omitting the miracle. But in truth the moral of parable and miracle is one and the same. The parable intimates that the people of Israel, represented by the fig-tree, is in danger on account of its unfruitfulness; the miracle proclaims that the danger threatened is near and inevitable. The merciful Intercessor would be glad still to plead for a respite, but he knows that it is now too late.

---

* Luke xiii. 6–13.

VII.

THE GOSPEL MIRACLES IN RELATION TO THE WORKER.

To such as feel the modern aversion to the supernatural it comes as a surprise and a disappointment that Jesus had anything to do with miracles. Miraculous pretensions, in their view, savour of charlatanry, but how could the Sage of Galilee have aught in common with the charlatan? As a teacher was He not conspicuous not merely by His wisdom and moral elevation, but by the severity of His attitude towards pretence and unreality in religion? What more remarkable in the Gospels than the scathing exposure of Pharisaism with its sham morality and its sham sanctity! How hard to think of this vigorous denouncer of counterfeit holiness playing the sorry part of a thaumaturge! John, it is written, did no miracle. That fact the children of the *Zeitgeist* would set down to his credit. They wish the same thing had been recorded of Jesus. Therein the Baptist seems superior to his great contemporary. He was nothing but a prophet, a stern, fearless, impartial preacher of righteousness, who proved his sincerity and earnestness by martyrdom. If Jesus, in some respects, rose far above him—in range of thought, in geniality, as the inaugurator of a new era, not the mere reformer of an old era—did He not, in so far as He intermeddled with thaumaturgical arts, fall far below him? Nay, does He not sink even below the level of Mahomet, who, with all his faults, had sincerity enough to keep steadily clear of miraculous pretensions?

There are two ways in which unbelievers in the super natural may escape this painful sense of incongruity in connection with the public character of Jesus. One is to re gard the miraculous element in the Gospels as for the most part, if not wholly, the legendary creation of a later generation. This is the method adopted by Strauss. The other is to regard the thaumaturgical side of Christ's career as an unwelcome rôle imposed upon Him by the age in which He lived. This is the way preferred by Renan, who has expressed his opinion on the point with much frankness in his famous *Vie de Jesu*. "Many circumstances," he observes, "appear to indicate that Jesus became a thaumaturge tardily and unwillingly. Often he performed his miracles only after prayer, with a sort of bad humour, and reproaching those who demanded them from him with carnality of spirit. . . . . One would say, at times, that the rôle of thaumaturge is disagreeable to him, and that he strives to give as little publicity as possible to marvels which spring up, as it were, under his feet. . . . . It is therefore permissible to believe that his reputation as a thaumaturge was imposed on him, that he did not resist it much, but that he also did little to aid it, and that in any case he was sensible of the vanity of opinion on the point."* The brilliant *savant* finds it necessary to make this apology for his hero, because he has no doubt that actions, which would now be considered signs of folly, did really hold a prominent place in His life. His historic conscience does not allow him to listen too much to nineteenth century repugnances, and to attempt to rescue the character of Jesus by suppressing facts which in the judgment of contemporaries were of the first importance. But, indeed, he does not feel that there is any

* *Vie de Jesu*, p. 264.

occasion for solicitude about the character of Jesus. The thaumaturgic aspect of His public career is after all but a spot on the sun. Who would think of sacrificing to that unwelcome phenomenon the sublime side of such a life? It is enough to say that "the miracles of Jesus were a violence done to him by his age, a concession extorted from him by a temporary necessity. The exorcist and the thaumaturgic have passed away, but the religious reformer will live for ever." *

This is very pretty and very magnanimous; only it is contrary to fact to say that the attitude of Jesus as a worker of miracles was one of reluctant submission to an external pressure. If we may judge from the recorded utterances of Jesus, it can neither be said, with Strauss, that He worked no miracles, nor, with Renan, that He worked them *à contre cœur*. Witness the message to John: *the blind receive their sight, and the lame walk, the lepers are cleansed, and the deaf hear, the dead are raised up*, the message having for its object to prove that He who sent it was the Christ. Witness again the woe pronounced on the cities of the plain because of their unbelief, notwithstanding "the mighty works" done among them. It is enough to allude to the famous discourse delivered in self-defence against the charge of casting out devils by the aid of Satan. Then once more there is the striking word recorded by Luke, spoken in reply to the advice of false friends to get out of Herod's way: "*Go ye and tell that fox, Behold I cast out devils, and I do cures to-day and to-morrow, and the third day I shall be perfected.*" † These sayings all bear the unmistakable stamp of genuineness. Strauss seems, indeed, half inclined to doubt the authenticity of the first, referring to it cautiously as a

* *Vie de Jesu*, p. 268.

† Luke xiii. 32.

saying ascribed by the Evangelists to Jesus.* But the whole chapter in Matthew's Gospel, in which the message to the Baptist occurs, produces an impression on the candid reader of quite exceptional originality. It is full of striking thoughts, strikingly expressed, which could proceed only from one quarter, and which combined present to our view a remarkable autobiographical picture. The speaker appears as a man who is a puzzle to his best friends, and who disappoints those who have cherished the highest expectations regarding him. He is singularly patient towards their honest doubts and speaks generous, magnanimous words concerning the Baptist whose hesitating attitude has just been reported to him. At the same time he is a sharp critic of his age, perceiving clearly its littleness and unreasonableness, and exposing these in language expressive at once of contempt and of pity. The men of his time appear to him like children playing at being righteous and religious, and incapable of appreciating true righteousness and wisdom under whatever guise it presents itself. He enjoys the repose and peace of faith amid the humiliations and apparent failures of life. Communion with God and the sincere attachment of a few simple disciples amply compensate for the forfeited favour of the wise and understanding. Against their cold disdain he knows how to assert his dignity and importance as the Bearer of the revelation of the Father. Yet He is full of sympathy and sweetness towards the burdened sons of men, and His final word is, "Come to me and I will give you rest." Here surely is a portrait from the life! But to this historic character is added one more trait not less historical. The man who is thus self-pourtrayed by His utterances claims to be the *Christ*, and offers to

---

* *Leben Jesu*, ii., pp. 47, 61.

doubters His credentials, which are, in short, that He works miracles and preaches a gospel to the poor.

In view of the message to the Baptist, and the other sayings above referred to, the apology of reluctant compliance appears altogether beside the mark. Jesus, it is manifest, worked miracles willingly, with a good conscience, as one acting under divine inspiration, and regarded those acts as manifestations which laid men under obligations and gave Him a claim on their faith. These conclusions are confirmed by the further consideration that Jesus appears in the records as working miracles with discrimination. He did not do all sorts of mighty works, and especially not those which popular predilection most wished Him to do. As a matter of fact, He did not yield to the pressure of His generation, but firmly and successfully resisted it when His moral sense disapproved of its spirit and tendency. One of His hardest and sternest sayings was directed against the contemporary *penchant* for miraculous signs. He spoke as severely of that as of the religious hypocrisy of His time, regarded it indeed as a feature of the latter portentous phenomenon. "A wicked and adulterous generation seeketh after a sign,"* He remarked, evidently deeming this hunting after signs as one of the darkest omens of a God-forsaken state. Thus His prophetic sincerity was active within the miraculous sphere. If He worked miracles, He did so as one who was all the time aware that in connection with the miraculous much baseness, falsity, and superstition might manifest itself.

There must, therefore, be some way by which a voluntary and even enthusiastic activity in the performance of miraculous deeds can be reconciled with all else that we know

---

* Matt. xii. 39; xvi. 4.

and value in Jesus, with His prophetic sincerity and with His humility, wisdom, and goodness. We cannot be content with anything short of a real reconciliation, yielding a true unity of character. We may not say, Jesus was a sage, a saint, and a thaumaturge, and leave apparently incom patible attributes in mere external juxtaposition. We may deal thus with an Apollonius of Tyana, who is a purely eclectic character, put together artificially in imitation of Jesus Christ by a Pagan philosopher, who has it in view to take the wind out of Christ's sails by showing that He is not unparalleled.

Where, then, shall we look for the principle of reconciliation and unity? Considering the apologetic use it was meant to serve, and that it was sent to a man whose whole past history and present situation demanded that he should not be trifled with, we should expect to find in the message to the Baptist the key to the understanding of the public character of Jesus as we know it; the character of a man who is on the one hand sternly truthful and passionately opposed to all pretence, and on the other, undoubtedly, avowedly, and extensively identified with an ostensibly miraculous activity. That message contains two announcements, that Jesus is the Christ (for that is implied, though not expressed), and that the Christ is signalised by fulness of love. Let us consider the import of these two propositions in their bearing on the question of miracles.

Jesus was a prophet, but He was more: the bringer in and King of the Messianic Kingdom. In this capacity He was expected to work miracles. Why? The reply that comes readiest is, because Old Testament prophecy pointed to that as one of Messiah's functions. The answer touches the surface only, but it does touch the surface, and sufficiently accounts for popular expectation. This expectation according to Strauss, gave rise to miracle-legends. This theory goes on the assumption that the Messianic honours of Jesus were posthumous. But the Gospel records in general, and the message to the Baptist in particular, shows clearly that Jesus claimed to be, and allowed Himself to be regarded as, the Messiah. Baur frankly admits the fact. He even goes so far as to say that there was no option left to Jesus but to claim or accept the title if He wished to succeed in His aim as the introducer of an ethical and universal religion. Christianity had to clothe itself in the Jewish form of the Messianic idea in order to get started on its world-conquering career. Not otherwise than through the medium of the Messianic hope could anything claiming to be the *summum bonum* take a firm root in Jewish soil.* If this view be correct, then the same popular expectation which, according to Strauss, created the miracle-myths, must have been active in the lifetime of Jesus, requiring Him as the reputed Christ to play the part of a miracle-worker. From the view-point of naturalism this amounts to saying that Jesus was doomed to an impossible task, had to seem to be what in the nature of things He could not be. That is to say, the great ethical reformer and teacher of highest wisdom, the Introducer of the universal, absolute, perennial religion, was under the necessity of being a charlatan! An unwelcome necessity, we may well believe, and Baur admits. Christ's claims to the Messianic title and to miraculous power, from the Tübingen point of view, were both alike extorted from Him by the necessity of His position. He had no real liking for either; in both He simply accommodated Himself to circumstances. It was a supreme example of the cunning of the Idea which

---

* Baur, *Kirchengeschichte der drei ersten Jahrhunderte*, p. 36.

compels its instruments to employ the beliefs of an old era to gain currency for new truths destined to sweep the old era and all its beliefs away into oblivion. Surely the Idea is a hard Master! And surely these Hegelian phrases which make the deceit of the individual the impersonal sin, or virtue perhaps, of the world-spirit, gloze over rather than solve the difficulty presented in the public character of Jesus! The truth is, it is insoluble on the principles of naturalistic philosophy.

But there is a difficulty to be dealt with even for believers in the supernatural. What makes the problem insoluble for Naturalism is the assumption that miracles are impossible. But even granting the possibility of miracles, there remains this problem to be solved: how to reconcile the Messianic and miraculous rôle of Jesus with His spirit. That rôle seems to remove Him from our sympathies, and to injure the humility if not the sincerity of His character. The difficulty can be surmounted only by penetrating to the heart of the Messianic idea as conceived by Jesus, and viewing rightly the relation between that idea and the exercise of miraculous gifts.

That there was much in the current Messianic idea with which Jesus was not, and could not be, in sympathy, there can be no doubt. It is the fate of many religious ideas to undergo degeneracy, and this fate had overtaken the idea in question. It had become vulgarised and falsified, and was associated with false opinions, vain hopes, ambitious passions, and sham sanctities. With a belief so debased, however popular or orthodox, one endowed with the insight and sincerity of Jesus could not even pretend to be in agreement. It must either be utterly rejected or completely transformed. The former alternative Jesus could not adopt because He believed in God and in His promises uttered by the mouth of prophets. He had not attained unto that degree of enlightenment which can clearly discern that the Messianic idea is simply Aberglaube, extra belief, a fairy tale which noble men told themselves, being very much in earnest about righteousness, and despairing of seeing their deal realised in the ordinary course of human affairs. He believed with all His heart in a Divine Kingdom and a Messianic-King, and devoutly expected both to come. But His conceptions of kingdom and king were not those current among the Jews of His time. And that was the reason of His remarkable reticence regarding His own claims to be the Christ. That reticence is not rightly accounted for by saying that the Messianic idea in every form was distasteful to Him, and therefore He had as little to do with it as possible. The true explanation is that He was conscious that the word "Christ" did not mean the same thing for Himself and for His hearers, and that it was difficult to use it without fostering opinions He did not share, and encouraging hopes He knew to be delusive. The Messianic idea of the populace was conventional; His own idea was transformed.

What was the nature of the transformed Messianic idea cherished by Jesus? It seems to have been formed chiefly from two prophetic oracles: one being that which according to the testimony of the third Evangelist was the text of Christ's discourse in the synagogue of Nazareth, the other that quoted by the first Evangelist in the twelfth chapter of his Gospel. "*The Spirit of the Lord is upon me, because he hath anointed me to preach the gospel to the poor; he hath sent me to heal the broken-hearted, to preach deliverance to the captives, and recovery of sight to the blind, to set at liberty them that are bruised. To preach the acceptable year of the Lord.*"* "*Behold my servant, whom I have chosen; my beloved*

---

* Luke iv. 18, 19.

in whom my soul is well pleased: I will put my Spirit upon him, and he shall show judgment to the Gentiles. He shall not strive nor cry; neither shall any man hear his voice in the streets. A bruised reed shall he not break, and smoking flax shall he not quench, till he send forth judgment unto victory. And in his name shall the Gentiles trust."* These and other Old Testament texts of kindred character appear to have been the source of Christ's Messianic idea. That both the passages quoted were much in His thoughts we have good reason to believe. Even if we were to concede that the prominent place occupied by them in the Gospels is due to the Evangelists, and that they express, strictly speaking, only the sense in which they understood the Messianic vocation of Jesus, we should still not be left without evidence that Matthew and Luke have herein reflected truly the mind of the Master. The closing words of the message to the Baptist: *the poor have the gospel preached to them,* are clearly an echo of the first cited oracle, and the voice from heaven, uttered at the Jordan and on the Mount of Transfiguration, *thou* (*or this*) *is my beloved* (*chosen* †) *Son,* is not less clearly an echo of the second, and that voice again, conceived of as spoken in the air, was but an echo of a still small voice in the Baptized and Transfigured One's heart.

What kind of Messianic idea, then, do these prophetic oracles, manifestly favorites of Jesus, embody? That of a loving, sympathetic, gentle, sage Messiah, who bears the sins and miseries of men as a burden on His heart, gains power by meekness, and through His wisdom gives light to the dark world. Love is the Messianic charism pointed at in the text quoted by Luke, the meekness of wisdom is emphasized in that quoted by Matthew. The spirit with

* Matt. xii. 18–21.

† ὁ ἐκλελεγμένος, The reading of ℵ. B. in Luke ix. 35.

which according to the one, Messiah is anointed is the spirit of fellow-feeling with all the victims of the world's varied woe. The spirit which, according to the other, God puts upon him as a garment, is a spirit of gentleness towards opponents, aud of humility in shunning vainglorious display. It is utterly contrary to the spirit of the world, which pursues the policy of self-assertion and self-advertisement in order to gratify personal ambition, and has recourse to the methods of conflict and ostentation, by the one striving to overcome obstacles, by the other courting public applause. Messiah calmly lets His light shine, neither hiding it in fear, nor obtruding it in vanity, and so becomes the sun of the world.

In a Messiah of this sort, passionately sympathetic, meekly wise, Jesus could earnestly *believe*. In such a Messiah we can all believe. A Messiah who is the friend of the sinful and miserable, who meets the deepest wants, not of Jews alone, but of mankind; who is patient, gentle, hopeful, as one confident of the ultimate triumph of truth and righteousness; a humane, universal, spiritual Messiah, answering to a divine kingdom of kindred character, is worthy of all acceptation, and can never be superseded, but must remain an Eternal Christ, the same yesterday, to-day, and for ever.

Such a Messiah Jesus Himself *was*. It was the close correspondence between the prophetic ideal and the historic reality exhibited in the public ministry and personal character of Jesus that led the Evangelists to quote the above cited prophetic oracles as apposite. Such a Messiah, moreover—and this is the point with which we are specially concerned—Jesus could believe Himself to be *without prejudice to His humility*. Attempts have been made to explain the genesis of Christ's Messianic-consciousness. No solution of the problem can be accepted which does not respect His lowliness. He did not elect Himself to this honour. "No man taketh this honour unto himself, but He that is called of God"; no man free, as Jesus was, from all selfish, ambitious passions. How then was Jesus led to think of Himself as the Christ; through what channel did the divine call come to Him? Through the consciousness of sinlessness, it has been replied.* Through the deep, intense love to man with which His heart was filled, I prefer to say. The call coming thus, the Messianic vocation might be undertaken without suspicion of presumption. For thus coming it would appear a call, not to honour, but to service, yea to suffering. Through the love which filled His heart His Father said to Him, Go forth to heal, to bear, the world's sin and woe; and what could He do but loyally obey the command, walking by faith as to the truth of His calling and expecting confirmations that He had rightly interpreted the divine will? And all through His public career, while faithfully performing Messianic functions, He was not indulging high thoughts, but simply learning obedience to Heaven's behests by the things which He suffered. Never did a moment occur when He could say complacently to Himself, I am the Christ; but there were many moments when He was tempted to say, would that I had never undertaken Messianic tasks! The contradictions and slanders of hostile classes jealous for their position, reputation, and influence; the misunderstandings of men well affected like John; the grievous misconstruction put upon His very love the ingratitudes of those on whom He had conferred benefit—all seemed to whisper: how much better to have remained an obscure carpenter than to have entered on this thorny path!

---

* So Weiss, *Das Leben Jesu*, i., 290.

These observations help us to understand how Jesus could regard Himself as the Christ without detriment to His moral simplicity and purity. They are neither fitted nor intended to rob Jesus of His Messianic dignity. Believers in Him can have no such desire. They regard Him with a faith and love chastened by reverence. They know that His spirit while humble was also imperial, that He was born to wear a crown, and that He has well earned the honour.

Having solved one-half of our problem we shall find little difficulty in disposing of the other, and showing how Jesus could find the performance of miracles such as those recorded in the Gospels congenial work. The simplest and most satisfactory view to take of these miracles is to regard them as the forthflowing of that love which, according to prophetic oracles, was the chief Messianic charism. This view may not be applicable to all the Gospel miracles without exception, but it holds true of the healing miracles, which form by far the larger proportion of the whole. Of these we may say that they had the same origin as the preaching of the Gospel to the poor—the deep well of love in Christ's heart. Jesus was as much in His element in the one department of labour as in the other. In both alike His human sympathy found outlet. Here again we have occasion to admire the spiritual insight of the Evangelists. We stumble over their petty inaccuracies in trivial details; we should be better employed in noting the many indications in their pages of that spiritual discernment which is the true proof of their inspiration. Matthew, to one of whose Old Testament citations I have already adverted, makes another very pertinent one in connection with Christ's healing ministry. The text which that ministry suggests to his mind as most apposite is the beautiful one: "surely He hath borne our griefs and carried our sorrows." Therein he gives us the key to Christ's miraculous activity, as in the other text already quoted he gave us the key to His Messianic consciousness. Who can doubt that the key fits the lock, and that nothing more appropriate could be said than this: "Himself took our infirmities, and bare our sicknesses." * All indeed have not been content with Matthew's simple explanation, and enquiries have been instituted as to the motives which led Jesus to perform individual miracles. In these enquiries it has been overlooked that what we have to account for is not the few miracles recorded, but the vast multitude of healing miracles, recorded or unrecorded, amounting in all to hundreds or thousands. The first and most radical explanation of these is love, sympathy: "surely He hath borne our griefs"! There may be more to be said, but that must be said in the first place, and emphatically. Even when some more special explanation seems to offer itself it really amounts to the same thing. Thus, for example, in the case of the Sabbatic miracles, we might be inclined to think that the motive was to vindicate the true idea of the Sabbath. But that is rather the motive of the recorder than of the worker of the miracle. But even if we allow that a desire to rectify Pharisaic notions concerning the weekly rest had some place in Christ's motives, the admission is quite compatible with the view that love was the supreme motive. In those Sabbatic miracles Christ's love was simply overflowing the embankments of custom. It was daring to do well when current opinion said it should do nothing. It was only one of several ways in which the deep, strong, original love of the Son of Man set at defiance conventional limits. Another of its most notable and most censured eccentricities was keeping

* Matt. viii. 17

company with the social abjects. In both cases the action of Christ's love was spontaneous. He acted as He did, not from desire to be eccentric, or to provoke remark, or in a spirit of controversy, or with a polemico-didactic aim. He associated with publicans and sinners not to be singular or to spite the Pharisees, but because He loved them. He healed the man with the withered hand, and the man afflicted with dropsy, and the woman bowed down with a spirit of infirmity, for the same reason.

While disregarding inhuman class prejudices and arbitrary legal definitions, the sympathy of Christ did not claim to be exempt from all restrictions. It was not an unreasoning passion taking no counsel with wisdom. To conceive of it thus were to destroy the very unity of character which we seek to establish. In the spirit of Jesus love, humility, and wisdom were linked together in unbroken harmony. We are, therefore, prepared to find that, while giving free scope to His benevolent impulses in healing the sick, as in associating with the sinful, He acted as one conscious of limits and subject to law. And it is important to note the fact, and to ascertain as far as possible the nature of the limits. Failing to do so, we might form an idea of the possible scope of Christ's miraculous activity altogether fantastic. Thus, *e. g.*, we read in the Gospels of certain healings at a distance. It seems not unnatural to enquire, If Christ could heal at the distance of a few miles, why not also at the distance of a thousand, or ten thousand? Why should there be any space-limits to His beneficent ministry; why should not the whole earth get the benefit? And if space-limits are to be abolished, why not also time-limits? Why should not the great Physician save to the latest generation as well as to the uttermost ends of the earth, and so bring about the total abolition of disease?

Looking into the Evangelic records, then, we discover that in the exercise of His sympathy in healing acts, Jesus acknowledged Himself subject to control in various directions. In the first place He regarded Himself as restricted in the sphere of His ministry to the Jewish people. "I am not sent," He said, "but to the lost sheep of the house of Israel." * This was the reason He assigned, according to the account of Matthew, for refusing at first to grant the prayer of the Syrophenician woman, and though the word is not found in Mark, we can have little doubt it was spoken, for it supplies the needed explanation of His behaviour. Jesus certainly must have uttered the saying at some time or other, and no more fitting occasion for its utterance could be imagined. A pagan mother asks Him to heal her daughter, and He passes on unheeding, and on His disciples interceding on the woman's behalf, He excuses Himself in the manner aforesaid. The reply was earnestly meant, and was no mere ruse for drawing out the suppliant. It expressed a conviction on which Jesus had all along acted, and continued to act to the end of His ministry. From first to last He was simply a minister of God to Israel; the few exceptions only proved the rule. This self-restriction within the limits of the chosen people is perfectly compatible with the view that Jesus expected and desired the movement He had originated to spread into the Gentile world, and assume the character of a universal religion. The way to conquer the world was to begin by gaining a sure footing in Judæa. The Saviour of mankind must not only die in Jerusalem, but live in and for Palestine. If, as Baur tells us, the universal religion must commence its world-subduing career by clothing itself in the form of the Messianic idea, it is not less true

---

* Matt. xv. 24.

that the founder of this religion, however far-reaching His aims, must devote Himself exclusively to the Messianic people. This accordingly He did, with full comprehension, we may be sure, of the reasons for adopting this policy. He respected the law of development, and was content to bear the obscurity which is connected with all beginnings. He kept within His appointed lot in all departments of His work, in His teaching not less than in His healing ministry. He sought impartially to communicate spiritual instruction to all classes of His countrymen; to the social outcasts, to the simple provincials, to the learned students and strict observers of the law, speaking to all what they needed to be told, in the manner most fitted to influence them; but it was for His countrymen that He let His light shine. Doubtless light is self-diffusing, and wisdom cannot be confined within geographical boundaries; and the teaching of Jesus is, except in form, altogether unprovincial, cosmopolitan, as good for Gentiles as for Jews, for westerns as for orientals; and, again, except as to form, better understood and appreciated among Aryan races and in these late ages, than it was by the Semitic people to whom it was first addressed. Nevertheless to that unworthy people the treasure was first offered. And if Jesus was wise for the Jews, we cannot wonder if He was also sympathetic for them. What we rather admire is the loyalty with which He exercised a self-restraint that was a most real part of His earthly humiliation. The self-restraint was, we can well believe, more severe in connection with the forthputting of His love, than with the emitting of His light. How severe it was we can guess from the heartiness and even eagerness with which escape was made from the restrictions imposed, on good cause shown. Jesus was evidently delighted when it appeared that He could make the Syrophenician suppliant for help an exception without breaking the spirit of the rule. What a relief it was to Him to find that this Gentile dog was a distinguished child of faith, and therefore entitled not merely to a dog's morsel, but to the children's bread! "O woman, great is thy faith," He exclaimed, as one set free from bonds, who could now at last let His large human heart have full scope.

The absence of that quality which was so conspicuously present in the case of the woman of Canaan, supplied another restricting influence tending to limit the healing ministry of Jesus. According to the records our Lord wrought cures chiefly, if not exclusively, where there prevailed a mood of believing recipiency. He does not seem to have been at all exacting as to the degree of faith, or to have given any narrow theological definitions of the kind of faith requisite. A little faith apparently sufficed; for it was not His way to break the bruised reed, or to quench the smoking taper. Conspicuous examples of faith, bright-minded, quick-witted, like those presented in the cases of the centurion and the Syrophenician woman, gave Him exquisite delight; but the weakest, most commonplace faith He would recognise and respond to. It was not necessary that it should express itself by act or word; it was enough if there appeared in the eye or in any feature the slightest sign of an expectant or recipient mood; and it may be assumed that faith to this extent at least existed when no mention is made of the faith of the parties benefited. He even took into account vicarious faith, blessing one for the sake of another who loved Him and believed in his stead; witness the cases of the palsied man, and the sufferers for whom the Capernaum centurion and the Canaanitish woman interceded. But some little spark of faith somewhere He desiderated. Where that quality was wholly lacking He did not manifest His power. It was not merely that He would not, but that He was not able. "He could there," it is written, "do no mighty work, save that He laid His hands upon a few sick folk, and healed them."* That was at Nazareth, His native town, where receptivity was least likely to be forthcoming, according to the maxim that a prophet is without honour in his own country. Nazareth, unhappily, was in this respect but an exaggerated type of Israel in general. Jesus declared that He could not find anywhere in Israel faith like that of the Roman centurion, and doubtless He had the same feeling in reference to the faith of the Syrophenician woman. Sad state for a people to come to who had such a history to look back on, and so many examples of faith among their forefathers to contemplate! But if heroic faith was scarce in Israel, commonplace faith was to be found among the humble people of the provinces to such an extent as to make it possible for Jesus to give ample expression to His sympathy with them under their afflictions by healing their diseases. Sometimes, however, as in Nazareth, even commonplace faith was wanting, and the result was that the low temperature of the neighbourhood froze the well of sympathy. A cold, critical temper paralyzed the mighty arm. We are not to imagine that Christ's power depended for its existence on the faith of those who received benefit. We ought rather to conceive of it as thrown back on itself by a chilling, unsympathetic attitude. As an orator is apt to fail when addressing an unsympathetic audience, as a skilful player on an instrument seldom succeeds in bringing out all its sweetness before a dull, irresponsive assembly, so Jesus was smitten with comparative impotence in the midst of a spiritually stupid population. His miraculous gift, like genius, was a shy, retiring thing which manifested itself only to faith and love.

* Mark vi. 5.

It seems to have been due to an extension of the same evil influence that the healing ministry of Jesus to a great extent ceased towards the latter end of His career. Such, so far as we can gather, was the fact. The halcyon days of these labours of love were the first months of the Galilean ministry antecedent to the Capernaum crisis, after which the populace, having discovered that Jesus was not going to be a Messiah after their model, speaking broadly "went back, and walked no more with Him." * Previously unbelief had been sporadic, manifesting itself here and there; then it began to be national, manifesting itself in greater or less virulence everywhere. Thereafter it was faith that was the exception. And in consequence the miraculous manifestation of Christ's sympathy appears to have been in the later period only occasional, intermittent, and on a comparatively small scale. There was, indeed, no sudden and total cessation at a certain period. To the end the will and the power to heal were in existence and in occasional exercise. In the later chapters of the Gospels occur some of those general reports of healing acts of which I had occasion to speak in a previous lecture. When Christ has finally left Galilee and gone to Peræa, He is still busy at His beneficent work. "Great multitudes," we read, "followed Him, and He healed them there." † The coasts of Judæa beyond Jordan were an outlying district, which He had not visited since His baptism, and at the close He revisits the scene of solemn memories, and gives it too an opportunity of being benefited by the spirit of love with which He had been anointed. The requisite recipiency, we may assume, was there forthcoming. Even in arid, cold, unbelieving Jerusalem, there seem to have been souls not altogether dead to the divine,‡

* John vi. 66. † Matt. xix. 12. ‡ Matt. xxi. 14.

for we read: "the blind and the lame came to Him in the temple; and He healed them." These notices bear witness that if Jesus worked fewer cures in the later months, it was not because He was weary in well-doing, or because fickleness and ingratitude had embittered His feelings, but simply because, as time went on, the faith on which from the first He had insisted, became an increasingly scarce commodity.

In these three respects, then, at least, our Lord's work of healing was subject to restriction. It was confined to the land of Israel, it was conditioned by faith even within that land, and it underwent an ebb as time advanced, due to a change in the mood of the Jewish people. But this is not an exhaustive statement. It must now be added that Jesus exercised His ministry of love in subordination to the interests of the Divine Kingdom. Bodily health is a blessing, but it is not the *summum bonum.* The kingdom and the righteousness of God are the chief end and the chief good of man. So Jesus ever taught, and He ever kept the fact in view in His own conduct. However deeply He might sympathise with the people burdened with disease and poverty, He did not imagine that if only men were well fed and clothed and in physical vigour all was well. In all He did as a temporal benefactor He acted under law to the maxim that life is more than meat and the body more than raiment. The ills of poverty He did not attempt to cope with directly. The sole consolations He offered the needy were companionship in want, and a gospel which to those who received it made hunger a light affliction. With disease He grappled more closely, but in His beneficent labour as a healer of the human body He remembered that the grand desideratum was a healthy mind. He wrought miraculous cures as a means towards that end. It was one of the ways He took to lift men's thoughts up to the kingdom He proclaimed. This appears from the fact that He equipped His disciples with similar powers when He sent them forth on their mission. "Go," He said, "preach; the kingdom of heaven is at hand. Heal the sick, cleanse the lepers, raise the dead, cast out devils."* The preaching and the healing were both to be used as means of securing for the kingdom the supreme place in men's regards. The healing, in fact, was only another kind of preaching. It was a kind obviously well fitted to arouse attention at the first. But it was also a kind very liable to produce wrong impressions. People would listen eagerly to what men had to say who were able with a word to charm away their ailments. But the very eagerness with which they listened would show what a risk there was of their dragging down the kingdom—the preacher's great theme—from heaven to earth. The physical benefit was only too likely to make them either neglect the kingdom as related to the realm of the spirit, or, what amounts practically to the same thing, entertain false notions respecting the nature of the kingdom. The latter seems to have been what actually happened. The healing miracles of Jesus made Him the object of popular admiration. The enthusiasm reached its height when miraculous healings culminated in a miraculous

* Matt. x. 8. The clause "raise the dead" is surprising. Raising the dead was quite exceptional even in the personal ministry of Jesus, and it is hardly credible that a commission was given to the twelve to perform systematically works of that kind. There is no evidence that anything of the kind happened in connection with the Galilean mission, though it may be assumed as certain that the twelve would have mentioned such events in their report on their return had they occurred. The clause in question occurs only in Matthew. Weiss thinks it has been introduced by the Evangelist from Matthew xi. 5. *Das Leben Jesu*, ii., 123. It is not inconceivable that the words are a gloss which very early crept into all the copies. To interpret them spiritually is inadmissible as out of keeping with the connection of thought.

feeding. Then the thought took possession of the multitude: here is a king worth having, one who can cure our diseases and fill our hungry mouths. Behold the golden age of prophecy come at last; lo, our Messiah is among us.

Thus a divine thing was on the point of becoming a very human thing. The danger imposed on Jesus the necessity for reserve and for great caution in the use of His miraculous power. The question suggests itself, ought not the danger to have been foreseen from the beginning, and in view of it would it not have been better to abstain from a line of action which, while most benevolent in aim, was probably fitted to do more harm than good? But the danger was foreseen; hence the prohibitions so frequently addressed to persons cured not to speak of the benefit they had received. These prohibitions, indeed, seem for the most part to have been very ineffectual in producing silence; often they appear to have acted rather as a provocative to freer speech, a result which can surprise no one acquainted with human nature. Probably Jesus Himself expected no other result, though He deemed it proper in certain cases to give the warning. The healing ministry can therefore hardly be justified by saying that precautions were taken against abuse which might reasonably have been expected to be successful. A better line of apology would be to say that with all its drawbacks the beneficent movement was worth the risks. It was meet that Messiah's advent should be signalised by such a movement. The fulness of His grace must be made manifest even at the risk of temporary misunderstanding. The manifestation of His sympathy, in all possible ways, will be a revelation of perennial value.

The foregoing discussion has had for its aim to show that the healing ministry of Jesus stood in a harmonious and congenial relation to His whole spirit and character. It now remains to consider briefly how far the same thing can be affirmed of the Gospel miracles which do not fall under that category. These consist of the miracles wrought on Nature. They are few in number, being at most nine in all, and if duplicates are admitted, seven. They are not only all that are recorded, but so far as our information goes, all that happened; herein differing from the healing miracles, the number happening, in their case, being out of all proportion to the number recorded. On this account they must be regarded as of quite subordinate importance to the class of miracles we have hitherto been considering. They are mere incidental occurrences, at rare intervals, in a career of activity of which healing miracles formed a standing feature. The question we have to ask is, can these stray incidents be brought into rational connection with the rest of Christ's public action, and with all that we know of His character? Or have we here something to be ashamed of, something to hide or explain away, something that we could gladly see expunged from the Gospel records?

The first of the group, the earliest of all the miracles, is undoubtedly the most difficult to construe. Whether we regard it as a miracle of Providence or as a miracle of Omnipotence, it is not easy to assign for it an intelligible rationale. It can hardly be regarded, like the healing miracles, as an act of humanity, for there was no urgent need to be met. If we think of it as a symbolic miracle, expressing by act a deep spiritual truth, we are met by the difficulty that the Evangelist, otherwise so copious in interpretive discourse, gives not the slightest hint of its didactic significance. In spite of this fact, the best solution that occurs to one is just that which has commended itself to thoughtful students in all ages, viz.: that in the miracle at Cana Jesus took occasion to foreshadow by a symbolic action the nature of the new era He was about to inaugurate: to say in deed what the Evangelist in the first chapter of his Gospel says in word: the law was given by Moses, grace and truth came by Jesus Christ.* The miracle that comes nearest to this one in character, the feeding of the multitude, is more easily accounted for. Compassion for the hungry crowd is expressly mentioned as a motive in the narratives of the second feeding, and may be assumed to have been at work in both. It does not indeed appear that the need on the earlier occasion was very urgent, as the disciples suggested that the people should be dismissed, that they might go and buy bread for themselves in the neighbouring villages. But a similar remark might be made even with reference to the healing miracles. It was not absolutely necessary that the sick should be cured. They could have contrived to endure their ailments till death came to relieve them from misery. There is indeed a wide difference between bearing hunger for a few hours and suffering pining sickness for weary years; still it is a question of degree. Yet one cannot help feeling that some other motive than compassion must have influenced the conduct of Jesus on that occasion. A crisis was at hand. The enthusiasm of the people for the Great Healer was approaching fever-heat. But it was an impure enthusiasm, having its source in selfish desires, and nursing foolish expectations. It was time that the mass of discipleship were sifted. The miracle of feeding supplied the means of sifting. It was a testing, critical miracle. It caused the popular enthusiasm to take definite shape in a proposition to make Jesus king, and it gave Jesus the opportunity of saying emphatically "A king such as ye

---

* John i. 17.

desire I decline to be."* Here therefore we see Jesus at once doing a characteristic deed of kindness, and guarding the high interests of the kingdom from the very dangers to which they were exposed by the abuse of His beneficence. He displays a truly Messianic generosity, and He exhibits a worthy jealousy for the purity of the Messianic ideal. If there were two feedings, these remarks apply only to the first. A Capernaum crisis does not repeat itself. The sole *raison d'être* of the second feeding was compassion. It takes rank with the healing miracles.

With one exception, all the other nature-miracles sprang from concern for the interests of the kingdom as centred in the disciples. The miraculous draughts of fish had for their aim to win Peter and his companions to the high vocation of fishers of men, and to keep them faithful to that vocation against temptations to revert to their original occupation of fishermen in the literal sense. In the storm incidents we encounter miracles which, whether providential or not in nature, were certainly such in aim. The object Jesus had in view in both cases was to guard against danger threatening the men with whom the fortunes of the kingdom were identified. Danger is expressly pointed at in the story of the stilling of the storm, and it is pretty plainly implied in the other narrative concerning the walking on the sea. In the curious incident of the stater we find Jesus again engaged in watching over the interests which lay nearest His heart, those of the divine kingdom; only this time the danger springs not from storms on the

* This view of the miracle will be found stated at greater length in *The Training of the Twelve*, chap. ix., section 1. A somewhat different view is taken by Weiss. He regards it as a symbolic miracle, proclaiming that Jesus is come in fulfilment of prophetic promises to help all the people's needs, to bring to them the fulness of blessing even in things relating to the bodily wants. Vide *Das Leben Jesu*, vol. ii., p. 197.

sea of Galilee, imperilling the lives of the twelve, but rather from tempests of ambitious passion raging in their own breasts. The point of importance in that narrative is not the poverty of Jesus, or His peaceful trust in the Providence of His Father amid earthly cares, or the extraordinary manner in which apparently His wants even on that occasion supplied, but the bearing of the occurrence on the dispute which had arisen as to places of distinction. The key to the meaning is to be found in the words "notwithstanding, lest we should offend." I might claim exemption and stand on my dignity, but I submit to the humiliation; let the tax be paid as it can; take home, my ambitious disciples, the lesson to yourselves—such is the moral of the tale.

The cursing of the fig-tree may be regarded as a prophetic act, foreshadowing the doom of the elect nation which had hitherto been identified with the Divine Kingdom, but had forfeited its privilege by moral degeneracy. It is a protest against the kingdom being regarded as the inalienable monopoly of any people or class.

It thus appears that all these miracles had a relation to the Messianic vocation of Jesus. Their relation thereto is less central than that of the healing miracles. In these we see the work of the kingdom actually going on, in the form of a copious display of Messiah's love. In most of the others we observe simply the occasional defence of the kingdom against the hazards to which it was now and then exposed. The earliest miracle has only the remote connection of an emblem. The last mentioned of the group vindicates the independence of the kingdom of all human instruments on whom lengthened occupancy may seem to have conferred prescriptive rights.

Thus far we have been considering the relation of the

miracles to the character and vocation of Jesus. Another topic now invites our attention. In what relation do the miracles stand to the natural endowments of the worker? This question is less urgent than the one which has hitherto occupied us. That bore on the character, this bears merely on the mental or bodily faculties of Jesus. The moral problem being satisfactorily solved, we could afford to leave the psychological one standing over. Yet the enquiry is not a merely idle or curious one; it has a bearing, as will appear, on our mode of conceiving the person of Christ and His relation to His Father. On this account, as also because it will give completeness to the treatment of the subject of this lecture, it will be worth while to go into the matter a little.

The miracle-power of Jesus is usually conceived of as a natural faculty resident in Him, which He used at will as ordinary men use their power of walking or practising a handicraft, or playing on an instrument. This view is not without apparent support. In favour of it is the constant, habitual use of the power in works of healing; also some of the phrases employed to describe its exercise. The people who witnessed the cure of the demoniac in the synagogue of Capernaum are reported by Luke to have said, What a word is this! for with authority and power (ἐξουσίᾳ καὶ δυνάμει) He commandeth the unclean spirits and they come out.* The formula employed in the cure of the leper, "I will, be thou clean," seems to imply that the will of Jesus is the source of the power. In the account of the mission of the twelve the power appears not only as one which Jesus could personally wield at pleasure, but as one which He could communicate to others. "He called His

* Luke iv. 36.

twelve disciples together, and gave them power and authority over all devils and to cure diseases."* The narrative of the woman with the issue of blood, as given by Mark and Luke, suggests the idea of a power resident in Christ's very body, which could be brought into play even without any exercise of will on His part. His whole person seems charged with the mysterious force, so that it can be elicited by the slightest contact, like electricity from an electric battery.† In some instances the power seems to be conducted from Jesus to the patient by some physical act, touching, spitting, anointing with clay, or by the utterance of a word. In other instances, as in the case of the centurion's servant, it appears as if these media could be dispensed with, and the power could be exerted at a distance, like the force of gravitation. There are, however, other things which suggest the idea of a power not indwelling but transcendent, called into play by the prayers and faith of Jesus. He represented Himself as casting out devils by the finger of God.‡ He looked up to heaven before working one cure, as if recognising the source of His strength;§ He thanked His Father for hearing His prayer in connection with another.‖ The reflections of beholders are not decisive either way; some can be cited on this side as well as on the other. The people, we read, gave praise unto God for the opening of the blind man's eyes at Jericho.¶ They glorified the God of Israel, we are told by another Evangelist, in connection with a multitude of cures they had the privilege to witness,** as if they regarded not Jesus but Jehovah as the true worker.

* Luke ix. 1.

† *Vide* also Luke vi. 19: "The whole multitude sought to touch Him, for there went virtue out of Him and healed them all."

‡ Luke xi. 21. § Mark vii. 34. ‖ John xi. 41.

¶ Luke xix. 43. ** Matt. xv. 31.

Distinct from both these views is the hypothesis that the healings recorded in the Gospels were the result of the combined action of the faith both of the healer and of the healed. This is a naturalistic theory which recognises no real miracle-power either in Jesus or in God. Faith in this theory does not call into action a divine power distinct from itself; it is itself the power, and its virtue lies in the force of imagination. The sufferers fondly believed that Jesus could help them, and the hope fancy-bred was half a cure. Jesus, in the intensity of His sympathy, fondly believed that His love could not be impotent, and this conviction, sincerely cherished, raised to a maximum that power of moral therapeutic which lies dormant in human nature, and which seems to be specially strong in some exceptionally endowed men.*

Of the two modes of conceiving the miracle-power of Jesus, the former seems to harmonise best with the high idea of His Person, according to which He is to all intents and purposes God upon earth. On this view the one Miracle is that of the Person; all other miracles become the natural acts of a miraculous Personage. The other view seems most in accord with the human conditions of Christ's life on earth, which in reference to the divine aspect was a depotentiated life subject to *κένωσις*, and in reference to the human aspect, a life of dependence and faith. On this ground it is likely to be preferred by all who are much in earnest in maintaining the likeness of Jesus in all things to His brethren. The completeness of that likeness depends largely on the extent to which Jesus had to walk by faith. But He cannot be said to have lived by faith in a signal degree if important departments of His public career,

* Such is the view of Keim, vide *Jesu von Nazara*, ii., 157.

such as His Messianic vocation and His healing ministry were exempted from faith's scope. It seems necessary, therefore, to hold that even with regard to these He had to exercise habitually trust in His heavenly Father, looking to Him for evidence that He was not mistaken in regarding Himself as the Christ, and for help to do His Messianic works. Confirmations of faith in either direction would aid faith in the other. Every assurance Jesus received that He was indeed the Father's elect, well-beloved, anointed one, would give Him increased confidence of success in His ministry of love; and on the other hand success in that beneficent work would be to Him the best proof of His Messianic vocation. Walking by faith, in reference to these high matters, does not necessarily mean walking with hesitating steps. We are not to think of Jesus as at any time tormented with doubts, such as visited John in prison, as to whether He were indeed the Christ; or as uncertain, when each new case of sickness was brought under His notice, whether He would be enabled to cure it. The fellowship between Him and His Father was so complete that a cloud of doubt as to His Messianic vocation, or as to unfailing support while faithfully discharging Messianic functions, never cast its shadow on His path. He knew that the Father heard Him always, and that He had delivered all things into His hands, among them power to do Messianic works. He was ever assured that His Father regarded Him as the Christ, and the thought supported Him when His claim was rejected by the world. Nevertheless this knowledge was that which comes through faith, and the faith of Jesus, though never shaken, was often severely tried. There were times when He was tempted to think He was mistaken in regarding Himself as the Messiah, or in His conception of the Messianic office. The antagonism of the reputedly wise and holy, the doubt of the Baptist, the enthusiasm of the populace buoyed up with vain hopes, the cross appearing in the horizon, were all temptations to such doubting thoughts. There were times, also, when He was tempted to think that His Father was deserting Him in the midst of His beneficent labours, as at Nazareth when He could not do mighty works. Doubtless a satisfactory explanation of the fact is given in the records when it is ascribed to the unbelief of the inhabitants. But it is one thing for us to read that explanation in a book, a very different thing for the actor to whom it refers to realise its truth, and so possess his soul in peace. To the outward appearance, and in the view of the world, it was a failure; and though a self-confident man might find it easy to comfort himself by blaming others, and offering as an excuse for all miscarriages, "unbelief," thoughts of a less flattering description might intrude themselves on a humble mind.

These observations tend to show that Jesus wrought miracles in the exercise of a most real and sometimes sorely-tried faith. They do not, however, therefore prove that He possessed no native miracle-faculty, but was as dependent on God in the performance of His mighty works as were His disciples, or any other ordinary men. The two ways of regarding these works, as wrought by faith, and as wrought by an indwelling power, are not mutually exclusive. They are rather mutually complementary;* and this

---

* Beyschlag, *Leben Jesu*, i., 288, remarks; "That the thoroughly religious conditionedness of his (Christ's) miraculous working, which makes it an action of God through him, does not remove from him the feeling that he carries in himself a nature ground of the miraculous powers which therein reveal themselves, is shown by the history of the temptation. The temptations presuppose that he could in his own strength do supernatural things, and they fail only because it is his unbending principle to will no miracle without an understanding with his Father."

being so, it is only what was to be expected that the miracles should be exhibited in the records now in the one light, now in the other. There are, indeed, certain classes of miracles which appear more easily conceivable when viewed simply as works of God in response to the faith of Jesus—those, viz., referred to by Strauss under the titles, *cures at a distance*, and *involuntary cures.* The *healing of the centurion's servant* may be taken as the type of the one, and *the healing of the woman with a bloody issue* of the other.

Assuming that in His miraculous works Jesus drew upon divine power by faith and prayer, the view to be taken of the former of these miracles is this: Jesus did not by an act of will cure the sick boy at a distance, but by faith surely counted on God restoring him to health, believing that it was His will thus to honour the Christ before the eyes of a Gentile who had formed such an exalted conception of His power.* The cure does not thus cease to be miraculous, but the peculiar difficulty of power exerted at a distance disappears, for distance does not exist for God. In the other class of miracles the difficulty to be disposed of is the idea of a curative influence emanating from Christ's body without His knowledge or will. If the seat of the power was not Christ's person, but God's will, we can conceive how the woman might experience physical benefit on touching Christ's garments without His co-operation. It might please God thus to honour faith, even though the faith took the superstitious form of imagining that the mere touch would suffice for a cure. Christ's part in the matter in that case would simply be to assure the woman that her cure was the reward of her faith. And this is the view suggested by Matthew's account. The woman furtively approaches from be

* So Weiss, vide *Das Leben Jesu*, i., 422.

hind, thinking she can steal a cure by an unnoticed touch. Jesus feels the touch, turns about, and having ascertained (how not explained) from whom it proceeded, tells the sufferer that her faith has saved her.*

All here is quite simple. But the trouble is that it is hard to bring the accounts given by the other Evangelists into harmony with this view. According to Mark the woman approaches with the same intent as in Matthew, touches and is forthwith healed. Jesus turns and asks, Who touched my clothes? the Evangelist explaining the question by the remark that Jesus knew in Himself that virtue had gone out of Him. The disciples represent that in such a crowd an individual touch can hardly be thought of; but Jesus, knowing better, looks about for the hidden one, who at last reveals herself. In Luke all proceeds as in Mark till Jesus puts the question, Who touched me? Then all around there is denial, and the disciples back the denials of the crowd with a general apology. Unmoved, Jesus declares in persistent tones, Some one touched me, giving as His reason for being so positive: I perceived that virtue had gone out of me. The main difference between Mark and Luke is, that in Mark consciousness of virtue going forth is ascribed to Jesus by the Evangelist, in Luke Jesus ascribes it to Himself. Common to both is this view of the order of events: Jesus first feels virtue issuing from Him; then infers a touch; then enquires who touched. The order implies that the forthgoing of influence is involuntary, for Jesus is in ignorance whence the movement proceeds, is, as it were, taken by surprise, and cannot, therefore, rationally concur. The usual way of escape from the unwelcome conclusion is to say that the ignorance was feigned; that Jesus in reality knew all

* So Weiss, vide *Das Leben Jesu*, i., 545.

about the woman, and asked the question merely to draw her forth from her hiding-place.* If this solution, exegetically unjustifiable and docetic in doctrinal tendency, were the only one possible, there would be no recourse left for an unbiassed interpreter but to choose the least of two evils, and ascribe error to the Evangelists rather than to impute an unworthy view of His own healing power to Jesus. But another alternative can be suggested. The ignorance may be conceived of as partial, and the course of events thus represented. The touch is immediately felt, and discerned to be the touch of one who desires to be healed. Jesus consents to the wish of the unknown one, and then proceeds to find out the person, that he or she may be brought to confession, and so receive the larger blessing.† This is a perfectly credible view of the occurrence. It is quite credible that the quick sense of Jesus should promptly detect the nervous, eager touch of a suffering human creature trembling with emotion, and that He should at once divine its meaning; that He should thereon instantly sympathise with the unknown sufferer, and consent to his or her relief,‡ and that He should then proceed to ascertain who the person benefited was. Only at one point is the hypothesis in conflict with the texts: in reference, viz., to the connection between the touch and the forthgoing of virtue. The hypothesis implies that the felt touch led up to the willing consent to cure. The texts seem to imply that the touch was inferred from the sense of liberated virtue; at least it is not easy to put any other construction on them.§

* So Olshausen, and after him Trench. † So Lange.

‡ Τίς ὁ ἁψάμενός μου (Luke viii. 45), implying ignorance of the sex.

§ Godet in his commentary on Luke comes indefinitely near recognising the automatic character of the cure which seems to be implied in the narratives of Mark and Luke. He says: In every miracle there are two poles, the receptivity of the cured, and the activity of Jesus. To the

Granting that there is error at this point, it is important to note the narrow limits within which it is confined. It does not affect the main incident, but merely the order of certain links in the chain of events. The mistake, if there be one, relates not to the miraculous fact, but to the manner in which it took place. It points to no uncertainty in the tradition as to what happened, but only to some not unnatural theorising as to how it happened. The mind of the apostolic church seems to have been exercised on the same question which now occupies our attention. If their theory of such cures as that of the woman with the issue was a little crude it is not to be wondered at. Facts well accredited seemed to suggest that healing virtue resided in the very body of Jesus. They heard how people brought their sick folk to Him and besought Him that they might only touch the hem of His garment, and how as many as touched were made perfectly whole.* In inferring from such facts a spontaneous curative power inherent in Christ's body they only overlooked one important circumstance, viz., that He was a consenting party to the cures. Permission to touch was asked and granted. The touch of the sufferers in such cases served the same purpose as the touch of Jesus Himself in other cases; it was an aid to faith, a sign, not a cause, of cure. The oversight is very pardonable, all the more that it can be utilised for apologetic purposes. If the infant church theorised crudely, their mistake at least shows that there was something to theorise about, marvel-

maximum of the action of one of these factors can correspond the minimum of the other. In the case of the blind man of Bethsaida the receptivity of the healed is a minimum and the action of Jesus a maximum. In the present case the reverse holds. The woman's receptivity, as it were snatches a cure, and Christ's action is reduced to that continual will to bless which ever animated Him.

* Matt. xiv. 35, 36.

lous facts to be accounted for. That is one lesson we learn from it. Perhaps there is another, even this, that it is best not to commit ourselves too decidedly to any theory as to the connection between the power exhibited in the healing ministry and the person of the Agent.

One other observation on this topic may be added. In the farewell address to His disciples, as reported in the fourth Gospel, Jesus is represented as promising that those who believed in His name should be able to do greater works than those done by Himself.* This promise may seem to harmonise best with the view that Christ's miracles were properly not His but God's. If God is always the real worker there is no reason why He should not work more mightily through an ordinary Christian than through Christ, unless, indeed, it be that it seems meet that the Christ should be honoured by having His name associated with the greatest displays of miraculous power. The sole question in that case would be whether the interests of the divine kingdom required more signal manifestations of power at a more advanced stage than at the initial period. But the promise referred to has really no bearing on the subject now under consideration. For even if the miracles of Jesus were wrought by a power resident in Himself, and the miracles of the apostles by a power delegated to them by their Master, it is conceivable that the latter might eclipse the former. The view to be taken then would be that the ascended Christ thought fit to give larger measures of power to the apostles than He exercised Himself when on earth, reckoning that this increase would redound to His glory as the exalted Lord. This is the view naturally suggested by the reason given for the increase in the words "Because I go unto my Father."

* John xiv. 12.

VIII.

THE GOSPEL MIRACLES IN RELATION TO THE CHRISTIAN REVELATION.

FOR all believers in the miraculous the question is vital, What is the function of miracles, what purpose do they serve? They must have an urgent *raison d'être;* they cannot be idle, superfluous occurrences without use or aim. The question, *Cui bono?* therefore, is one which cannot be put aside, and which no believer has ever sought to evade. And all believers are agreed in finding the justification of miraculous events in a service rendered in connection with Revelation. There is not entire agreement as to the nature of the service, some regarding miracles chiefly as evidences annexed to a Revelation supposed to be already complete in its substance, while others regard them as constituent elements of the Revelation itself. Which of the two modes of viewing the relation between miracles and Revelation is the more correct, or whether the two may not be combined, are questions internal to faith on which the schools of apologists are divided. A more radical question is whether miracles can be of any use at all in connection with Revelation, whether as evidences or as media. The position taken by Spinoza on this question is well known. He maintained that from miracles we can learn nothing either as to the being, the essence, or the character of God. In expressing this opinion he acted as the spokesman for all who do not believe in a living God. Miracles for Atheists, when not fables, are simply prodigies, unusual events whose causes are not known. Therefore, they can be of no avail to refute Atheism. They cannot prove the being of a God; they can only tell us something about a God already believed in.

Theism being assumed, miracles may make God better known. They may communicate to men a knowledge of God's character and purposes higher in degree than, if not different in kind from, that derived from the ordinary course of nature. Thus, regarding the ten plagues as miracles, we can see how they would serve to make God known with special clearness as the Deliverer of the oppressed; so accentuating a lesson taught more or less distinctly by the ordinary course of Providence. They showed God making special efforts in behalf of a down-trodden, helpless people. The mode in which they did this is not generically distinct from that in which ordinary Providence reveals the divine character. The method as well as the substance of the revelation is the same in kind. Our knowledge of God's ways and purposes is gathered from the common course of events by induction. We take a wide survey of human history, and we read there in legible, though somewhat indistinct characters: "God is good to all, and His tender mercies are over all His works." Many isolated events tend to suggest doubt whether God be either merciful or just, but a connected view of history expels the sceptical mood and confirms the belief that "Truly God is good to Israel." Even so may we conceive of the bondsmen in Egypt arriving at an assured conviction that Jehovah was their friend through means of the miracles wrought in their behalf. While they suffered under the Egyptian task-masters, it would seem hardly credible that the God of their fathers cared for them. The first miracle would light up in their dark hearts a ray of hope. But it might be an accident, they could not yet be sure. But as the plagues followed each other, the purpose of grace would shine forth with increasing clearness; and when the series was complete all doubt would be at an end. It was now a certainty that God was on their side, and was about to deliver them from bondage.

In this case the miracles evidently embodied the revelation. It was not, however, adduced for the purpose of forestalling the question as to the precise function of miracles, but merely to show how we might claim for them a real value as a source of knowledge concerning God, without exaggerating their importance. In passing now to the more special question, I remark that, assuming the reality of miracles, the presumption is altogether in favour of the view according to which they enter into the very substance of revelation, and are not merely signs confirmatory of its truth. For this view guarantees at once their standing and their character. Miracles forming an essential part of revelation are as important as the revelation itself. The two stand and fall together. On the other hand, miracles attached to a revelation as evidential signs assume the position of detachable and dispensable accidents. This indeed is denied by the Evidential school of apologists, who maintain that a doctrinal revelation worthy of the name cannot dispense with miracles as proofs of its claim to be from God. Thus one of the most vigorous representatives of the school, Dr. Mozley, says: "If it was the will of God to give a revelation, there are plain and obvious reasons for asserting that miracles are necessary as the guarantee and voucher for that revelation. A revelation is, properly speaking, such only by virtue of telling us something which we could not know without it. But how do we know that that communication of what is undiscoverable by human reason is true? Our reason cannot prove the truth of it, for it is by the very supposition beyond our reason. There must, then, be some note or sign to certify to it, and distinguish it as a true communication from God, which note can be nothing else than a miracle." * This passage defines very clearly both the writer's idea of revelation, and his view of the function of miracles. A revelation consists of a body of truths not discoverable by reason, and also not verifiable by reason. The function of miracles is to certify that it comes from God, and therefore may be accepted as infallible truth. The author illustrates his position by applying it to Christ, the chief agent of Revelation. Enumerating the most startling of the declarations Christ made concerning Himself, such as that He was the only begotten Son of God, he asks: "If this person made these assertions about himself, and all that was done was to make the assertions, what would be the inevitable conclusion of sober reason respecting that person? The necessary conclusion of sober reason respecting that person would be that he was disordered in his understanding." † Put briefly the position is, that one calling Himself the Son of God must work miracles to prove that He is, on pain of being pronounced a madman if He do not. The truth of this statement is not apparent. All that you can demand of one calling Himself the Son of God is that He be Godlike in His manners. The question is, what are Godlike manners? In some respects they are very different from those of men, the Scriptures being witness. Thus a Hebrew prophet declares that God's ways differ from men's very markedly in respect to the magnanimity of His forgiving mercy.‡ One might expect, therefore, to find an unexampled, unearthly love a prominent feature in the character of one truly claiming to be the Son of God. And just because His love was unearthly and

* Bampton Lectures, p. 6. † Bampton Lectures, p. 13.

‡ Isaiah lv. 6–9.

Godlike, one would also not be surprised to find that men refused to believe in His claim. In case He did happen to work miracles, one would not even be greatly surprised to find men persisting in an unbelieving attitude, His miracles notwithstanding. Thus it might turn out that miracles were unavailing for those who saw not the divinity of His love, and on the other hand they might be unnecessary as evidence for those who had insight to discern that nothing could be more divine. It is probable that such a Person, when He appears, will work miracles, for it is as easy and as natural for a Divine Being to do wonderful works as it is for ordinary men to perform ordinary actions. But we should not expect Him to work miracles for an evidential purpose, to show Himself to be the Son of God ; but rather in the more divine manner of the spontaneous play of His power in the service of great and Godlike ends. That He should be called on to work purely evidential miracles to justify His pretensions is every way likely, especially among such a people as the Jews, for they were a people who sought after signs : except they saw signs and wonders they would not believe. But if the Son of God should decline to comply with the demand, and say in effect, Look at my life as it unfolds itself before you, and draw your own conclusions, we should be disposed to accept that as a more reliable mark of His divinity than if He were to perform the most unparalleled miracles to gratify the cravings of the sign-seekers. And even if He wrought no miracles of any kind, it would not follow that it was for want of power, or that He was not the person He claimed to be. It might simply be because He did not deem them necessary or expedient. In that case men might still have believed in Him most rationally ; nay, faith might then have been of the highest and purest quality, as resting solely on insight intc the spiritual worth of one unique in wisdom, holiness, and love.

The concession is made by Dr. Mozley that a perfectly sinless character, itself as great a miracle as any that could be conceived, would suffice to prove a revelation, if only it were itself proved.* But the great moral miracle, it seems, can only be proved by physical miracles. These prove the divinity of the worker, and thence it is inferred He must have been sinless. Now, it must be acknowledged that to establish the absolute moral worth of any character by an inductive process is difficult, if not impossible; not, however, for the reason given by Dr. Mozley that real goodness depends on the inward motive whose perfection is not proved by the outward act.† It is possible to be satisfied by inspection as to a fellow-man's purity of heart, for moral simplicity is transparent and self-evidencing to every ingenuous soul. But from relative to absolute goodness faith takes a leap which it cannot easily justify by reasoning based on observation. But by whatever process faith arrives at its transcendental conclusion, it does not seem to be by the roundabout method indicated by Dr. Mozley. The Gospels supply us with both a positive and a negative experiment bearing on the question. On the one hand, the disciples seem to have arrived at the conviction that Jesus was the Holy One through an intimate knowledge of His character made possible by habitual companionship; on the other, the conventional saints and sages of the time, giving heed to the miracles, and specially to those which seemed most fitted to evince the holiness of Jesus, were not only not convinced thereby, but arrived at the opposite conclusion. "We believe and know that thou art the Holy

---

* Bampton Lectures, p. 14. † Ib., p. 14.

One of God,"* said the companions of Jesus, expressing the honest impression made on their minds by all that they had witnessed of His conduct in the past; and in the strength of that conviction they were prepared to abide by Him at a trying crisis when many forsook Him, and to accept His teaching as the words of eternal life, even when they did not comprehend them. "This fellow doth not cast out devils, but by Beelzebub the prince of the devils,"† said the Pharisees, in presence of those miraculous works in which Jesus claimed to be most obviously and emphatically acting by the inspiration and power of God. In drawing this contrast, I do not forget that the disciples also were witnesses of the same miracles which the Pharisees so grievously misinterpreted, and of all the other works of healing wrought by their Master. And I know that these works were among the things through which the character of Jesus gradually manifested itself to them in all its spiritual beauty. The point to be observed is that their method of studying that character was the reverse of the Pharisaic. The Pharisaic method was to begin at the outside. Starting from the data of miraculous signs viewed abstractly as mere wonders, they tried to read the heart, and they failed. The method of the disciples was to start from within and reason outwards. Discerning the spirit of Jesus with the clear vision of an honest heart, they read in the light of it all His outward conduct, and saw in all His acts, miraculous or otherwise, the self-manifestation of the Christ, the Son of the living God.

This, then, is the first point in favour of the view which regards miracles as vehicles of revelation, and not merely as evidential adjuncts. It guarantees their standing, gives

* John vi. 69. † Matt. xii. 24.

them a secure position in connection with revelation. The other is that it guarantees their quality. This mode of viewing miracles requires them to possess characteristics congruous to the nature of the revelation with which they are associated. If it is a revelation of grace, the miracles also must be gracious. Any kind of miracles will not do; a definite ethical character is indispensable. They must tend directly to advance the interests of the divine kingdom. If, on the other hand, the sole purpose of miracles were to serve as evidences of a doctrinal revelation all miracles would be alike good, provided only they were miraculous. Or, if any preference were to be given, it would be in favour of those miracles which were of the nature of naked signs, stript of every attribute except conspicuous, staring, undeniable miraculousness, the sort of miracle which the Jews seem to have desiderated when, unsatisfied and unconvinced by the beneficent works of the healing ministry, they demanded a sign from heaven; or, let us say, miracles of *the pen changed into a pen-wiper* order. It is unnecessary to remark on the irreverence displayed by Mr. Arnold in selecting a hypothetical miracle of this frivolous type to represent the miracles of the Gospel.* But as against the advocates of an extreme evidential theory he has shown tact in selecting as his typical miracle one which makes the theory appear ridiculous, yet cannot be complained of as a mere caricature. The case supposed is certainly trivial, but it is not irrelevant. If miracles were meant only to serve as evidential signs, then the thaumaturgical element is the only thing of value. Utility, dignity, ethical character may make them more worthy of respect, but they do not add to their probative force. The *pen-wiper* miracle,

---

* *Literature and Dogma*, p. 128.

however, it must be added, is an irrelevance as against those who assign to miracles more than the single function of evidential signs, and recognise them also as constituent elements of revelation. Such may say, there are no such miracles in the Gospels as that of the pen changed into a pen-wiper, because the miracles of Jesus were intended to serve a twofold purpose, and to be at once media and evidences of the Christian revelation. For the former purpose ethical character was indispensable, and in that connection it is the thing to be emphasized. When they are considered in the light of evidence, on the other hand, it is their miraculousness that must be accentuated. That element must be abstracted from all others, and made the sole object of attention. In a similar way may insistance on the evidential value of the predictive aspect of prophecy be reconciled with recognition of its essentially ethical character. The procedure of the apologist in both cases is analogous to that of the Protestant dogmatist when he strenuously insists on assigning to faith the function of a mere hand in the matter of justification. He knows that a faith which is a mere hand is an abstraction, and that all real faith is more than a hand to lay hold of pardoning grace, even a mighty power working towards sanctification; nevertheless he deems it not only legitimate, but even vitally important, to leave the latter function out of view in stating the doctrine of justification.

Apologetic writers have not always been careful to discriminate between the two aspects of miracles, and to give to both equal recognition. A polemical aim has commonly led them to lay a one-sided stress on the evidential as distinct from the revealing function. The traditional conception of the nature of revelation, moreover, has made it impossible for such as accepted it to do justice to the revealing function of miracles. Revelation, according to that conception, consists of a body of theological truths undiscoverable and unverifiable by reason. Miracles may be very necessary in connection with such a revelation as means of attesting the divinity of its source, but it is not easy to find a place for them in it as vehicles. Words, not miraculous acts, are the appropriate channels through which to communicate a dogmatic revelation. Bringing this conception with us to an examination of the Gospels it is easy to see how we must deal with the contents. We look to the *words* of Jesus exclusively in endeavouring to ascertain the nature of the Christian revelation. "*The Son of Man came to give His life a ransom for the many.*" "*As Moses lifted up the serpent in the wilderness, even so must the Son of Man be lifted up, that whosoever believeth in Him should not perish, but have eternal life.*" "*I and the Father are one.*" "*I am the resurrection and the life; he that believeth in me, though he were dead yet shall he live.*" These and the like texts setting forth the doctrines of the atonement and of Christ's divinity and of the resurrection from the dead, are the data from which we form our notion of the revelation which came through Jesus Christ. We look next at the miracles, and ask ourselves what construction is to be put upon them. We perceive that they stand in no intrinsic relation to the doctrines we have collected from the texts. In a few instances, indeed, the miracles appear to exemplify the doctrine taught, as in the case of the raising of Lazarus, which showed that Jesus did indeed possess the life-giving power which He claimed. But for the most part the relation of the miracles to the doctrines seems to be as extrinsic as that of a seal to a will. What then, we ask again, can be their function? We reflect that the doctrines gathered from Gospel texts are very important and very mysterious, not easily verifiable, very momentous if true. At length the use of the miracles dawns upon us. They were wrought to show that He who taught those transcendental doctrines came from God, and that therefore all His teaching about God, man, and Himself, however strange or hard to believe, may be implicitly accepted as true. Such is the view to be taken of the miracles collectively; presumably, also, in detail. If we find in Matthew's Gospel a group of miracles following immediately the great Sermon on the Mount, we may accept the miracles as seals of the doctrine, proofs that the Preacher was entitled to enunciate with legislative authority the laws of the kingdom of God.* If an epileptic patient is cured in the synagogue of Capernaum the event is designed to make those present regard what they have heard spoken as the discourse of one who has a commission to speak to them in God's name. The miracle may appear to be an accidental occurrence, but Providence arranged that it should happen just then, and with that end in view.

The foregoing is an ideal sketch, but it describes correctly in the main the traditional manner of handling the miraculous element in the Gospels and in the Bible generally. The penalty of all one-sidedness is neglect, and it is not surprising that a theory at once so artificial and so superficial should have fallen into general discredit. The evil is that one extreme leads by reaction to another, its opposite. The recent tendency has been, not to substitute for one view of the Gospel miracles which has been found defective, another more in accordance with fact, but to turn away from them

* So in effect Jerome, and after him Trench. Jerome remarks: Recte post prædicationem atque doctrinam signi offertur occasio, ut per virtutum miracula, præteritus apud audientes sermo firmetur. Comment. in Matthæum.

altogether as a thread-worn topic which can yield no satisfactory apologetic results. Even in the case of apologists of too well-balanced judgment to be guilty of totally neglecting the argument from miracles, the influence of reaction is apparent in a marked preference for other lines of argument. Thus the favorite theme for some time past has been the *moral* miracles of Christianity, the very title implying a disparaging reference to the physical miracles which form the basis of so much elaborate reasoning in older apologetic treatises. A recent Bampton lecturer, of a very different school from Dr. Mozley, who has rendered important service in connection with this new field of enquiry, assigns reasons why the moral miracles should take the place of prominence formerly occupied by the physical. The chief are that the moral miracles are present facts, not merely facts of the distant past, like the miracles of Scripture; that they satisfy the modern requirements of verifiableness; and that the argument based on them is one which can be appreciated by men of ordinary intelligence and information.* The relevancy of these allegations will be apparent when it is explained that by moral miracles is meant the effects produced in the history of the world by the appearing of Jesus Christ and by the religion bearing His name. Christ Himself is the first great moral miracle, and all the other miracles belonging to the same category consist of the influence which He has exercised upon the moral and social condition of mankind within the bounds of Christendom. The results which have flowed from that influence are called miracles, because it is believed that they rise above the effects which have been produced or can be produced by the teaching lives, or character of mere men however great, and

* Row, *Christian Evidences viewed in relation to Modern Thought* pp. 30–38.

can only be accounted for by superhuman agency. They are present miracles, because the effects referred to do not merely lie in the past, but continue to this hour. They are verifiable by all who study history, or who even make a good use of their eyes.

That this new field of investigation is fitted to yield valuable and wholesome apologetic results is already apparent from the contributions of those who in recent years have adopted it as their chosen department of labour.* The phenomena appealed to are such as make it easily possible without straining to prove the excellence, even the incomparable excellence of the Christian religion: to show that it is indeed a Tree of Life which has borne many good fruits, and whose very leaves are for the healing of the nations. If the tree is known by its fruits, the study of the facts connected with the history of Christian civilisation cannot fail to produce a most favorable bias in favour of Christianity and its Author on the mind of every candid enquirer. But whether it is fitted to do more than this, and to take the place of the main argument in support of the Christian religion to be the one religion divinely given, and therefore absolutely perfect, is another matter. The argument is certainly not so easy as some seem to imagine. It cannot serve the purpose of "Portable Evidences" of Christianity adapted to the capacities of the unlettered. It involves a wide comparative study of history which the plain man has neither the ability, the learning, nor the leisure to prosecute. He must find his evidences in a much narrower sphere: in the adaptation of the Gospel to his needs, and in its regenerating influence on his spirit and conduct. The argument

---

* Among the works which have recently appeared on this subject may be mentioned Brace's *Gesta Christi* and Storrs' *Divine Origin of Christianity*.

further demands careful discrimination between improvements in the condition of the world, which are the direct consequences of Christianity, and those which merely came into existence subsequently to the commencement of the Christian era. It is further complicated by serious differences of opinion among Christians as to what are the effects apparently traceable to the advent of Christ, on which the world has cause to congratulate itself. What diverse shapes the argument will assume according as it is wielded by a Catholic or by a Protestant! To the former the church of which the Bishop of Rome is Head, is the one grand effect of Christ's appearing, the proof of His Divinity, the perpetuation of His incarnation; a perennial miracle, possessing indefeasibly, and exercising daily all manner of miraculous gifts. To the latter the Church of Rome is the great opprobrium of Christianity, the great trial to faith, that which makes it most difficult to believe that Christianity is any exception to the law according to which all religions beginning in comparative simplicity and purity undergo degeneracy, and end in superstition and priestcraft. If one happens to be not merely a conventional Protestant, but one who protests against ecclesiasticism in all churches, he will be inclined to regard the Christian Church throughout its history as on the whole a most disappointing, disenchanting phenomenon, and to ask himself how it came to pass that so fair an ideal found so abortive a realisation. Jesus Christ is beautiful, His teaching is beautiful, the ideal church of the New Testament is beautiful; but where in church history can one see any approximation to that divine beauty except in select saintly souls, in obscure corners, in favoured periods of too short duration? To indulge in such reflections might seem querulous and pessimistic, but there is just enough ground for them to tempt men of earnest spirit, and thoroughly loyal to Christ, to see in the church little else than an incubus which has prevented Christianity from having a fair chance, and of which it must yet rid itself in order to live and thrive. On the most dispassionate estimate the amount of evil that has been wrought by those bearing Christ's name, and acting officially in His stead, is so great that large admissions have to be made by all who wish to be listened to in the endeavour to show how much the world owes to Jesus.

Once more, even if the effects of Christ's action were all demonstrably good, it would not be easy to prove that they were superhuman. Many effects unquestionably good can be and have been specified. Christ's doctrines of the Fatherhood of God, and the brotherhood of man, have borne blessed fruits in the emancipation of slaves, the restriction of paternal power, the elevation to her rightful place of woman, the diffusion of philanthropic feeling towards the poor, the sick, the helpless, the aged. These and many other familiar features of Christian civilisation are genuine *Gesta Christi*. But are they necessarily superhuman effects imperiously demanding a superhuman cause? The argument requires them to be such, as will be apparent from the following statement of it by one who has most forcibly plied it: "As an event manifesting purpose, for which the action of the forces of the material universe is unable to account, is a physical miracle, and proves the presence of a power different from those forces, so an event in the moral and spiritual worlds, for which the forces that energise in man are unable to account, must be a moral miracle, and must prove the presence of a superhuman power. I claim on behalf of Jesus Christ that His character and action in history constitute a manifestation of such a power the presence of which admits of an actual verification in the history of the past and the facts of the present."* In form and method the argument does not differ materially from that of the old apologists. Nothing indeed is changed but the substitution of moral in place of physical miracles, the change being justified by the superior verifiableness of the new order of miracles. The stress of the argument does not lie on the morality of the miracles, but on the circumstance that it is more easy to prove their miraculousness. The miracles might conceivably be of another kind, intellectual, or artistic, for example. If it were possible to cite artistic effects traceable to Christ's influence and demonstrably superhuman, they would suffice to prove that He was superhuman quite as well as moral miracles. But *de facto* the effects on which the argument turns are moral And the point to be proved is that they are miraculous superhuman, facts "for which the forces that energise in man are unable to account." The appeal, of course, is to history. The contention is that from the pages of history telling the story of mankind for thousands of years, we can learn the limits of human power in all departments of life, and that outside Christendom no such influence has ever been exercised on men, as Christ can be shown to have put forth in those who bear His name. Where, for example, it is asked, can you find anything to parallel the devotion of Christians to Jesus as their Lord, or the means employed by Jesus to produce that devotion? No believer will be disposed to question either the relevancy or the force of this appeal; but what we may legitimately doubt is the cogency of the argument viewed as addressed to unbelievers. It is not easy to prove a universal; to show that certain things not only have never been done by men, but

* Row, *Christian Evidences*, p. 91.

never will or can be done. Then granting that the uniqueness of the effects of Christ's action on the world, stamps them as superhuman and points to a superhuman cause, must all unique effects be held to point in a similar direction? In that case might it not be plausibly contended that through Greece was given to the world a divine revelation in art, as through Judæa a divine revelation in morals and religion? Nothing useful, says Origen, comes into the world without the Providence of God.* In that sentiment all devout minds will concur. Every good gift is from above, coming down from the Father of lights. The difficulty is to prove that the gift is so supremely good, so absolutely perfect a boon, as to be nothing short of a miracle.

If the world has ever received from above a gift which may without exaggeration be described in these terms it is the Lord Jesus Christ Himself. The effects which He has produced in history may or may not be demonstrably superhuman; but He, the Source of Christian civilisation, is certainly the most remarkable moral phenomenon which has appeared in the whole history of mankind. The study of effects is useful as tending to raise a presumption in favour of the divine origin of Christianity, or to confirm a belief therein already existing; but the most direct road to faith is open-eyed, open-hearted contemplation of the Founder, in whom some have been constrained to recognise a moral miracle, who refuse to believe in any other miracles. This great moral miracle will be our theme in the next lecture. Meantime we are to learn how the physical miracles of the Gospels served to illustrate the Moral Miracle, to show forth His glory: for this, as John hints in the close of his narrative of the first miracle, was after all their chief use.

---

* *Contra Celsum*, i., 9: οὐδὲν γὰς χρηστὸν ἐν ἀνθρώποις ἀθεεὶ γίγνεται.

The Gospel miracles all served as vehicles of the Christian revelation, but not in the same way or to the same extent. There is a broad difference here between the nature-miracles and the miracles of healing. All relate to the kingdom of God, the grand theme of Christ's preaching; but the former teach general lessons concerning the kingdom, while the latter give us insight into its inmost nature. The nature-miracles proclaim two truths concerning the kingdom: its supremacy, and the certainty of its realisation. The kingdom of heaven is the *summum bonum*, and it shall surely come—such are the two foremost lessons to be learnt from the miscellaneous group of incidents included under that title. Other lessons readily suggest themselves and have often been drawn. The nature-miracles seem to prove in a conspicuous manner the Divinity of Christ by exhibiting His divine attributes in exercise; the miraculous draught of fishes, and the finding of the stater showing His omniscience; the change of water into wine, and the feeding of the multitude proclaiming His creative might; the walking on the water, and the stilling of the storm, announcing the Lord of nature superior to its most unvarying laws, master of its wildest elements; the cursing of the fig-tree bearing witness to one who, besides being the Maker of the world, is also its judge. These theological inferences, however, do not unfold the main significance of the incidents in question. The point to be emphasized is not the Divinity of Christ, but His absorbing concern for the Divine kingdom and His firm faith in its destinies. In these nature-miracles He says in deeds, what at other times He said in words, that the kingdom is the chief end of life, and that it is not a mere dream. They are, so to speak, pictorial illustrations of the two great mottoes: *Seek ye first the kingdom of God and His righteousness; Fear not, little flock, it is your Father's good pleasure to give you the kingdom.*

These truths, however, while very important, are but formal generalities. The vital question is, What is the kingdom which is declared to be supreme, and destined to victorious establishment? For a contribution to the answer to this question we must fall back on the main body of the Evangelic miracles, those connected with the healing ministry. These enter into the very heart of the Christian revelation, whether we view it as a revelation of Jesus Christ Himself, or as a revelation of the nature of the kingdom He preached. The two aspects, while formally distinct, virtually coincide.

The healing miracles, then, were an important contribution to the *self-revelation of Jesus Christ, in the fulness of His grace.* They were not, it is unnecessary to say, a solitary contribution. Jesus manifested the grace that was in Him along several lines of action; the chief being, preaching the Gospel of the kingdom to the poor, kindly intercourse with social and moral outcasts, and the ministry of love in the cure of disease. In the first department of activity He uttered "words of grace," which at Nazareth and elsewhere excited admiration; in the others He wrought works of grace equally impressive, equally with the words a forthflowing from the deep well of love within His heart. The effect of those gracious works as a revelation of sympathy is much enhanced when they are viewed in connection with that systematic antagonism to Pharisaism through which Jesus manifested the truth that was in Him. By that antagonism He declared what the righteousness of the kingdom was not; by the other lines of conduct He showed what it was. His habitual bearing towards the Pharisees was a protest against sham sanctity; his beneficent relations with the people of the land revealed a new kind of holiness, whose essence and inspiring soul was love. The wide prevalence of the counterfeit made it needful that He should not only be very emphatic in express condemnation of it, but also very painstaking in the exhibition of genuine goodness. Every means must be employed to make the difference as marked as possible. Humanity must be displayed as broadly as the inhuman type of virtue which paraded its merits so ostentatiously before the public eye, that an adequate comment might be supplied on the prophetic oracle, "I will have mercy and not sacrifice." Jesus performed the difficult task most thoroughly, so that all men had it in their power to compare the two moral types. What an amazing, eloquent contrast was presented to their view! On one side the Pharisees, scrupulously observing the petty rules of the Rabbis as to Sabbath-keeping, fasting, washing, tithe-paying; but utterly heartless, caring only for their own reputation, living apart in sanctimonious pride, and regarding all outside their coterie with indifference or abhorrence. On the other side Jesus, neglecting the religious fashions, and laying Himself open in many ways to the censures of those who practised piety *à la mode* (though for no breach of God's law), but showing Himself in all possible ways as the friend and brother of the people, preaching to them on the highway the Gospel of God's Fatherly love, visiting them in their homes, taking food with them, healing their sick, only drawing closer to them in fraternal sympathy when His intercourse with them was impugned, and even misconstrued in the most brutal manner. It is a romantic story; we are tempted to think it a mere poetic idyl, a picture altogether too beautiful for real life. The protest against false sanctity we have less difficulty in accepting as historical, for many prophets and sages have said such things against hypocrisy, and pride, and ostentation, though none have said them so well.

But how many do little more than protest! It is so easy to expose and denounce the false, so hard to exhibit in one's own life the true. But the glory of the Gospel story is that the tale of love is as true as the record of prophetic sternness. Its truth is guaranteed by its utter originality. Such sternness as Christ's had been witnessed before in the Hebrew prophets, but such love never. It was an absolutely new thing, whereof prophets at their utmost stretch of inspiration had been just able faintly to dream.

In the revelation of this new love to man the healing works played a prominent part. They are entitled to be associated, as means for that end, on equal terms with the preaching to the poor, and the social intercourse with the outcasts. All proclaimed aloud one grand profoundly significant fact, the human sympathy of Jesus. All taught by obvious implication one momentous blessed truth, the infinite importance of man, body and soul, in God's sight; of man in any circumstances, and in the worst samples, destitute, diseased, depraved. This doctrine concerning man, taught by deeds more than by words, is one of the most distinctive in the Christian revelation. It is the complement of the doctrine of the Divine Fatherhood so prominent in the teaching of Jesus; and these two together form the foundation of the Christian theory of the universe. When we consider the share which the miracles of healing had in launching this doctrine, we perceive what a mistake it were to treat them with neglect, and to turn to the so-called moral miracles as a more attractive and instructive subject of study. To abandon, as antiquated, the artificial views of apologists as to the uses of the Gospel miracles may be right and proper, but the miracles themselves can never be wisely treated as of little, or at most of only subordinate moment. To turn from the primitive manifestations of the spirit of Christian Humanity to later developments, in quest of proof that that spirit is Divine, is to forsake the pure fountain of living water as it gushed forth from the heart of the Son of Man for the impure stream of common philanthropy. There is no respect in which the preference can be justified. Is it that the earlier miracles were physical? But they were moral in significance if not in immediate effect. They formed an integral part of Christ's ministry of grace; they contributed towards the revelation of His love; they were one of the means by which the distinctively Christian doctrine concerning God, man, and their relations was promulgated. Or is the plea for preference that the import of the argument from the later philanthropies of the Christian era can be more easily appreciated by the common mind? But what can be more intelligible than the lesson of the Gospel miracles. "He healed them all." Why? Because He was a lover of men; such love is of God: behold the simple logic of the matter in a few words, which a child can understand. The argument can be elaborated at pleasure and made to cover the whole wide field of Christian philanthropy, and enriched with illustrations drawn from all the Christian centuries. But in essence it is in the Gospel miracles, as in a nutshell, intelligible to the "babes" who have neither talent nor time to master the teachings of history. But the drawback of the Gospel miracles may be that they *are* miracles, the like of which do not happen now, therefore unverifiable, and gravely to be suspected by all who are imbued with the scientific spirit, stumbling-blocks to the "wise and understanding." But the value of the healing works of Jesus as media of revelation does not at all depend on their miraculousness. Their value as evidences of the Divine origin of a doctrinal revelation does depend on that, and the fact constitutes a grave objection to that mode of viewing them. On the old theory of miracles their miraculous character has to be settled at the outset. You must satisfy yourself as to the credentials of the supposed revelation before you look into its contents; for only in case those are satisfactory can these be accepted as divine. Such a stipulation practically dooms all to whom a miracle is a stumbling-block to permanent ignorance and unbelief. But take the healing works not as evidences but as media of revelation, and you may learn much that is of vital importance in Christianity, and be in important respects a Christian in faith and practice while your judgment is in suspense on the whole subject of miracles. Whether they be miracles in the strict sense, or only marvels, or not even so much as marvels, they serve the purpose of making manifest the sympathy of Christ equally well. Their lesson is independent of all theories as to how they happened. We do not need to verify them as miracles, but only as facts. We do not need to know by what power Jesus did these things, but only that He did them. If He wrought them by the power of God brought into play by prayer, He prayed without ceasing, and prayed effectually, as only he can whose prayers are inspired by fervent love. If He wrought them by a power inherent in Himself, and peculiar to Himself, He used His singular gift to the uttermost as one filled with the enthusiasm of humanity. If He wrought them by a power common to Him with other men, He employed the common talent in a most uncommon way, evincing a most extraordinary zeal in well-doing. Look at them as you will, these works of healing are a Revelation of grace, a worthy inauguration of the era of grace. As such they claim the attention and respect of all. None of the excuses for inattention that might be pled in reference to other views and arguments are relevant here. To the old apologetic argument from miracles men of naturalistic proclivities might reply: the cogency of the argument turns on the miraculousness of the events, and that is precisely what cannot be verified. To the new apologetic argument from moral miracles a similar reply may be returned by the philosopher; and the rustic for his part may say that he has not time to go into historical researches. Against the view now presented these excuses are pointless. To the philosopher we can say, Miraculous or not, the healing works are facts; consider what they mean. To the rustic we can say, The facts are few, all the relative narratives can be read in a single Sabbath evening: read them attentively, and note the impression they make on your mind. To both classes they will proclaim the presence of a love altogether unique, if not of a power altogether miraculous; a moral miracle without doubt, whatever we may think as to the alleged miraculousness of the events in which it is embodied. A service, this, surely not to be despised! What more important in the interest alike of a pure religious faith, and of an elevated standard of morals, than that the love of Christ should take its place as a fundamental article in the catholic creed of Christendom; that Jesus should stand out to the eye of the whole world as the one man who loved the human race with all His heart? If that desirable result has been achieved, we owe it in no small measure to the Evangelic miracles.

In the foregoing observations I have been viewing Christianity in its most general aspect as the *religion of Humanity*, and have found that in this connection the healing ministry performed a direct revealing function. But in its more special aspect Christianity is the *religion of Redemption*, having in view as its chief end the cancelling of moral evil. In one of His pregnant parabolic utterances Jesus called Himself by implication a Physician; but the connection in which the word was spoken shows that He regarded man's soul and not his body as the proper subject of His healing art. His vocation was not to perform ordinary medical cures, but, as He Himself said, "to call sinners to repentance." If He did, nevertheless, work many cures of physical maladies, it is reasonable to suppose that, besides serving the immediate purpose of manifesting sympathy, they also served an ulterior end in connection with the higher spiritual ministry. We have something more to go upon here than our own conjectures. The mere fact that faith in some form and measure was required as a condition of cure raises the healing works of Jesus above the level of the cures wrought for their own sake by an ordinary physician in the pursuit of his calling. The complaint against the cities of the plain implies that an end had been aimed at in the mighty works performed in their midst which had not been reached, in consequence of moral shortcomings on the part of the inhabitants. Their diseases had been healed, but they had not "repented"; they had not made the kingdom and righteousness of God their chief good and end, and therefore their benefactor was dissatisfied, and felt that His beneficent labour had been in vain. It seems as if He had intended the cure of their physical maladies to lift their thoughts to maladies of another kind with which it was more properly His business to deal.

In connection with the redeeming work of Christ the revealing function of the healing ministry was only indirect. Herein it differed from the evangelisation of the poor, and the intercourse with the socially and morally degraded, in both of which we see Jesus directly engaged in the work of His calling as the spiritual Physician. The immediate aim of the preaching was to inspire faith in a heavenly Father's love, and of the eating and drinking with publicans and sinners to bring the fallen under the recuperative influence of purity sympathetic with impurity. The miracles of healing also made for these ends, but only by a circuitous path; on which account they must be regarded in this connection as subordinate in importance to the other two departments of our Lord's public activity. Their significance here is that only of symbols or parables. They are a system of signs, hinting a lesson they do not expressly teach, which many therefore might fail to learn. That Jesus sympathised with suffering they said plainly to all; that He was the physician of souls they said in mystic language which only the more thoughtful could interpret.

Yet the miracle-parables were not much more abstruse than other parables. The signs were not hieroglyphics legible only by a privileged caste, but a demotic alphabet adapted to the popular understanding. The key to their meaning was to be found in the connection between disease and sin, a connection which was not only real for the popular mind, but was the subject of exaggerated and superstitious opinion, the prevalent notion being that sin was not merely in general the cause of disease, but that particular sins were the causes of particular diseases. There is nothing in the Gospels to show that Jesus either shared or encouraged that view; on the contrary, there is positive evidence that He regarded it as mistaken. But while He gave no countenance to the idea that for every physical ailment there was a corresponding moral ailment related to it as cause to effect, He did believe that there was a close connection between the two kinds of evil, and He took advantage of a similar conviction in the minds of the people to lift their thoughts from the lesser to the graver kind

He healed their diseases that they might think of their sins and seek deliverance from them. In this point of view the whole healing ministry was one grand parable of Redemption. Jesus dealt with the physical effect, the evil of which all could appreciate, to advertise Himself as one prepared to deal with the spiritual cause, to the evil of which many were insensible. He healed disease with an unsparing hand that the presence of the Spiritual Physician might be the better known, and to proclaim a plenteous redemption.

The latent parabolic import of the healing ministry came to light in the particular instance of the healing of the palsied man. In that case Jesus expressly spoke of that which was always more or less in His thoughts.* "Son, thy sins be forgiven thee," was the first word He uttered to the sufferer; "arise and take up thy bed," only the second: the order of the sayings intimating the relative importance of the spiritual and physical benefits in the view of the healer. It has, indeed, been supposed that some special reason existed for the reference to sin in this case, and conjectures have been made as to its nature. One of the most plausible is that of Paulus, that the assurance of forgiveness facilitated a cure by removing mental depression and awakening hope. On this view the pardon of sin is reduced to a medical expedient, and the health of the soul is subordinated to the health of the body as a means to an end. Without calling in question that some unknown circumstances may have made express mention of sin and forgiveness natural and desirable just then, I believe that Jesus on this occasion proclaimed in the hearing of the multitude

* Reference to sin occurs, also, in the narratives of the healing of the impotent man at the pool of Bethesda (John v. 14), and of the healing of the man born blind (John ix. 2, 3).

the emblematic significance of all His healing acts, saying in effect: "In compassion for your sufferings I heal your bodies, but what I chiefly desire is to heal your souls. He that hath an ear let him hear." It may be asked, If this was the lesson intended to be taught why was it not more frequently inculcated? Without insisting on the fact that the miracles recorded in the Gospels are only a few typical instances selected from a great number, so that the healing of the palsied man may, for aught we know, have been only one of many cases in which sin was alluded to, I ask in reply, Was not the ministry of healing closely associated with the ministry of preaching? Christ's habit was to preach and at the same time to heal. Thus we read that He "went about all the cities and villages, teaching in their synagogues and preaching the Gospel of the kingdom, and healing every sickness and every disease among the people."* The records show that He was engaged in preaching to a great crowd when the friends of the palsied man brought him to Him to be healed.† And what was the burden of His preaching then and at all times? Sin, repentance, pardon, the life of peace and purity accessible to all through faith in a heavenly Father's gracious love. The preaching thus made the understanding of the miracles which followed easy. The parable embodied in the healing acts needed no further interpretation. None but such as were very slow to learn could imagine that their benefactor meant them to go home and enjoy their restored health without thought of anything higher. It is not likely that all or even the majority of the healed entered on the new life; but they were dead indeed in sin and worldliness, if they did not at least feel that their cure was a summons to moral amendment.

* Matt. ix. 35.

† Mark ii. 2.

In some instances the summons might come home with special power because the disease healed possessed peculiar significance as an emblem. Possibly all diseases of the body might be employed with some measure of appropriateness as emblems of spiritual states, but in the case of such diseases as leprosy and blindness fitness for emblematic uses is exceptionally apparent. It is not necessary to suppose that lepers were cleansed and blind eyes opened for the express purpose of typifying Christ's power to remove the defilement of sin, and to dispel spiritual darkness; but we can readily conceive the common moral of all the healing miracles presenting itself with peculiar vividness to the minds of such as had been delivered by Christ's power from the maladies referred to. In the homiletic treatment of the miracles the emblematic significance of leprosy, blindness, and certain other diseases is taken for granted as self-evident. We may credit lepers cleansed, and blind men to whom vision had been restored, with the talent to preach homilies to themselves, and we can believe that it was their benefactor's desire that the talent should not be buried in a napkin. To say more than this, and to represent Christ as working miracles expressly to give instruction in the nature of His redeeming work—to exhibit it as delivering from a moral disease loathsome as leprosy, weakening as palsy, destructive of all the spiritual senses, were to play into the hands of those who resolve such narratives as the healing of the leper into figures of speech originally employed to describe Christ's work as a spiritual healer and afterwards converted into literal physical miracles.*

* This view is hinted at by Dr. Abbott when he speaks of Providence preserving "through records of physical miracles the truth that Jesus was the worker of spiritual miracles." *Oxford Sermons*, Introduction, p. lvi.

It will help us to guard against this tendency if we remember that the healing ministry did not merely serve as a parable of a purely spiritual redemption. It pointed to a redeeming work of a comprehensive, many-sided character, embracing within its scope the whole of human nature. It was a prophecy of the redemption of the body as well as a parable of the redemption of the soul. In this point of view the miracles of healing are in entire harmony with the whole attitude of the Christian religion towards the material side of man, as contrasted with that of Paganism. The idea of the body being redeemed or sharing in the future life was utterly foreign to Pagan habits of thought, as exhibited especially in the literature of Greece. The hope of the Pagan was the immortality of the soul. The hope of the Christian, on the contrary, is eternal life for man, involving the resurrection of the body. The difference in this respect has its root in widely diverse ways of regarding matter. To the Greek philosopher matter was something essentially vile, evil, incurably bad, the seat of sin, and making sin inevitable for man as long as he lived in the flesh. To the Christian, taking his inspiration from the New Testament, the human body not less than the human soul is God's creature, therefore in itself good—evil only by accident, and capable of being delivered from evil, and destined to be raised into a state of incorruption beyond the reach of disease and death.

In a very prominent department of the healing ministry, the cure of demoniacs, we seem to see Jesus actually at work as the Redeemer of souls. With reference to this part of His work Jesus Himself said, The kingdom of God is come unto you; and it seems as if it could not come more effectually than through the expulsion of demons from the unhappy children of men in whom they had taken up their abode. Yet this work, however beneficent, was rather a prelude to the proper work of redemption by which men were delivered from sin, than an instalment thereof. It prepared the way of the Lord, but it did not of itself bring the Lord into the heart. The kingdom of God came very nigh to a demoniac emancipated from subjection to a strange power, but dispossession of the demon who kept him in thrall did not constitute him a citizen of the kingdom. The seat of demoniacal possession was not the innermost core of man's being, the spirit, but rather the physical and psychical parts of his nature. The proper concomitants of possession were not immorality, vice, wicked feelings, ungodliness, worldliness, but epilepsy, insanity, and the like morbid physical and psychical states. The publicans and harlots were addicted to sensual sins, but they were not demoniacs. Judas Iscariot and the Pharisees were great sinners in another way, and might most legitimately be described as children of the devil, but neither were they demoniacs. Jesus spent much of His time among the "publicans and sinners," seeking to redeem them from the power of sin, but His work among them was not of the nature of exorcism. Nor was the effect of His work in the two cases the same. In the case of the publicans and sinners it was to bring them to repentance and a new life of purity. In the case of demoniacs it was to restore them, not to sanctity, but to sanity, physical and mental. The demoniac of Gadara, after he was healed, was found by his fellow-countrymen sitting, clothed, and sane. The poor sufferer whom they had formerly known as restless, nude and mad, they now saw to their amazement, quiet, decently attired, and in his right mind.

The healing work among demoniacs was thus strictly viewed, like the healing ministry in general, only a parable of redemption. Our Lord actually drew a parable from demoniacal experiences to illustrate the moral condition of the Jewish people, comparing them to a demoniac from whom one devil had been expelled, and who was afterwards taken possession of a second time by the same demon, accompanied by seven others more wicked than himself, making the last state of the man worse than the first.* It is a very graphic description, but it is parabolic, ending with an, Even so shall it be also unto this wicked generation. It is an illustration of a truth relating to the moral sphere, drawn from another sphere distinct though closely akin.

It remains to add that the cure of demoniacs, like all the healing miracles, besides being a parable of spiritual redemption, bore witness to the many-sidedness of Christ's redeeming work. If the healing of ordinary physical maladies testified that the body was destined to share in that work, the cure of the peculiar class of diseases comprehended under the title of demoniacal possession proclaimed impressively that the mind also fell within the range of Christ's redemptive influence. Thus viewing the healing ministry as a whole, in combination with the preaching ministry, we learn to regard Jesus as the Redeemer of man, body, soul, and spirit. He means to do the work on which He is sent thoroughly. When we consider to whom He specially preached His Gospel, and how liberally He dispensed the benefits of His healing power, we see that He aims at universality as well as thoroughness. Everything bespeaks a plenteous Redemption.

The redemption is very complete in intention and plan. What then? Does it proceed along two lines, manifesting itself, as in Christ's own lifetime, on one side as a regenerat

* Matt. xii. 43–45.

ing force in the spirit of man, and on the other side as a healing ministry in connection with the diseases of the body? Was it Christ's purpose that it should assume this dual form in parallel streams of spiritual and corporeal blessing running as rivers of life and health throughout all the Christian ages? In the foregoing statement it has been implied, though not expressly affirmed, that the cure of disease, though very prominent in our Lord's public ministry, was not co-ordinate with, but subordinate to, His work as the Saviour from sin, and that it served once for all certain purposes in connection with the Christian revelation, revealing the grace and sympathy of Jesus, exhibiting the genius of the religion of humanity, supplying a system of acted parables of spiritual redemption. But it may be asked, why should the manifestation of Christ's sympathy with human suffering be a mere fact of past history, why should it not go on now as of old in the same benignant way, resulting in the extensive, signal, supernatural healing of disease in answer to the prayer of faith? Why should not a healing ministry of the exalted Christ form an integral, perpetual part of the work of the kingdom? Would it not serve the important purpose of showing that Christ in glory still remembers the woes with which His eye was familiar during His sojourn on the earth, and worthily exhibit Christianity to the world as having for its twofold aim the extinction at once of disease and of sin?

The Church has at no time in any of her branches so viewed the plan of redemption. Not even the Catholic portion of the Church, in which belief in the continuation of miracles has ever been much more prevalent than in Protestant Christendom, has so understood the matter. Miraculous healings abound in Catholic annals, but these have ever been regarded rather as honours conferred by God upon saints, or as notes of the true Church than as an ordinary normal part of the Church's functions. How has it come to pass that the whole Christian Church, speaking broadly, has allowed the healing of the body to fall into abeyance in comparison with the saving of the soul? Apparently the explanation is this, that it has been generally felt that disease is not on the same level with sin; that physical evil in general, of which bodily disease is only one form, cannot be co-ordinated with moral evil as of equal importance, and that while the divine plan of redemption contemplates complete deliverance from all evil, each part comes in its own order, spiritual deliverance first as most urgent and important, physical deliverance in the end, coming at last after long waiting in answer to the longing of the whole creation.

Some, however, in our day regard this view as mistaken, and hold that the cure of disease ought to be placed alongside the pardon of sin as a part of the present heritage of redeemed humanity, and contend that if the Church rightly understood her Lord's will and her own duty and privilege, and acted up to these, cures would be as common as conversions. Such a doctrine, if true, ought to have Scripture support. It is found in the prophetic oracle quoted by Matthew, "Himself took our infirmities, and bare our sicknesses,"* interpreted to mean that Jesus as Redeemer of the world bore human disease in the same vicarious manner as He bore human sin; and in the promise recorded in the close of Mark's Gospel, "These signs shall follow them that believe: in my name shall they cast out devils; they shall speak with new tongues; they shall take up serpents; and if they drink any deadly thing it shall not hurt them; they shall lay hands on the sick and they shall recover," † which is held to be an unrestricted promise to believers in all ages.

* Matt. viii. 17.

† Mark xvi. 17, 18.

On which side does the truth lie? Before answering, it may be well to note the true state of the question. The question is not one as to the possibility of remarkable and even supernatural cures being wrought now, as in Christ's time, in answer to the prayer of faith. This is believed in by all who sincerely pray for the healing of sick friends. Neither is it a question as to the reality of alleged faith cures, whether of the present or of any past time. A Christian man has no interest in obstinately denying their reality. On the contrary, he can only hope that all cases of the kind are as real as the most enthusiastic advocates of modern miracles could desire, and devoutly wish that their number were greatly multiplied. What missionary would not be glad to be endowed with the power to heal diseases conferred by Jesus on His disciples when He sent them on their Galilean mission? I know the feeling well. I spent a part of my apprenticeship as a preacher as a missionary in a once prosperous, but then decaying village in the west of Scotland, filled with an impoverished and exceptionally disease-stricken population. There I daily saw sights which awakened at once intense sympathy and involuntary loathing. There were cases of cancer, strange demoniac-like forms of insanity, children in arms twenty years old, with the face of a full-grown man and a body not much larger than an infant's. I returned home ofttimes sick at heart and unable to take food. What would I not have given to have had for an hour the charism of the Galilean Evangelists, and how gladly would I have gone forth that day, not to speak the accustomed words about a Father in heaven ever ready to receive His prodigal children, but to put an end to pain, raise up the dying, and to restore to soundness shattered reason! Or had I found some day, on visiting the sufferers, that they had been healed, according to their own report, in answer to the prayers of some saintly friend, I should have been too thankful to be at all inclined to be sceptical.

But the question is, Ought the Church to put the healing of disease on the same doctrinal foundation as the pardon f sin, and to announce it systematically as an essential part of the Gospel? Ought believers in Jesus to make it their business to heal diseased bodies not less than to save sinful souls, pursuing the one end not less than the other exclusively by faith, guarding against the use of medical skill as carefully as against self-righteousness? I for one cannot believe it. This theory unduly magnifies the benefit of merely physical health. It may be doubted if it would have entered into the mind of any one to advocate such a theory, had the healing of disease not occupied so prominent a place in the ministry of Christ. The exegetical basis of the theory is very slender. The inference drawn from the prophetic text cited by Matthew—that Christ suffered vicariously for the diseases of the world not less than for its sins—can commend itself only to minds prepossessed in favour of the theory, or addicted to a very prosaic method of interpretation. Christ bore men's sicknesses as He bore their poverty, and all other ills of human life which moved His compassion, and the cure of disease is no more a part of His Gospel than is the cure of pauperism. There is no need or call to make a specialty of this benefit; it belongs to the category of physical, temporal, or social ameliorations, and must be dealt with on the same principles as all other benefits of the same class. Christianity is not indifferent to human health and wealth; on the contrary, it tends in many ways to promote these But it has not these for chief ends. Its chief ends are the kingdom and the righteousness of God. To those who with singleness of heart seek these, health and wealth are added, as far as a benignant Providence deems needful, or as far as is compatible with the effective prosecution of higher interests. The two interests—the lower interest of the body and the higher interest of the spirit—are not completely compatible in this present state of things. To a certain extent one must be sacrificed to the other. Supreme consuming devotion to the Divine Kingdom often means shattered nerves, premature age, death before the natural time. The treasure is in an earthen vessel. The outward man perishes, not only while, but because the inward man is renewed day by day.*

---

* I have taken my account of the views entertained by advocates of the Faith-cures theory from *The Ministry of Healing*, by A. J. Gordon, D.D., Boston, and *Gospel Parallelisms Illustrated in the Healing of Body and Soul*, by the Rev. R. L. Stanton, D.D., Buffalo. Bushnell also was a believer in modern miracles, and faith-cures in particular, but his interest in the subject had a different origin. He longed to see new outbursts of supernatural powers as a witness to a living God, and as a welcome interruption to the dreary depressing reign of naturalism. He pled for the continuation of miracle as one animated by a philosophic concern for the cause of Theism, not as the advocate of an eccentric theory based on a crude interpretation of a single text.

IX.

THE GREAT MORAL MIRACLE.

To the faith of the Church Jesus Christ is sinless in spirit and conduct, unerring in spiritual insight, original as a religious teacher; in the strictest sense a moral miracle. His character is the one miracle vitally important to faith. Believers could part with the physical miracles of the Gospels if science or exegesis demanded the sacrifice; but if a sinless Christ were taken from us on the plea that the moral order of the world knows only of imperfect men, all would be lost. Nothing less than a sinless, infallible, incomparably original man is demanded by the titles and functions ascribed to Christ. The Son of God must be holy as God is holy. The Redeemer of sinners cannot Himself be a sinner. The Light of the world can have no share in the world's darkness. The Inaugurator of the new era of grace cannot be a commonplace man, the creature of His time, in all His thoughts a mere echo of current opinion. We could not believe such a man to be the Messiah—officially great, personally insignificant. A Messiah must be remarkable in His own intrinsic merits; only when these have been fully recognised can there be a question as to His Messianic claims.

Was the Christ of history such as the creeds require Him to be? Was the ideal of a sinless, infallible, original man realised in Jesus? Opinion is divided on the momentous question, but there is general concurrence thus far that the real Christ approximates the ideal. By common consent Jesus sustained the character assigned to Him by believers marvellously well, and was, if not perfect, at least unique in goodness and wisdom. And, indeed, no one competently acquainted with the facts, and capable of forming a just estimate of them, can come to any other conclusion. It is not necessary here to go into elaborate detail; a rapid outline will suffice to justify the statement.

The comparative sinlessness of Jesus is acknowledged even by those who deem it not impossible to detect in His conduct some traces of moral imperfection. The faults charged against Him are chiefly infirmities of temper, compatible with great moral excellence, and springing out of intense zeal for righteousness. The most outstanding is excessive severity in exposing Pharisaism. If there was any defect in Christ's conduct here, it was not an isolated act, but a habit, for stern denunciation of counterfeit piety formed a standing feature of His public action. But there is room for very legitimate doubt whether what some account a vice was not rather a virtue. If ever anger was justifiable it was in connection with an effort to expose the real character of a pretentious system which claimed to be a perfect embodiment of the Divine Will, and which in truth was the deadly foe of all sacred interests. In any case it was a fault which very decidedly leant to virtue's side. In nothing is Christ's essential goodness more conspicuously apparent than in that department of His conduct in which an undue passionateness of temper is supposed to have revealed itself. His antagonism to Pharisaism meant zeal for the great matters of the law, justice, mercy, and faith, neglected under a system which devoted exclusive attention to the petty rules of the scribes; for the honour of God, whose character was fatally misrepresented by men who claimed to be in specially intimate relations with the Divine Being; for the well-being of the people tyrannised over by religious guides who laid on their shoulders burdens grievous to be borne, and cursed them when they refused to bear their yoke. It reveals the purity of Christ's spirit that He discerned so clearly through all plausible disguises the essentially immoral, ungodly, and inhuman character of Pharisaic righteousness; it marks His passionate love of true righteousness that, regardless of consequences, He had the courage openly to express His convictions; and it shows the depth of these convictions that He persisted in giving utterance to them with ever increasing intensity of language till death on the cross sealed His testimony.

Along with intense abhorrence of counterfeit righteousness, the negative side of goodness, Jesus exhibited in His public conduct its positive side in the form of an ardent love to man, especially to the poor, the suffering, and the sinful. It was a prominent part of His teaching that love fulfils the law, and if that be a true doctrine He must be allowed to have satisfied the law's requirements. No fault can be found with Him here. Faults, many and grave, were found in His behaviour as the friend of man while He lived, but these faults are now seen to be to His honour. It was simply because His love was so new and unparalleled that He was blamed. It overflowed conventional barriers, and men exclaimed, "Behold, a man gluttonous, and a winebibber, a friend of publicans and sinners!" Love in Judæa, as in all other lands, was deemed a good thing within certain limits. But love exceeding these limits had against it the law of public opinion and average attainment. It was wrong to love social and moral outcasts and unclean Gentiles. Jesus demonstrated at once the originality and the greatness of His love by disregarding all such artificial restrictions. If He did appear to submit to restriction in reference to Gentiles, the limitation of His love to the Jewish people was not in His heart, but only in His public action. He loved Pagans not less than Israelites, and the alleged traces of narrow Jewish prejudice are simply the imaginary discoveries of those whose philosophy requires them to convict Him of imperfection. In His heart the wall of separation between Jew and Gentile was already broken down, and the sunny isles of Greece shook hands with the barren hills of Palestine

These two qualities, hatred of spurious goodness and love of mankind, suffice to attest Jesus as a moral Hero. But the characters of moral heroes, sincere, brave, and generous, are sometimes stained by private faults, more or less grave. Was Jesus an exception in this respect? Naturalism replies, we have no means of knowing, our information being defective. "We possess only fragments of His biography, and fragments relative to His public life; that is, to that which is best in the history of a man devoted to the good of others."* But there is one most significant fact to be taken into account here: the entire absence of all traces of any consciousness of sin on Christ's part. Jesus, as we see Him in the records, bears Himself as one who has no personal acquaintance with sins either of the flesh or of the spirit. He appears to enjoy habitually the peace of a good conscience. Nothing in His manner or moods suggests the thought that He has passed through tragic experiences, or that He has ever had occasion to exclaim with Paul, "Oh, wretched man that I am"; or to confess that the good He would that He did not, and the evil He would not that He did. He has indeed a very close relation to sin which visibly affects His spirit, but it is a relation of sympathy. Sympathy with the sinful in His case takes the place of the sense of personal sin in other men. Thereby He knows

* Pecaut, *Le Christ et la Conscience*, p. 240.

what an evil, bitter thing sin is; thereby, apparently alone, yet very thoroughly, insomuch that He almost feels as if the sins of men were His own. Even as, though so far as we know, having no experience of sickness, He so sympathised with the victims of disease that He might truly say, "With them that are sick I am sick," * so, though apparently knowing no sin as His own deed, He so sympathised with the slaves of evil desire and habit that He might truly say, With them that sin, I am a sinner. It was a case of extremes meeting, true holiness just because it was true, having for its essence pure, unselfish love, identifying itself with the unholy, and bearing their sin as a burden on its heart; the keen, sympathetic sense of the sins of others being itself the most convincing proof of personal sinlessness.

This sunny serenity of conscience appears all the more remarkable when we consider how delicate were the moral perceptions of Jesus, and how high and exacting His ideas of right conduct. Think only of that one word in the Sermon on the Mount, Whosoever looketh on a woman to lust after her hath committed adultery with her already in his heart.† What manner of man is He who dares to enunciate this stern law? Certainly not one whom personal shortcoming requires in sincerity to lower His tone. But neither is He one, this also is notable, who affects Pharisaic prudery in His relations to woman. The Pharisee, when he became conscious that he was in the neighbourhood of a woman, turned away from her as if the mere sight of womankind were defiling. But Christ's bearing towards woman was courteous, kind, and cordial to a degree that was sometimes surprising to those who were closely associated with Him. The sisters in Bethany were His intimate friends; the soci-

---

* *Philochristus*, p. 104.

† Matt. v. 28.

ety of disciples that gathered around His person and followed Him in His wanderings embraced in its membership many women; He did not shun even women of evil repute, though Pharisaic critics drew sinister inferences, and even His chosen companions marvelled.* It was the behaviour of one in whom the one master passion was gracious, redeeming love, and who in this quiet way was inaugurating a social revolution. It was the action of an exceptionally holy man, and of a great Initiator, the pure lover of woman, and her redeemer from social indignity.

In some men the tranquil unconsciousness of sin I have ascribed to Jesus might not possess much significance. A Greek, for example, might be guilty of certain sins, especially sins of impurity, yet wear a smiling, happy air which was but the reflection of a lax public opinion. But Jesus was a Jew who had inherited from the stern legal discipline to which His race had long been subjected, a highly educated conscience peculiarly sensitive just at those points where Gentile morality was most at fault. It must, however, be admitted that all Jews were not characterised by the sensitiveness which was the proper fruit of their national training. By the law rightly used comes the knowledge of sin, the faculty of shrewd discernment between right and wrong, and a deep sense of moral obligation. But by the law wrongly used might come ignorance at least of personal sin, a conscience sophisticated in its moral judgments, a spirit prompt to find fault with a brother, but prone to self-satisfaction. These were common characteristics of the Jews in Christ's time, and they appeared in the most exaggerated form in the Pharisees. The typical Pharisee was a self-complacent man. He had no consciousness

* John iv. 27.

.f sin. He considered himself as touching the righteous ness of the law blameless. He was very ready to condemn others, but he was equally ready to justify himself. But that did not signify that he was comparatively sinless. It only meant that he was in the habit of looking merely at the outside aspect of conduct, entirely overlooking the inner region of motive and disposition. All was well for him that looked well and gained the good opinion of men; even the whited sepulchre, though within it was full of dead men's bones and of all uncleanness. And just such a whited sepulchre he was himself; fair in appearance, bad at heart, vain, proud, selfish, greedy. But Jesus differed from the Pharisee precisely in this, that He placed the seat of true morality in the heart, and judged character by the spirit and not by the outward act. And He was on this very ground the ruthless exposer of Pharisaism, tearing off its decent disguise of scrupulous legalism and holding it up to the detestation of the world in all its hollowness and poverty and baseness. The good conscience of such a man has nothing in common with Pharisaic self-righteousness.

The serenity of Christ's spirit might from the naturalistic point of view be supposed to arise out of His own personal faith in the gospel of forgiveness which He preached to the sinful. Why, it may be asked, might Jesus not be happy in spite of shortcomings, just as every Christian is who truly believes in a heavenly Father's forgiving love? To penitents He was wont to say: Go into peace, speaking in the confident tone of one who was fully persuaded that that was possible, that the memory of the evil past might be completely obliterated, that the cold mists of an evil conscience might disappear before the warm beams of Divine mercy, that the repentant sinner might henceforth live in perpetual summer sunshine. What if His confidence was based on His own experience? Though the question is a painful one, we must admit its legitimacy on naturalistic principles. But even if we were to admit the plausibility of the suggested solution, there is one fact which excludes it as inadmissible. It is that Jesus claimed to be the *Judge* of men. The claim implies at least that He who makes it regards Himself as the moral idea realised. It is a claim which could not without presumption be advanced by one who had been Himself a sinner, even though He were a sinner completely delivered from both the guilt and the power of sin through the mercy and grace of God. The claim is a fact which cannot be denied, and which has to be taken into account by all who attempt to form an estimate of the character of Jesus. It does not of itself prove sinlessness, for absurd pretensions have often been made. But it greatly complicates the problem of accounting for the character of Jesus on the principles of naturalistic philosophy. We do not expect absurd, not to say blasphemous, pretensions from men of indubitable and acknowledged worth and wisdom. That a sinless man should say, I am Judge of the world, is conceivable and credible; that a man essentially good, yet faulty as other men, should say it, is indeed hard to credit.

The wisdom of Jesus, not less than His goodness, has awakened universal admiration. Here, also, of course, naturalism is qualified in its praise, contending that Jesus, while a man of remarkable spiritual insight, shared the ignorance and errors of His time and country, not only in matters morally indifferent, but even within the religious sphere, as for example in reference to demoniacal possession. But even if all the deductions insisted on were allowed they would amount only to a few dark spots on the sun. Jesus would still remain the light of the world if not a perfect sun, the best sun yet vouchsafed to mortals. To be satisfied as to the legitimacy of His claim to this supreme place we have but to open our eyes to His illuminating influence. The sun is known by the brightness of his beams; no one who has seen both day-light and night-light can mistake the moon for the sun, or the sun for the moon. Even so, simply by looking at Jesus, and walking in the light of His teaching, we discern Him to be the great luminary of the spiritual world. The Pure One, as was to be expected, is the one who most clearly sees and shows the nature of God, and of man, and of righteousness. The clearness of His vision is another proof of His purity; for the source of His knowledge is not books or the schools, but His own heart. In Him is the true light, because in Him is the true life. But the point at present insisted on is that the light of Jesus is true, genuine, sunlike. Who can doubt it? What better, more reasonable, more acceptable doctrine concerning God ever has or ever can be taught than His doctrine of the Divine Fatherhood? Compare with it the doctrine of the man who most resembled Jesus in spirit—Buddha, the "light of Asia," which was virtually that there is no God distinct from the order of the world. Doubtless the verdict of modern philosophy may be that Jesus spake the more poetically, but Buddha the more truly. But even philosophers may yet come to see that poetry and truth here go together, and that where the subject of thought is the Eternal Source and Centre of the universe, the highest, noblest, most beautiful things we can think are likely to be the truest. Judged by that test nothing can be more credible than Christ's doctrine of God. Kindred in character and equally worthy of acceptance was His doctrine of man, which was in effect that human nature is made in the Divine Image, and that man at his worst is still God's son, redeemable and worth redeeming. Here, also, He may be thought to have taught rather poetically or pathetically, than truly, and to have spoken of man in a way that does credit, indeed, to the kindness of His heart, but does not reveal deep insight into truth. But here again the heart is seen to be the most reliable guide to truth, and love to be the mother of wisdom. The loving heart of Jesus told Him that the people who were given up as helpless by the reputedly wise in Israel were not irrecoverably lost to God and righteousness. It even emboldened Him to believe that the last might become first, the greatest sinner the greatest saint; that from the very scum of society might come the most devoted citizens of the divine kingdom. To the Pharisees such ideas appeared wild absurdities. But after all who was right; the Son of Man or His critics, who so often enquired, Why doth He eat with publicans and sinners? The insight of Jesus has been justified by the history of Christendom in which His doctrine of the worth of man has borne much beneficent fruit, by the long roll of saints which includes many who loved much because they had been much forgiven, by the course of all great social movements which, as Renan has pointed out,* have germinated amid the so-called corruption of great cities, and by the tendency of modern politics to transfer power from the privileged aristocracies of wealth, blood, and culture, to the great masses of the people.

In teaching these two doctrines Jesus was not only a true light, but in the strictest sense a light of the world. For they are the fundamental truths of a universal religion; they constitute together a Gospel of Hope for entire Humanity. They are not only free from all particularistic elements, but they exclude these, and involve the abrogation

* *Saint Paul*, p. 334.

of all such envious distinctions and restrictions as happen to exist. God in relation to man a Father, man as such His child—in what country could these simple yet momentous propositions be either unintelligible or unwelcome? And what people has a right to arrogate to itself a peculiar interest in the good tidings they embody? A Father-God is not the God of Jews any more than of Gentiles; for Gentiles, whatever faults may be imputed to them, are still men. Nor can Jews, whatever their prerogatives may hitherto have been, have any right to attach to the worship of the Father-God any incongruous or inconvenient conditions, arising out of their national customs, which shall make it uncongenial to the rest of the world. The worship of the Father must be free as the air—a worship in spirit and in truth, unclogged by antiquated rites and local limitations.

It has been doubted whether Jesus was fully aware of the universalistic tendency of His own teaching and action. The doubt has been entertained, not so much by naturalistic critics like Baur, as by orthodox critics of the type of Weiss, who have cherished too severe ideas as to the connection between the teaching of Jesus and the letter of Old Testament prophecy. The river that rises in the mountains is unconscious of its destiny to mingle its waters with the waves of the great ocean. Even so is it thought that the Christian religion, while intrinsically fitted and destined to become a world-wide faith, nevertheless took its rise in the mind of a man who deemed Himself merely the Messiah of Israel, having it for His vocation to set up in the holy land the theocratic kingdom of Hebrew Prophecy, embracing among its citizens all men of Jewish birth, and as many from the Gentiles as were willing to become proselytes.* This view

* Such is the view which pervades Weiss's *Leben Jesu*.

makes Jesus the slave rather than the fulfiller of the prophetic oracles, denies in effect His originality, and represents Him as a commonplace man, while assigning to Him the very uncommon position and functions of Messiah. It is a view in itself intrinsically improbable, for who can believe that the man who could discover the two fundamental truths aforesaid, and perceive that they were fundamental, could not also understand their implications and consequences, especially one so obvious as that of religious universalism? Nay, may we not ask, How could He have had insight into these truths unless He had first had a vision of a kingdom of God not confined to one land or nation, but cosmopolitan in character, opening its gates to all on equal terms? What had hitherto prevented men from seeing the Father and from acknowledging all mankind as their brethren, but the acceptance of arbitrary distinctions of race, custom, and religion, as final and absolute? Once more the view now combated is contradicted by the universalistic drift of Christ's whole teaching and conduct, and by not a few express sayings such as those which represent His disciples as the light of the world and the salt of the earth.

In His teaching concerning the nature of righteousness Jesus well sustained the character of the True Light. His doctrine here is characterised by the insight of genuine wisdom alike on its negative side as an exposure of Pharisaism, and on its positive side as an exposition of the righteousness which is worthy of the kingdom, and belongs to all true citizens. In the former aspect Christ's doctrine is much more than a fierce prophetic denunciation; it is an exact, calm, artistically finished analysis of a false system which offered itself to the world as a genuine article, and which it was the duty of the true guide of men to detect as a counterfeit. No one who has not carefully studied the relative utterances of Jesus can have any idea how thoroughly this duty was performed. The Pharisaic righteousness is shown to have just those faults which were to be expected in a system having for its original aim to put a fence about the law. From this apparently good aim were likely to arise in course of time: multiplication of by-rules to make the written law cover the whole ground of human conduct, rules growing ever more minute as they increased in number; contrivances for evading rules unduly multiplied and vexatiously minute, and so easing the pressure of an intolerable yoke; neglect of the very commandments of God which it was the professed design of the system to fence, through undue preoccupation with the fencing process; externalism, exclusive attention to outward conformity with the rule; wherefrom followed inevitably certain spiritual vices—ostentation or vanity, all turning on the outward appearance, self-complacency, the letter of the law being duly observed, censoriousness towards others whose conduct showed disregard of precepts and practices deemed by the censor of vital importance. All these faults were rampant in the Pharisaism which fell under the observation of Jesus, and He has photographed them for the instruction and warning of all ages in clear, sharp outline. The huge accumulation of scribe-made law, forming a heavy burden to the shoulders; the Jesuitical evasion, as in reference to gifts and oaths; the substitution of the hedge in the place of the law, tithing, mint, anise, and cummin, to the neglect of justice, mercy, and faith; the cup and platter clean without, within full of extortion and excess; the prayers said at street corners and the alms given to the sound of the trumpet; the thanks rendered for being a paragon of virtue and piety, and the contempt of publicans and all base, wicked people—who that has read the Gospels does not recognise the familiar features of the typical Pharisee? There he stands in the pillory a byword to all generations, and sufficient, one would say, by the very hideousness of his distorted, sanctimonious countenance to scare men in all ime from the devious courses which issue in such disfigurement, if human nature were not so inveterately prone to the sins with which he is chargeable.

With equal insight and felicity Jesus depicted the true righteousness of the kingdom. It appears, of course, in His delineation, inward, having its seat in the heart, consisting in a right spirit, not in conformity with rules. The citizen of the kingdom is recognised not by phylacteries, but by Godlike dispositions sadly lacking in the men who wear these: humility, meekness, quenchless aspiration after goodness, love, simplicity. As towards God the true righteousness consists in childlike trust showing itself in a peaceful, blessed life, free from care like that of the birds and the lilies. That life of trust, described in the Sermon on the Mount in a few sentences which read like a lyric poem might well appear too ethereal for this world if Jesus Himself had not exemplified it, thereby making another notable contribution to the realisation in His own person of the ideal goodness. As towards men the true righteousness consists in imitating in our relations with them the chief divine virtue charity; loving enemies, blessing them that curse, benefiting them that do evil, praying for persecutors, so approving ourselves to be the children of the Divine Father who maketh His sun to rise on the evil and the good, and sendeth rain on the just and the unjust. As towards ourselves the true righteousness consists in realising our dignity and felicity as God's children, bearing ourselves in all ways as becometh sons; submitting cheerfully to

God's will; trusting utterly in His good-will, so rising above the cloudy atmosphere of care into the serene region of perpetual sunshine, holding habitual fellowship with our Father, and finding in that fellowship our chiefest joy and our unfailing solace amid the ills of life; strenuously asserting, carefully guarding, our liberty, refusing to be made slaves in any form, to the world, to possessions, to men, to opinion, to custom. As towards the kingdom of God the true righteousness consists in self-devotion: soldierly promptness to sacrifice all personal interests, even life itself, to its supreme claims, whenever called on. In all these aspects of the true righteousness Jesus was a model. He not merely thus taught, but thus practised righteousness. He offered to His Father the homage of a perfect trust and reverence. He loved men when to love was hardest. He behaved Himself as a Son in all respects, rejoicing ever more, praying without ceasing, in everything giving thanks, so exemplifying the true filial temper; standing fast in His liberty, and asserting His spiritual independence at all hazards. He made the kingdom of God from first to last His chief end, and cheerfully endured all hardships its service entailed. Wherefore, lastly, the righteousness of the kingdom might legitimately be made to consist, as it was in His teaching, in imitation of Himself. "Follow me" might be given as a compendious direction to those who desired to practise true righteousness. So viewed, the righteousness of the kingdom is the righteousness of *discipleship*.

To expatiate on the *originality* of Christ as a religious teacher is wholly unnecessary. The mere statement of His doctrine suffices to prove it. His doctrine of God was new The application of the term *Father* to God was indeed not new; it occurs in the Old Testament; it is even as old as the Vedic Hymns. But the connotation was new. The

Vedic Indians, like the Gentiles in general, sought chiefly after food and raiment, and their Father was the sky; they worshipped the power that gave sunshine and showers, and through these fruitful fields. The Divine Father of the Old Testament is only the Father of the Hebrew nation or of its royal head; the paternal relation of God to the individual is not yet proclaimed. In the teaching of Jesus the conception of Divine Fatherhood is prominently ethical; it is its reference to the higher life of the spirit that is chiefly though not exclusively accentuated. The Father knows that His children need food and raiment, and provides these, but it is His kingdom and righteousness He would have them seek first, and these supreme goods He most loves to grant. And He desires to bestow them on all, and would have all men seek them. He reserves not His best gifts for a privileged class; He offers them to the million; He sees in the lowest types of humanity His prodigal children, and with paternal affection longs for their return, and keeps His door ever open to receive them.

Christ's doctrine of man was equally new. It was a new thing to say with passionate emphasis of the poorest, meanest man, He is a man. That is what Jesus did say by associating with the abjects. His manner of teaching was as original as the teaching itself. He taught the worth of the individual man, irrespective of possessions, position, or character, not by abstract propositions, but by loving the neglected, the people of no social account. He taught the equality of men all the world over in the sight of God, by the same means. He cancelled the religious disabilities of the Gentiles by befriending those in Israel who were as heathens to the proud advocates of Jewish privilege. His doctrine of the Fatherhood He also taught chiefly in this way. He affirmed God's paternal attitude towards such as might well be regarded as no more worthy to be called His sons in certain notable words, but mainly by being in His whole behaviour the brother of the prodigals, not after the manner of the elder brother in the parable. That genuine, genial brotherhood taught its own lesson to the dullest, bearing witness to a God very different from the one in whom Pharisees believed—a God who did not keep aloof from the sinful, but desired to make them partakers of His holiness; a God good and ready to forgive; a God who did not wish to be regarded as the patron of a conceited coterie of self-styled saints and sages, but rather as the wide-hearted Father of the people of the land; a benignant, gracious Being with whom a penitent publican had a better chance of favour than a self-satisfied religionist who scrupulously followed all the legal traditions. The novelty of the love by which Jesus quietly insinuated these new revolutionary doctrines concerning God and man is attested by the astonishment and scandal it created in Judæa, and by the echoes of these sent back from the Gentile world, as in the well-known complaint of Celsus concerning the preference of Christians for the bad;* who herein may be taken as the representative of Greek philosophy and Pagan sentiment in general. Buddha had indeed shown something of the same humane spirit centuries before in India. But Buddha's love was different from Christ's. It was acute, tender, but despairing sympathy with human misery, rooted in a pessimistic view of life, and prescribing as its sole remedy ascetic self-extinction. Christ's love was a hopeful, victorious love before which pessimistic theories disappeared like mists before the sun. The world of fact was the same for the two men, but the intenser, more heroic love of Jesus made the world

---

* Origen, *Contra Celsum*, iii., 59.

as it existed for thought in His case altogether another world from what it appeared to the sad, hopeless eye of Sakhya Muni—having a Father in heaven who careth for all, and an outlook in the future for the most miserable of the sons of men.

In the doctrine of righteousness Jesus is not so obviously original. Hebrew Psalmists and Prophets had gone before, and had said many beautiful things of which the words of the Prophet of Nazareth spoken on the Mount and elsewhere, may seem but an echo. But Jesus even here was more than an echo. His doctrine of righteousness is not a mere cento of quotations from David and Isaiah. In His exposure of false righteousness His attitude is the same as that of all the prophets, and His key-note, *I will have mercy and not sacrifice*, is taken from one of them. But what a rich, original descant He offers on this simple theme! In His unfolding of true righteousness we feel ourselves in presence of a fresh breeze of inspiration, blowing across the arid desert of four hundred years, during which the voice of prophecy had been silent. In Jesus the intuition of the kingdom is not merely restored, but reproduced with a widened range and superior clearness of vision. His eye sees further and more accurately than the eye of the most gifted Hebrew prophet. He occupies a different position towards the kingdom from that of ancient seers. To them it was a land afar off, dimly descried, and therefore described in confused outline. He stands within the kingdom, and speaks of all things pertaining to it, as matters with which He is thoroughly at home. Therefore, His words concerning the kingdom and its righteousness have a different value from those of Old Testament prophets. Their oracles stand written indelibly in the Hebrew Book, but they have become obsolete as descriptions of the Messianic kingdom, and are valuable mainly as witnesses to the existence of such a kingdom. They are like old maps of countries known to exist, but comparatively unexplored, superseded by new maps based upon information supplied by travellers who have passed through the once unknown lands in all directions. The words of Jesus are the new map of the divine kingdom, which supersedes all the old ones with their large blanks and crude outlines. They tell us truly of the King of that land, and of its citizens, and of their manners and customs, and of its physical geography. We shall never have a better account of these than they contain; therefore, they will abide for ever, not only in the letter of the Gospel records, but in the hearts of Christians, living and luminous; perpetually valid, unfading in their charm.

This contrast between Jesus and the prophets suggests the remark that His greatness grows as we extend comparison. How great He appears, *e. g.*, when compared with the Church, His own creation, in its ideal conception His fair, stainless spouse, and on the Catholic theory a perpetuation of His Incarnation! To contrast His moral purity with the sad, disenchanting mixture of good and evil presented in the Church's history may seem of little avail for our purpose, as only directing attention to a common law, according to which religions in the course of development undergo degeneracy, and even provoking reflections on the lack of foresight displayed by the Founder in originating a new society intended to embody the ideal of the divine kingdom, but destined in fact to reproduce in new forms all the moral and spiritual evils He had denounced. Certainly, when we think of the endless controversies and numberless divisions of the Church, the wide scope given to ambitious passions in ecclesiastical affairs, the rise and baleful career of priestcraft, the many masters who have had dominion over men's faith, the carnal weapons employed to propagate and defend the faith, not to speak of gross scandalous immoralities we must acknowledge that if the Church is to supply an argument for the divine origin of Christianity it must be on some other principle than that of resemblance. Instead of reasoning from divine effects to a divine cause, we must rather argue, How pure must have been the fountain whose waters can bear such extensive pollution, and yet remain a stream of life! But it is a small matter to compare Jesus with the Church at its worst: His lowliness with clerical ambition and pride, His sweet reasonableness and gentleness with churchly violence, His wise, meek patience with ecclesiastical intolerance. The point to be emphasized is the incomparable superiority of Jesus to His Church, even when it means well, and through its best members behaves heroically. Take as an example, the monastic system, which forms so conspicuous a phenomenon in church history. Hideous evils grew up in connection with that system, but of these let nothing here be said. Let the life of celibacy and poverty be looked on in its most favorable aspect, as a noble outgrowth of aspiration after a heavenly life, and of self-sacrifice in the pursuit of a cherished ideal. Even when so viewed it was the result of a one-sided morbid tendency, which has no justification in the healthy, human, though austere teaching and life of Jesus. For He was no ascetic, nor did He preach self-sacrifice as a mere matter of self-discipline. He was a soldier, the first soldier of the kingdom, not a monk like St. Francis de Assisi, to whom Renan is so fond of comparing Him,* and his so-called "Counsels of Perfection" are a summons to the soldier-life, and to cheerful endurance of its hardships.† They are in-

---

* *Vie de Jesus,* p. 183.

† Matt. xix. 10–26.

deed words uttered in unqualified terms by one accustomed to speak with prophetic intensity and poetic freedom, and addressed to the emotions rather than to the intellect ; words, therefore, liable to misconstruction when made the subject of prosaic theological interpretation. The best comment on Christ's words concerning self-sacrifice is His life. Who can mistake the genial Son of Man, who came eating and drinking, for a Jewish Essene, or an Egyptian anchorite ; for a Nilus of Constantinople, or a Simeon Stylites ; or for any typical monk known to history, with shaven crown and hairy garment, and intense but narrow spirit ?

Christian asceticism was an error, though a natural and perhaps an inevitable one. But how slowly was the error discovered ! It took more than a millennium to convince even a part of Christendom that the ascetic interpretation of Christ's words concerning wealth and wedlock was mistaken, and that the ideal of self-sacrifice set forth in His teaching is not incompatible with possessions and family relations. And this is but a single instance illustrating the rate at which the Christian Church is advancing from childhood to maturity. One step in a millennium ! At this rate how long it will be "till we all come in the unity of the faith, and of the knowledge of the Son of God, unto a perfect man, unto the measure of the stature of the fulness of Christ." Even yet, when we are approaching the close of the second millennium of the era of grace, we are only beginning to understand His doctrine of God and of man, and above all the spirit of His own life. There is much in the Church which is antagonistic to these, and which makes the comprehension of them difficult, and it is possible that the present institutions called churches may have to pass away like fading leaves, that the glory of Jesus may be manifested under some new form.

The greatness of Jesus appears when He is compared even with the apostle Paul, the man who best understood His doctrine, who did most to make Christianity a universal religion and who saw that it would take ages to unfold the riches of Christ's grace. Paul was great, but not immeasurably so. He had his limits and defects intellectually and morally. He was one-sided, theological, controversial, though that was more his misfortune than his fault. We can see round him, comprehend him, account for him. We can gather from his manner of reasoning that he has been trained in the Rabbinical schools. He is a Jew in thought; his mind is steeped in Jewish theology; he uses Jewish categories to establish Christian truth, and legal arguments to upset the law. We might even flatter ourselves that we could explain how he became a Christian, by the principle that extremes meet. How, we ask, can an intensely earnest Pharisee fail to discover that Pharisaism is a futility? At first he is occupied exclusively with externals seeing that all is right about fasts, ablutions, and alms, and Sabbath-keeping. But a man of exceptional moral earnestness cannot stop there, like an ordinary Pharisee who merely amuses himself in trying to be righteous. He must look within into the region of motive and disposition. Ah, it is not so easy to be right there! Evil thoughts, wild passions, malevolent affections cannot be controlled by Rabbinical rules. From the day the eye of this man's conscience is introverted Pharisaism is doomed; it is only a question of time when it will be given up, and the ex-Pharisee be heard exclaiming: Who shall deliver me? And so we think we can understand how Saul the Pharisee became Paul the Christian, more intent than any of the Christians to make grace all and law nothing.

Perhaps Paul is not so easily accounted for as we imagine

But be that as it may, who is so bold as to think he comprehends or can account for Jesus? His contemporaries, we are told, were of opinion that "when Christ cometh, no man knoweth whence He is,"* and on this ground they concluded he was not the Christ. But by this test he surely was the Christ. We know not this man whence he is, or who he is. He is a veritable mystery and wonder, and seems to come from the clouds rather than from Jewish soil. He is not a mere Jew, explicable by heredity and environment. In the Baptist we see the good fruit of Hebrew culture, and in the Scribes the evil, degenerate fruit, and he resembles neither. Neither is he of anti-Jewish type, a man of philohellenic proclivities, who has discovered the defects of Hebrewism and has opened his soul to the more genial influences of Pagan civilisation, circulating around Galilee. Least of all is he an eclectic who has picked out the best things in Hebrew books and Greek philosophy and pieced them together in his doctrine and life. Jesus has nothing in common with Philo. He is not to be accounted for in these ways, or in any ways that can be suggested. When I say that He is unaccountable and mysterious it is not meant that He is abstruse, unintelligible, or dubious in character. On the contrary, He is entirely luminous in utterance and spirit. He has this divine characteristic that He is light, and in Him is no darkness at all. Nothing so simple and so reasonable as His sayings, as there is nothing more charming in the manner of saying. But somehow we cannot define or label Him, or assign Him to a school or party or nation. He is simply human, catholic, cosmopolitan. His light is not chromatic, but white, a mixture of all the colours, as beseems the light of the sun.

---

* John vii. 27.

Comparisons have been made between Jesus and the philosophers. The subject is too wide to be gone into here, and it is hardly worth while. Hebrew wisdom is so very diverse from Gentile wisdom that the two things cannot very well be compared. But one feature in the wisdom of Jesus has often struck thoughtful readers of the Gospels, which, because it possesses moral significance, may here be noticed. The wisdom of most sages smells of the lamp. They can say very fine things if you give them time to study in their closets. The wisdom of Jesus is unstudied; He says *impromptu* the best possible things in the best possible way. His words are *jeus d'esprit;* inimitably felicitous, yet as profoundly significant as if they were the result of years of reflection. "Why eateth the Master with publicans and sinners?" "They that be whole need not a physician, but they that are sick." What a happy, spirited, convincing reply, and how pregnant with meaning. And so it is always. Jesus is never commonplace, never dull, never taken by surprise; always bright, always ready, always original, yet always simple, as if saying things which everybody knows. What is the meaning of this? Is it genius? Yes, and something more. It points to a high habit of spiritual life. Jesus speaks thus because He lives always in the unclouded region of truth. We labour and blunder and struggle in utterance, because we live low down in the valley of moral commonplace. We find it difficult to speak wisely, because our lives but seldom touch the heroic.

From all that has been stated it appears that Jesus was singularly noble, good, and wise. The facts suggest the thought of ideal goodness and wisdom. The historic Christ and the Christ of the Church's faith correspond. There is no perceptible breakdown in the historic personality which compels the admission that the reality comes short of the ideal to which it ever seems to point. But that the ideal of a perfect manhood is realised in Jesus in any respect, either in goodness or in wisdom, naturalism consistently denies. The sinlessness of Jesus it contests on the principle that everything real is relative, absolute goodness having existence only in thought and theory. Far from admitting the absolute perfection of Jesus, thoroughgoing naturalism is inclined to question even His claim to be the best of men, on the ground that it is *a priori* improbable that the first in a great historical movement should be greater than all coming after. For to naturalistic philosophy these two propositions are axiomatic: It is not the way of the idea to realise itself in individuals, but only in the totality of individuals, in the genus; and, the first in a series of developments cannot at the same time be the greatest. When these two axioms are employed to determine the moral position of Jesus they take Him down from the high pedestal on which faith places Him, and set Him on the ground to be jostled by the crowd; or at most, leave Him the honour of a place among the select few who rise somewhat above the common level. The first involves the denial of His absolute goodness, and His claim to be the one man who knew no sin. In truth, it relegates ideal moral excellence to the realm of imagination; for if the ideal does not realise itself in the individual, it does not realise itself at all. The second axiom implies that in the calendar of saints may be, yea ought to be, found better men than the Son of Man, whom all saints adore as their Saviour and Lord; as to which one can only say that the superiors of Jesus have not yet made their appearance, and that for the model Christian we must still have recourse, not to the lives of saints, but to the pages of the Gospels. Discreet naturalism, even at the risk of being inconsistent, will not care to dispute that these Gospels set before us an Example which is not likely ever to be superseded.*

While consenting, by way of compromise, to find in the Evangelic history the *Model* Man, naturalism cannot, without committing suicide, find there the *Ideal* Man. With regard to this its attitude is, A man realising the ideal is not possible, and if it were, the fact is unverifiable. It can never be proved that such a man existed, for all history yields only relative excellence. The real Christ cannot be shown to coincide with the ideal Christ by a process of historical demonstration; the identification of the two is an act of faith. Such in effect is the criticism of Baur on the Christology of Schleiermacher in which Jesus is regarded as the Ideal Man, that is as the man in whom the divine idea of humanity was for the first time realised, and in whom the God-consciousness was complete. This conception, says Baur, you do not get from the history, but from the Christian consciousness. It is a construction which faith for its own behoof puts on the facts. A Redeemer from sin must be sinless, therefore Jesus is credited with sinlessness, and as invested with this august attribute He is nothing more than the Idea of Redemption hypostatised in a historical personality.† This is acute criticism, but it does not settle the question at issue. Granting that the history does not strictly prove an ideal Christ, it points that way. The facts are remarkable and demand the attention of all. Faith does not put on them an absurd or gratuitous construction, but suggests a likely hypothesis; and it is for those who refuse the hypothesis of faith to offer a better, which shall not underestimate the significance of the facts as much as faith is supposed to overestimate them.

* *Vide* Ullmann, *Die Sündlosigkeit Jesu*, p. 159.

† Baur, *Die Christliche Gnosis*, pp. 643–56.

Some have thought to solve the hard problem by ascribing to Jesus the perfection of a single-minded devotion to the Divine Kingdom. "A life wholly spent for the sacred cause, devoted to it, possessed by it, without self-seeking and self-love, without receptivity to the solicitations of the senses and of the world, as manifested in the public ministry, this is what may be called historically His sinlessness. It consists neither in freedom from bad impulses and desires, nor in the completeness of all virtues; but in this, that He was out and out what it behoved Him to be, that He maintained His unity with God in moral effort and warfare, and realised in life whatever He knew to be true."* This is a high heroic character, but it does not differ materially from that which is ascribed to many in the Scriptures. There are two sorts of perfection spoken of in the Bible. One is the perfection of faultlessness, or absolute holiness, the other is the perfection of moral simplicity—of an undivided heart. The one is ascribed to God only, the other is predicated of men characterised by moral defects and infirmities, like Job and David. Of perfection in the second sense there have been many examples; if Jesus was perfect only in that sense He was not unique, but only one of a noble band of heroes who have sacrificed all for duty, a captain at most in the army of martyrs. That army is not completely equipped till it has placed at its head one who in the struggle with moral evil has been altogether successful, tempted indeed in all respects like the rank and file, "yet without sin." Such an one is fit to be *the Great Captain*, the one supreme leader of the war-worn host.

How the originality of Jesus as a religious teacher is undermined by the Tübingen criticism, is well known. Jesus

---

* Weizsäcker, *Untersuchungen*, p. 438.

we are told, simply gathered together and fused into one the moral and religious ideas that were in the air. The notion of a universal religion He got from the Roman Empire, in which political universalism was already realised; the spirituality of His doctrine, or the conception of man as a moral subject, with the associated truth of the worth of human nature, He borrowed from Socrates and the Greek philosophy; for the skill to extract from the Old Testament a pure ethical monotheism, purged from all Hebrew particularism, He was indebted to the allegorical method of interpretation invented by the philosophic Jews of Alexandria, and for the ascetic ideal of life embodied in His sayings, to the Essenes.* It is a brilliant generalisation, but it does not stand close inspection. In the first place the facts are partly imaginary. Christ's ideal of life was not ascetic, and His manner of interpreting Scripture was not fashioned after any school, Rabbinical or Alexandrian. In the second place, if it is implied that Jesus was a conscious eclectic or borrower, no assertion could be more destitute of historical foundation. If, on the other hand, what is meant is that Jesus, without having studied the history of philosophy, or travelled into other lands to sit at the feet of sages, had an intuition of all the best thought concerning religion and morals that had ever been uttered, that fact alone, even if He taught nothing absolutely new, would go far to establish His claim to be the light of the world. Socrates teaches one truth, Buddha another, Confucius a third, Philo a fourth; Jesus teaches them all. Surely they are but burning and shining lamps, and He is the Sun!

Even evolutionary science can make room for an original Christ, by conceiving of Him as a "sociological variation,'

* *Vide* Baur, *Geschichte der Christlichen Kirche*, i., pp. 2–21.

our modern scientific equivalent for a "man of genius. The very title implies unaccountableness; for all variations in all departments of life are admitted to be spontaneous, unexplained, ultimate facts for the theorist; not without cause, but due to the operation of laws hitherto undiscovered, perhaps undiscoverable. It also implies that the function o genius in promoting the onward progress of the human race, is analogous to that of variations in the lower departments of animal life in supplying the laws of natural selection with the means of giving rise to higher species. Whether the analogy holds, is a question on which opinion is divided. One eloquent expounder of the creed of science maintains that the civilisations of humanity have not been accomplished by natural selection, as the Darwinian doctrine implies. The development of the human spirit, he thinks, "has come from an inner revelation to certain privileged individuals, a revelation of truth, of insight, of inventive power, of duty, of beauty; visiting the soul unsolicited, coming none can say whence, not even the possessors, further than that it is from the unknown, from the Purpose of the universe, that thus means and wishes to declare and develop itself—from God and not from chance."* Mr. Fiske, on the other hand, replying to another advocate of the same view, contends that recognition of the influence of great men is perfectly reconcilable with the Spencerian doctrine, which ascribes social changes in large measure to environment, and generally to what may be called impersonal forces. The reconciling formula he offers is that social changes are due to those individual initiatives and decisions which are selected for preservation by the contemporary environment, the abortive ones that are crushed out or held in check, go

---

* Graham *The Creed of Science*, p. 72.

ing for nothing.* Whatever the truth may be as to the general question, it would seem that the category of variation, as applied to Jesus, fails to do justice both to His personal character and to His influence. Its chief value in this connection is that it serves to bring faith in the moral miracle embodied in these into accord with current scientific habits of thought, and in that view it may be accepted by apologists as true and useful so far as it goes.† But to regard Jesus as a very remarkable sociological variation, does not involve belief in Him as the greatest of the sons of men that have been or shall be, even in the moral and religious sphere, not to speak of the intellectual. The most that can be conceded from the evolution point of view is that in Him was exhibited the maximum variation possible in His time and country. That may well on strictly scientific grounds be regarded as probable. But that the maximum sociological variation in Judæa nearly two thousand years ago should be the maximum for all time and for all peoples, can hardly appear likely to the disciple of Mr. Spencer. With more than the Baptist's doubt, he will ask the Christ of history, Art thou he that should come, or do we look for the absolutely greatest religious genius in the far distant future? Then as for the extraordinary influence of Jesus on the subsequent history of the world, it seems at least *prima facie* irreconcilable with Darwinian principles. Instead of being selected for preservation by His environment, this sociological variation who appeared in Judæa eighteen

---

* Fiske, *Excursions of an Evolutionist*, p. 185.

† It is so accepted by Mr. Curteis in the following words : "The way in which the law of variation works is by the unexpected, yet from all eternity prepared appearance, of some exterior agent, some divergent force, some new strain ; in the animal sphere some fresh departure, among mankind some dazzling 'genius,' who turns the world upside down." *The Scientific Obstacles to Christian Belief*, pp. 133–4.

centuries ago was crushed out, and the strange thing is that the crushing out was what gave Him His power. His crucifixion was His exaltation to the throne of a world-wide dominion.

Striking testimony to the power of Jesus to command the free homage of ingenuous souls is supplied in the unreserved confession of the moral Miracle by certain theologians whose attitude towards the miraculous in general is sceptical or negative. As one instance, may be cited Schleiermacher, whose bias is to reduce the miraculous to very small dimensions and to strip it of significance; who, nevertheless, confesses the sinlessness of Jesus, and worships Him as the Ideal Man. A more pronounced example is Dr. Abbott, who resolves the miraculous elements in the Gospels either into natural events (as in the case of the healing miracles) or into legends (as in the case of the birth from a virgin), or into visions (as in the case of the resurrection), yet retains unabated his faith in a sinless Christ, a miracle in the spiritual sphere.* The position taken up by the English theologian has this peculiarity and interest, that it is not speculative or theoretical, but purely empirical. He does not say miracles are impossible in the physical sphere, possible in the moral and there only; he simply says, Jesus was sinless and He did no miracle. But the empirical position suggests the theoretical one, and is weak without its support, and the support which the latter yields is itself very weak. The thesis Jesus was Himself a moral miracle and could do no physical miracle is open to two serious objections. In the first place, from the speculative point of view, miracle is equally inadmissible in all spheres; rupture of continuity in the moral order must be rejected not less than rupture of continuity in the physical order. It may be

---

* Vide *Philochristus, Onesimus,* and *Oxford Sermons.*

pled that the rupture in the one case is not so violent as in the other. We see in other men approximations to the moral perfection realised in Jesus; we do not see anywhere approximations to the feeding of five thousand persons with five loaves and two small fishes. But what we see everywhere in the moral world is at most only approximations to the ideal and these by no means close, and the obvious inference on naturalistic principles is that there is nowhere anything else to be found; in other words, the sinlessness of Jesus must be denied. In the second place, the tacit distinction between the moral miracle and the physical miracles, on the ground of which the former may be deemed more admissible than the latter, viz., that the one is purely in the region of spirit, while in the other there is contact with matter and its laws, does not exist. That such a distinction should be supposed to obtain is natural, equally so that it should be supposed to justify a faith in spiritual miracles which cannot be accorded to physical ones. It is, as we know, the exact position taken up by Baden Powell. But in the case before us it is a position which a little reflection shows to be untenable. For sinlessness is not a purely spiritual miracle; it involves contact with matter and its laws, not less than resurrection or birth from a virgin. The sinless life was a life in the flesh, and the flesh as known to other men is the seat of evil desires and the too successful tempter to evil habits. How came it that Jesus was an exception to this universal experience? Naturalism says He was no exception, and could not be. Those who maintain the contrary must recognise in the holiness of Jesus not only a moral miracle, but a miracle having physical relations and aspects.

Of the miracles of the beginning and the end above alluded to, the birth from a virgin, and the resurrection from the dead, I cannot speak at length. They do certainly belong to the miraculous element in the Gospel history, and might very appropriately be made the subject of a special study. But they can only be briefly referred to here as congruous accompaniments of the Moral miracle. Their connection with the latter is so close that few who earnestly believe in the absolute moral worth of Christ's Person will be disposed to deny the truth of the Evangelic narratives relating to the manner of His entrance into and exit from the world. It is indeed possible with a show of reason to distinguish between the initial and final miracles on the one hand, and the miracle of the Person on the other, as to their relative value to faith. Thus Schleiermacher maintains that the birth from a virgin and the resurrection on the third day after the passion are of no importance to faith, but are at most mere matters of fact received on the authority of the Evangelists; therefore belonging more properly to the doctrine of Scripture than to the doctrine of Christ's person. That a supernatural creative activity of God was necessary to the origination of a sinless life is admitted, but it is contended that through that activity the result could be secured even though the birth of Jesus took place in accordance with the ordinary laws of generation, and that it could not be secured by any miraculous setting aside of these laws such as is reported to have occurred. In like manner it is held that while faith must conceive of Christ as victorious over all evil, glorified, and ever present with His people, these precious truths are in nowise dependent on a literal resurrection and ascension.* From denial of the value of facts to the denial of the facts themselves there is but a step, and that step has been taken by Dr. Abbott. Those who wish reasons for denial can easily

---

* *Der Christliche Glaube*, ii., pp. 67, 84, 85.

find them. Thus it may be alleged that the two genealogies seem to take for granted that Jesus was the son of Joseph as well as of Mary. Or the silence of John respecting the miraculous birth may be emphasized as very significant. Or stress may be laid on the fact that the narratives concerning the birth and the resurrection do not occur in the common Tradition, but only in the Supplement; that is to say, in the later less reliable accretion which gradually gathered around the early, well-accredited nucleus of the Evangelic history.* What does this mean, it may be asked, but that these narratives are simply legends born of faith and reverence, the aureole which an adoring church placed on the head of the Holy One? This sceptical attitude may be further justified by a reference to the style of the narrations. The poetry with which the Gospel of the Infancy abounds, and the angels who play so important a part in the Gospel of the Resurrection, may be cited as conclusive evidence that we are in the cloudland of legend, not in the substantial world of historic fact. All things may be taken hold of by two handles, and while the world lasts faith and unbelief will put antagonistic constructions on these portions of the sacred story. All depends ultimately on the attitude we assume towards Christ Himself. If we receive Him as the great moral miracle we shall receive much more for His sake. All other Gospel miracles appear natural to one who believes in the Incarnation, and sees in Jesus the true eternal Son of God, and the perfect Son of Man. If, on the other hand, this supreme miracle be rejected, the miraculous element must disappear entirely, and nothing will remain but a Christianity from which all miracle has been expurgated. What sort of phenomenon this will be shall next be considered.

* So Dr. Abbott, vide *Onesimus*, Third Book, §7.

X.

CHRISTIANITY WITHOUT MIRACLE.

To enquire into the character of a Christianity without miracle may appear very superfluous. You feel instinctively that it cannot amount to much. What, you ask, can it be but the ghost of the Catholic faith, the dim light in the evening sky after sunset, which so soon fades away into darkness? The prejudice is not unfounded; yet it may be worth our while patiently to weigh the merits of a non-miraculous Christianity, were it only that we may learn the better to appreciate that which we are asked to throw away. To whom shall we go? asked Peter, in reply to the anxious enquiry of his Master, Will ye also go away? and the clear perception that there was no eligible alternative, helped him to remain where he was.

The term Christianity may be used in two senses. Lessing distinguished between the religion of Christ and the Christian religion. By the former he understood that religion which the man Jesus Himself recognised and practised; by the latter that religion which assumes that Jesus was more than man, and makes Him as such the object of worship.* Availing ourselves of this distinction, we might define Christianity, either as the religion of Jesus the worshipper, or as the religion which worships Jesus. The question to be considered in that case would be how far Christianity in either of these senses would remain after every particle of the miraculous element had been removed

* Vide *Die Religion Christi*, in Lessing's Werke.

how far we could still worship with Jesus, and how far we could still regard Him as an object of religious affection. This method of treatment being as convenient as any other, I propose now to follow it, only giving to the second aspect of Christianity, as the more important, the precedence.

It is manifest that the nature of the Christianity which survives the abandonment of the miraculous must depend on the character of the Christ left us when miracle has been eliminated. That, therefore, must be first ascertained.

Now here we have to deal not with certainties but with possibilities. We cannot, in the case supposed, determine what the actual history of Jesus was, but only what an unbeliever in miracle might admit it to have been. The reputation of the Gospels for historicity is fatally damaged when once it is conceded that all that savours of miracle belongs to the region of myth and legend; but it is still possible to say how much might be recognised as historical in consistency with naturalistic principles. We can construct a *credible* Christ. This is the task attempted by all naturalistic writers on the life of Jesus. The image which comes forth from the critical fires is not always the same in its features. The tendency of a Strauss is to minimize the possible; that of a Keim on the other hand is to widen its range. Fairness requires us to follow the latter tendency, and to make it our business to ascertain what a Christ without miracle can be at most. To this task accordingly I now address myself.

Of course the non-miraculous Christ was born in the ordinary way, subject to the usual infirmities and imperfections of humanity. He was simply one of the sons of men. But He was one of the fairest, if not the absolutely fair; a man of singularly beautiful nature and of exquisite religious genius. He was not sinless, but He knew less than most of the conflict between flesh and spirit which assumed such a tragic character in the experience of a David, a Paul, or an Augustine. To do good seems to have been natural and easy to Him. As a public man He was characterized by certain outstanding features, prominent among which were an intense abhorrence of counterfeit piety, and an equally intense sympathy with the weak, the suffering, and the sinful. Both qualities are remarkable, but the latter is the more novel feature. Jesus is conspicuous in history as a man of boundless, passionate benevolence. He seems to have felt as if He would and could cure all the sin and misery in the world. It came as natural to Him to love, and labour, and suffer, and deny Himself for others, as it comes to most men to be selfish. He loved mankind as a devoted mother loves her babe. He bore Himself as one who had a solemn call to be a Physician in all senses. In that capacity He did some remarkable things. By His wondrous sympathy He brought about some surprising moral changes in the spirit and life of persons who had previously seemed dead to all good, and who after their conversion rewarded His kindness by a warm and steadfast attachment. He appears, also, to have wrought physical cures on the bodies of the sick; by what means cannot easily be determined. Perhaps He possessed some peculiar physical endowment, or in a high degree curative powers latent, more or less, in all. Doubtless His benignant spirit had no small influence in making sufferers feel better. The diseases healed appear to have been of the class in which bodily and mental states are closely connected, and in which "moral therapeutics" can be brought into play. From the Gospel narratives it might be inferred that He healed indiscriminately all the sick who were present in the crowds that gathered around Him, and who had been brought by their friends for that purpose. But this, doubtless, is an exaggeration. We may assume that in passing through a crowd He saw at a glance what cases were curable, as also who had the faith to receive the necessary mental influence.*

Besides being a denouncer of spurious righteousness, like the Hebrew prophets, and a lover of men, like Buddha, Jesus was also an ethical teacher of rare merit and originality. He uttered many golden moral aphorisms such as those which pass by the name of the Beatitudes. In particular He taught a new method of attaining to happiness, and a new secret for getting possession of that which all seek but few find. The method was inwardness, and the secret self-denial. Seek, said Jesus, happiness not in outward goods, but in the state of the heart, and bring thy heart into blissful conditions by taking up thy cross. Simple teaching and now commonplace, but fresh intuitions then; and then, now, and always of imperishable value.

Jesus could not, of course, be the Messiah; for the Messianic hope was but a Jewish hallucination—beautiful and pathetic, doubtless, and valuable as poetry, but having no place in the realm of reality. Nor can we readily believe that so wise and good a man earnestly regarded Himself as the Messiah. But it is quite credible that He cherished a purified and transformed Messianic idea, and He might even give Himself out for the Christ *cum grano salis.* He is reported to have said of the Baptist, "If ye will receive it, this is Elias, which was for to come."† In like manner He might have said of Himself, "If ye will receive it, I am the Christ who was to come," speaking with a certain ironical humour, and meaning, "I am all the Messiah you will ever have, though not such as ye desire." In this sense He not only

* Such is the view of Dr. Abbott, vide *Philochristus,* p. 97.

† Matt. xi. 14.

might rationally claim to be the Messiah, but as the introducer of a new religion, fitted by its purely spiritual character to be universal, He could not help doing so. He was a Jew, and it was His appointed lot to work among Jews, while working consciously or unconsciously for the world; and in that situation it was necessary to offer Himself as a religious benefactor, under the specific title of Messiah. Not otherwise could He gain a footing for His doctrine in the holy land, which was the indispensable first step towards the conquest of the world.* Having served the temporary purpose of a cradle for the universal religion, the Messianic idea might be discarded as of purely local significance.

Such a Messiah as Jesus was not at all to the taste of His countrymen. In His whole spirit and ways He ran counter to popular expectation. At first indeed by His works of healing, and by His preaching of the kingdom, He excited enthusiasm among the common people. But by and bye, when they understood better His aims, they grew cold and ceased to follow after Him. He never gained the confidence of the influential classes. At the outset He awakened in them suspicion and dislike, which as time went on deepened into hatred. He paid the penalty by enduring crucifixion. He died a faithful martyr for truth and righteousness and humanity. He was buried in a tomb provided by love, from which He never rose again, though fond disciples fancied they saw their old Master on several occasions; whence sprang the legend of the resurrection so fruitful of results in the history of Christianity. The visions were the creations of a heated brain, or at most appear-

* Such is the well-known view of Baur, vide *Geschichte der Christlichen Kirche*, i., 37.

ances like a body produced by the still living Jesus to assure friends that it was well with Him in the spirit world.*

Jesus was remarkable for a happy, hopeful temperament, which affected all His thoughts. Hence came His bright views of God, whom He ever spoke of as a Father, and implicitly trusted with an unfailing confidence that banished from His heart care and fear and gloom, and flooded it with a great tide of joy. Hence came also His hopeful, genial views of man as redeemable, and at the worst worth redeeming. In virtue of these thoughts of God and man, and of the sweet nature out of which they sprang, His presence was as summer sunshine, and the company of Galilean peasants that gathered around Him was gay and buoyant as a bridal party.

Jesus was not infallible, even in the sphere of religion, any more than He was sinless. No man, however original or enlightened, can altogether escape paying tribute to his age; and Jesus paid the tribute by holding many opinions current among His Jewish contemporaries, which in this advanced epoch can no longer be tolerated. The list of popular errors with which He is chargeable, even as drawn up by His most indulgent critics, is a large one; embracing a crude idea of God with a heavenly throne, and surrounded with angels and guardian angels, a sensuously-coloured Messianic idea, faith in a kingdom of Satan and in demoniacal possessions, expectation of a speedy end of the world, belief in the verbal inspiration of the Old Testament, and the perpetual obligation of the Mosaic law.† Nevertheless, He was to a surprising extent in advance of His time; His thoughts of God, man, and the world, considering His environment, are

* The last mentioned hypothesis is the view of Keim, vide *Jesu von Nazara*, vol. iii., p. 601.

† Keim, *Jesu von Nazara*, iii., p. 631.

truly marvellous, and still command, if not the assent, at least the respect of all intelligent readers of His memoirs.

From this short recital it appears that the Jesus of history was a man of very extraordinary character. That such a man should have become the object of a cultus is not wonderful; that a supernatural legend should grow around His history was almost a matter of course. The same thing has happened to other great men, as for instance in the case of Buddha. Even when the miraculous nimbus has been removed, and the true man stands before us, as He actually lived and taught in Judæa, may not we moderns, with all our rooted aversion to the antiquated superstitions of Christendom, still, without degradation or inconsistency, pay Him a kind of religious homage?

Thus far naturalism has been spokesman, and we have now to consider what reply is to be given to the question with which its discourse ends.

Obviously, then, naturalism cannot consistently make Jesus in any strict sense the object of a religious cultus; for only when a historical personage is invested with ideal qualities can he become the basis of a positive religion. In order to be the proper recipient of divine honours Jesus would require at least to be exalted to the position of the Ideal man. Short of that He can only be the object of a sentimental Hero-worship, having for its motto *Ecce homo*, and manifesting itself in a more or less enthusiastic admiration, and an imitation severe or easy according to the taste of the disciple.

Such worship might be based on three grounds and assume three forms:

Jesus might be honoured as the great Hero of moral Sincerity, as the Prince of Philanthropists, and as the Paragon of Ethical Teachers.

In the first capacity the claims of Jesus to homage are beyond all question. The world knows of no greater moral hero, no more faithful witness to truth, no more passionate hater of falsehood, no man of purer heart or superior singleness of mind, who could say with better right, The prince of this world hath nothing in me. A passion for right and hatred of wrong, injustice, hypocrisy, pride, tyranny, are characteristic of all prophets; but in these qualities all prophets and noble men known to history are second to the prophet of Nazareth. He has most completely exposed false righteousness in theory, and most perfectly avoided it in practise. Of Him it cannot be said as of many, His doctrine was exceptionally high, but His life was pretty much like that of other men. With Him was no prudential silence from fear of consequences, no trimming and time-serving, no courting of popularity by insincere compliance with customs secretly despised, no obsequious deference to unrighteous power or to ill-founded reputation. His faults, if He had any, lay in the opposite direction; they leant to virtue's side, they sprang out of a consuming zeal for a lofty moral ideal, incapable of compromise, scorning selfish calculations, and blazing out on occasions into irrepressible bursts of indignation. The cross, endured after three short years of conflict with spiritual wickedness in high places, is the conclusive proof of His almost spotless fidelity, and His best title to be accepted as the Captain of all who fight against odds for the true, the good, and the fair. While He lived He was faithful and true; in righteousness He judged and made war; His eyes were as a flame of fire, burning up all counterfeit sanctities; at His passion He was clothed with a vesture dipped in blood; and the armies of the martyrs clothed in fine linen, white and clean, gladly follow His banner.

For those who worship Christ as the moral warrior, His great achievement was His conflict with Pharisaism, and His main utterance the Sermon on the Mount. That famous discourse, a sort of antipharisaic manifesto, is wholly to their liking. For the philanthropies of Jesus, possibly, they do not much care, for free-thinking Christians, not less than orthodox, are apt to be one-sided ; but in that magnificent proclamation of a morality of the heart, and that stern denunciation of a religion of ostentation, they take unfeigned delight. They cordially sympathise with the feelings of the multitude who heard the sermon, who were astonished at the preacher's doctrine, perceiving that in matter and manner it was wholly diverse from that of the scribes. Even yet, at the distance of eighteen centuries, the murmur of applause that ran along the hill-slopes awakens an echo in their hearts. In practise this worship takes the form of criticism of the moral and religious views of the worshipper's age. The Christianity of the Deists consisted in the unwearied cursing of priests as the author of all the evils that had overtaken mankind. The Christianity of Thomas Carlyle consisted in the ruthless demolishing of shams of all descriptions—mercantile, political, moral, spiritual. His books are the best modern commentary on the gospel of sincerity. The Christianity of some powerful organs of public opinion in the present time consists largely in hostile criticism of the Church as to a great extent a modern reproduction of Pharisaism, and of the clerical class as the descendants and heirs of the Rabbis and the scribes. Let it not be supposed that this species of Christianity is here alluded to in a spirit of contempt or sneering. When it appears in isolated form, indeed, as a mere everlasting No hurled at all moral and religious counterfeits, it is apt to become a rather barren and monotonous thing. No protest can have weight which is associated with wholesale unbelief, with blindness or indifference to the good mixed with the evil in systems, institutions, customs, and characters, and, above all, with conduct not much if at all higher in its moral level than that which is the subject of censure. But protest against all that is false and unwholesome, especially in religion, is ever most needful. A counterfeit presentation of Christianity, bringing it into affinity with Rabbinism, is the true Antichrist; and it is a matter of life and death that it be unsparingly detected, and the work of detection should be undertaken by believing men if they do not wish it to fall into unholy hands. The danger is ever present. Pharisaism cannot be extinguished for ever by a single exposure, however thorough; the evil thing re-embodies itself in new forms, and the protest of Jesus stands recorded, not to save us all further trouble, but to remind us of our duty and to teach us how it may best be performed. The worship of Jesus as the true and faithful witness against ungodliness sitting in the temple of God is an indispensable element of true Christianity. A community called Christian in which it is lacking is a salt without savour, good for nothing but to be trodden under foot of men, as fate which will not fail to overtake it.

Not less worthy to be admired and imitated is Jesus as the Prince of Philanthropists, the inaugurator of the beneficent religion of Humanity. Here indeed Buddha came before Him, loving with a tender, yearning pity, not only man, but beast; and it may seem as if the earlier Hero had the prior claim to worshipful recognition. And certainly on the principles of naturalism no worship can be accorded to Jesus on this score which ought not also to be paid in measure to the Asiatic philanthropist. But the pre-eminence may be given to Jesus partly because He is better known, and partly because His love is of a more wholesome and beneficent type than that of Buddha. Beautiful words and deeds are ascribed to the saint of the far East, but at this date it is hard to tell what is history and what legend in the professed records of his life. The same difficulty in a minor degree presents itself, from the naturalistic point of view, in the biography of Jesus of Nazareth. But enough is certain to put His claim to the title, Friend of Man, beyond all question. Not even the most sceptical doubts that He associated with publicans and sinners with beneficent intent, that He preached the Gospel of the kingdom very specially to the poor, that He at least tried to heal many of their diseases, and would gladly have healed all. Buddha is reported to have said, "My law is a law of grace for all." It is certain that Jesus said that in deeds, if not in express words, and that He strove habitually by word and deed to make the kingdom of heaven with all its benefits accessible to all without distinction, and very specially to those whose antecedents might be supposed to exclude them.

The love of Jesus is the more worthy of honour because of its hopefulness. The love of Buddha, as was pointed out in last lecture, was despairing, pessimistic. It has indeed been asserted that Jesus was a pessimist not less than Buddha;* but this is, to say the least, a gross exaggeration. There are, doubtless, words of Jesus on which a pessimistic construction can be put by any one who has a mind; but the truth is that His view of life was neither pessimistic nor optimistic, but steered a middle course between the two extremes. He did not say existence is an evil, and the only way to bliss is to renounce the will to live, and to reduce conscious being to a minimum by the extirpation of desire.

* So Schopenhauer, vide *Die Welt als Wille und Vorstellung*, Viertes Buch.

Neither did He deny the presence of evil in the world, or seek to get rid of it by smooth phrases. He saw evils of every description all around Him, and painted them in sombre colours. But His habitual attitude in presence of evils, physical or moral, was not one of depression and despondency, but rather of cheerfulness and hope. He treated evil, disease, death, sin, as an accident, a thing that ought not to be, that might cease to be, yea, that would without fail eventually pass away. Be of good cheer, He was wont to say to sufferers and penitents. It was His motto in reference to all ill, and all the world: Be of good cheer, O earth, O mankind burdened with manifold woes; the burden shall be lifted off thy weary shoulders; the darkness shall vanish, and the day of joy dawn. How He came to be of this hopeful temper it is not necessary at present to enquire; the point insisted on is that the temper is good, because fitted to call forth the energies of love, whereby the miseries of the world must be greatly lessened if not wholly removed. In this view the philanthropy of Christ will always commend itself to the admiration of the active races of the West. But it may fare otherwise among the passive Orientals. Buddhism has possession of the Eastern world, and perhaps just because it is a religion of despair. It acts, as Bunsen graphically remarks, as "a mild dose of opium on the raving or despairing tribes of weary-hearted Asia."* Arise, said the Jewish Hero, and fight with brave heart the evil that is in the world, His voice sounding like a trumpet peal summoning a host to battle. Lie down and sleep and forget your sorrow, said in soft, plaintive accents the Eastern recluse. Europe and America listen to Jesus, Asia listens to Buddha, and the two philanthropists divide the world between them.

---

* *God in History*, i., 375.

It has been well for the Western world that it has adopted Jesus as its Hero. The "enthusiasm of humanity" with which He inspired His followers, has borne manifold blessed fruits of which Christian nations reap the benefit. But there is plenty of scope still for the display of its beneficent energies. Not even in Christendom have the new heavens and the new earth appeared for which faith looks with patient eye Poverty, disease, crime, sin, iniquity, injustice, oppression, discord, strife, are with us still. All hands to the work, is the urgent cry. It is a work in which all may join whatever their creed; those who believe in the Gospel miracles, and those who reject all miracle; those who worship Christ as God, and those who simply honour Him as the Friend of man. If the sceptics should be the foremost in the labour of love, let them have all due credit, and let it be acknowledged that a Christianity without miracle may be something to be thankful for.

The third ingredient in this Christianity is veneration for Jesus as an ethical teacher. Here Christ has formidable rivals in the sages of the Gentiles, Confucius, Buddha, Socrates, Plato, Epictetus. In some of His wisest utterances He had been anticipated, and in the manner of expression, some have thought that others excelled Him. Celsus was of opinion that what was good and true in Christianity had been said before and better by Plato or some other Greek author. The style of the Galilean sage appeared to him rustic in comparison with the elegance and refinement of the Athenian philosopher. "Resist not evil," said Jesus, "but whosoever shall smite thee on thy right cheek turn to him the other also." Celsus thought Plato put the doctrine of passive submission to wrong better when he made Socrates say to Crito, "We must on no account do injury; we must not even, as the multitude think, take revenge for evil done."* It

* Origen, *Contra Celsum*, vii., 58.

was the criticism of a pedant, and was well replied to by Origen when he remarked that the simple style of Jesus best suited a doctrine which concerned the million, while the ornate style of Plato could benefit only the few.* No competent judge of style would think of repeating such a criticism now. As regards the substance of Christ's teaching, great modern literary authorities, conversant with the wisdom of all ages and peoples, and nowise inclined to give the Galilean Master more than His due, have declared that nothing better, nobler, purer, ever has been said, or probably ever will be said, than the golden utterances preserved in the Gospels. It would seem, therefore that, prejudice apart, and according to the testimony of impartial judges, the first place among the ethical teachers of the world may be assigned to Jesus in strict consistency with naturalistic philosophy. Unbelievers in the miraculous, even in the moral miracle of an infallible guide, may take Christ's yoke upon them and learn from Him the way of life in preference to all other Masters.

It is superfluous to say that Jesus was incomparably superior to the Rabbis, the rival claimants to the honours of Mastership in His own time and land. He had them in His eye when He said, Come to my school; in current phrase, Take my yoke upon you, and learn from me. It was from their heavy burden of legal prescriptions He offered to deliver men; it was their galling yoke of mechanical rules, source of incessant irritation to reason and conscience, He undertook to remove and replace by a yoke that would sit easy. And He was quite entitled to invite men to forsake the Rabbis and come over to Him, for He was able to perform all He promised. Simply as an ethical teacher He was

---

* Origen, *Contra Celsum*, vii., 59.

a great deliverer from Rabbinical bondage. He taught His disciples a few great, broad principles in place of a multitude of vexatiously minute rules; He set before them a lofty ideal, and left it to work on them by its inspiring influence. His commands were not easy; on the contrary, they were difficult and high as Alpine mountains. Love your enemies, deny thyself, be as little children, be perfect as the Father in heaven is perfect: how the snowy summits of these precepts gleam in the clear blue sky! But high and difficult though they be, these precepts are not grievous. They are sweet to the taste and a joy to the heart, because they commend themselves to reason and conscience. Their very altitude gives liberty, because they lift one clear above the oppressive atmosphere of legalism with its mechanical routine and its small conventional moralities.

Such, from the point of view of naturalism, are the claims of Jesus to the homage of mankind. He was Prophet, Philanthropist, and Sage all in one, and all in a signal degree. If He had sustained only one of these characters well, He had been entitled to grateful adoring memory; uniting them in His person He stands before the world an incarnation of righteousness, love, and wisdom, before whom the greatest may bow. It is not easy to see how any one who knows His name and history can avoid giving Him some sort of recognition in His religious system. All may not be ready to hail Him "the chosen of God, the image, darling, chief agent, and world-artist of God in the history of humanity";* but none but a churl would refuse Him at least as much honour as is conferred on Him in a certain chapel in London where His name occupies the central place above the reading desk, supported on either side

* Keim, *Jesu von Nazara*, iii., 667.

by the names of Shakespeare, Socrates, Voltaire, and Moses.* It would compromise no man's dignity thus to confess himself a Christian, and certainly he would run no risk of forfeiting the esteem of his fellows who showed his right to the name by the practice of sincerity, charity, and all other virtues taught and exemplified by Jesus.

We have next to inquire how far the religion of Jesus Himself is likely to survive the complete elimination of the miraculous from His history and person. That religion may be described in a few words. He believed in a God who is a Father. He believed that this God shows Himself to be a Father by exercising a constant gracious care over all, and especially over those who make the divine kingdom their chief end. He trusted the Father in heaven utterly, and so was enabled to live in perfect peace amidst incessant trial and trouble. He prayed to His Father habitually, and especially and with peculiar fervour at critical periods of His life, seeking in such acts of devotion not only solace but light on His path. He regarded all men, even prodigals, as God's sons. He believed that towards the worst of men God cherished paternal affection. With such thoughts of God and man He naturally believed in life after death. From sonship He inferred immortality. God a Father, man His son, a benignant Providence, a power in prayer, a life beyond the tomb—behold the creed of Jesus shown to best advantage in His conduct. A beautiful creed, and good for Him, and good for all who can hold it. But there is the difficulty. Believers in miracle can take it on His word, and successfully resist all temptations to doubt arising from whatever in nature or in experience seems to give

* That of Mr. Moncure D. Conway. For an account of the worship carried on in this chapel, vide *The Contemporary Evolution of Religious Thought*, by Count Goblet d'Alviella, p. 119.

the lie to its cardinal propositions; for in Christ they recognise an infallible guide in all matters pertaining to religion and morals. But with miracle the infallible guide disappears, and there remains only a man with very charming views about God, man, and the universe; views for which He seems to have been indebted to a happy natural temperament, and which to men less fortunately endowed may be impossible and incredible. Not that these views are in themselves false or baseless; on the contrary they have commended themselves to many thoughtful men as at once intrinsically probable, and most worthy to be believed. But in a non-miraculous Christianity they are without authority, and must simply go for what they are worth. Certainty in regard to any of them is unattainable; they cannot have more than subjective personal validity. When miracle has been finally got rid of, the order of the day will be, Let him follow the religion of Jesus who can. There will always, probably, be some who find it possible. People of bright, buoyant temper, like Miss Cobbe and Theodore Parker, will hear their soul, for them the true oracle of revelation, saying to them, There is a Father above who is absolutely good; all men are His children; there is a Providence which careth for man and beast; and there is a heaven in store for every creature that lives. The same oracle tells them that prayer, at least for spiritual benefits, is both reasonable and useful and therefore incumbent.* But others, who also recognise as the highest guide in religion the inner light, but, like Rathbone Greg, are of more desponding disposition, follow haltingly behind. Their Christianity is of a very eclectic character. They may recognise Christ's doctrine of God as coming "probably as

---

* *Vide* Miss Cobbe's *Broken Lights*, and Parker's *Speculative Theism*

near the truth as the minds of men could in that age receive," or even as the best practical view of God that can be entertained in any age, though anthropomorphic and unverifiable. But as for His doctrines of Providence and Prayer and a Hereafter they stand gravely in doubt. What room for prayer in a universe governed by fixed law; what evidence that all things happen for the good of the individual; what probability that the mass of mankind, who scarce rise above the level of animalism, will survive the death of the body?* The mutual contradictions of the apostles of intuitionalism, and the discrepant oracles given out by the moral consciousness, their organ of spiritual knowledge, sufficiently show what slender hope there is of certainty even in regard to the most fundamental questions of religion where a Book revelation has been discarded in scorn, and men have ceased to believe in One who might say without arrogance, I am the Way, the Truth, and the Life. "I bless God," said Rousseau, following the guidance of *la lumiere interieure*, "I bless God, but I pray not. What should I ask of Him? That He would change for me the course of things, do miracles in my favour? I who ought to love above all the order established by His wisdom and maintained by His Providence, shall I wish that order to be disturbed on my account? As little do I ask of Him the power to do well, why ask what He has already given?"† Prayer, says Miss Cobbe, for physical blessings is indeed unphilosophical, but it is not irreligious or unreasonable to ask that God would perform His will in us.‡ Prayer, says Mr. Greg, is indefensible on rational grounds, but it springs

* *Vide* Greg's *Creed of Christendom*, concluding chapters on *Christian Eclecticism* and *The Great Enigma*.

† Vide *Profession de Foi du Vicaire Savoyard* in *Emile*, Livre iv.

‡ Vide *Broken Lights*, p. 177.

out of a natural instinct; it is a comfort to the weak and therefore is not condemned by the strong, though they know it is vain and therefore do not practise it.* Similar is the discordance all along the line. Which of the oracles is right? Is not the soul by these contrary voices discredited as a source of revelation; shown to be not a sun, but only at best a moon? What wonder if her claims should be as rudely set aside, as were those of a Book, or of a historical Person in her behalf, and the cry should be raised, Look not within but without; learn how to think of God and of man and of human destiny from the universe and its fixed laws; clear your mind of all fond illusions and sentimental beliefs, and accept as truth, however unwelcome, that there is no Father in heaven, that man is a comparatively insignificant being, and that the life beyond is a dream.

When this voice prevails it will be all over with Christianity in the sense of the religion which Jesus Himself practised. This gone, it will not be easy to retain the other kind of Christianity, which consists in doing homage to Jesus as the great hero of sincerity, philanthropy, and wisdom. For how can one make the lover of man his model if he cease to believe in the worth of human nature, and how can he accept as his guide one whom he regards as in error on the most essential questions of religion? At the utmost he can only continue to entertain a certain respect for the character of one who, however far behind the present age, was in advance of His own time, and who faithfully lived according to His light. When men have completely outgrown Christ's theory of the universe the time has come for them to ask themselves, "Are we any longer Christians?"

* Vide *Creed of Christendom*, chapter xvi.

This, accordingly, is one of the questions propounded by Dr. Strauss in his *Old and New Faith*, and answered with his usual directness. When he wrote his first *Leben Jesu* he thought it possible to find in Hegelianism a substitute for the Christ whom in his sceptical treatise he had crucified afresh. For an incarnation in an individual man he offered an incarnation in humanity, the latter being the philosophic idea (Begriff), whereof the former is the pictorial representation (Vorstellung). He counselled preachers to give the people the *Vorstellung* and to keep the *Begriff* to themselves. The story of Christian Märklin, so graphically told by the author of this advice, shows how hard it is for a conscientious man to act on it; Märklin having tried it for a year or two, and then found it necessary for his peace of mind to renounce a position in which he was required to speak as an orthodox churchman, while all the time he thought as a Hegelian. When he wrote his last book, Strauss had ceased to be a Hegelian and became a Materialist, and had grown weary of imposing on himself and others with fine phrases. In *Old and New Faith* he no longer pretends to be a Christian, and he gives three reasons for renouncing the name. First, we know very little about Jesus. The Evangelists have daubed His life-image so thick with supernatural colours that the natural colours can no longer be restored. The Jesus of history is simply a problem, and a problem cannot be the object of faith or the exemplar of life. It is the penalty He pays for being a God. He who has once been deified has irrevocably forfeited his humanity. Next, what is best known of Jesus shows Him in a light which makes it impossible to take Him for our guide. Nothing in the Gospels is more certain than that He expected shortly to appear in the clouds of heaven to establish on earth the Messianic kingdom. It was a fanatical expectation; and no fanatic, however worthy otherwise of respect, can wisely be adopted as a leader. He will conduct us into byways, if we do not subject his influence to the control of our reason. Once more, the bright side of Christ's character, His enthusiasm of humanity, was not peculiar to Him, neither will it die with Him. Buddha taught mildness and pity towards all living creatures five hundred years before Him. That we must help even enemies was a doctrine of contemporary stoicism; and a generation later, but quite independently, Epictetus declared all men brethren. Such truths lie in the direct path of the development of humanity, and at certain epochs reveal themselves necessarily, and to more than one.*

These are the reasons of one who is easily convinced. It is not difficult to suggest other arguments of a more cogent character pointing to the same conclusion. Thus: the historical Christ is far, far away, and is ever receding into a remoter distance. He may in some sense be the same yesterday, to-day, and forever; but He is not the same to us With the lapse of time His image grows ever dimmer, and His power fainter. We cannot always go back thousands of years for religious impulse; we urgently need a present source of inspiration if religion is not to die in us. Jesus Himself acknowledged the need when He said, Lo, I am with you always. But whatever His wish, He has not been able to fulfil His promise. He is not, cannot be with us now, as He was with the twelve. The only rational sense in which, without supernaturalism, He can be with us is through the four Evangelic memoirs, and the impression they produce on the reader, and through the Christian spirit present in greater or less force and purity in the community

* *Der Alte und der Neue Glaube*, pp. 76–86.

which bears His name. A spiritual, mystic presence through a person of the Trinity, called the Holy Ghost, is a super natural thing which cannot be believed in by those who have discarded miracle. And as for the Church, according to the Catholic theory a perpetual incarnation, making Christ ever present in the fulness of His grace through its services and sacraments, it is open to objection, not only on the score of supernaturalism, but even on the score of morality. We cannot accept the holy Catholic Church as a fulfilment of the promise of perpetual presence, because it is not holy. It is rather a second reason for dropping the name Christian in the interest of all in Christianity that is worthy of conservation. In the Church's creed, worship, and history, Christianity has become associated with so much that is incredible, unworthy, unchristian, and even antichristian, that it seems hopeless now to extricate the pure elements from the impure, the genuine from the counterfeit. It may be possible for the scholar, by careful study of the Gospel records, to discover for himself the Christianity of Christ, and to discern clearly the wide difference between it and ecclesiastical Christianity. But the distinction cannot be made valid for the multitude, which will always form its notions of the Christian religion from the actual Christendom by which it is surrounded. Instead, therefore, of labouring at the vain task of separating between the precious and the vile, the original and the adventitious, were it not better to begin anew, to cease calling ourselves Christians, and even when teaching or practising what is essentially Christian, carefully to avoid the use of a term which almost inevitably calls up misleading, uncongenial associations?

Thus reasoning from naturalistic premises may we arrive at the conclusion that the days of Christianity are numbered, that Christianity without miracle means Christianity ceasing to be a substantive religion, and becoming a mere unnamed element taken up, in so far as good, into some other modern religion bearing a new name, as the soil formed by decomposition of the vegetation of early geological epochs enters into the living plants of the present era. In short, the Galilean must be renounced, with or without regret, and some other divinity put in His place. It is not difficult to conceive with what diverse feelings such a religious revolution might be contemplated. Some would sympathise with the sentiments of one who, having undertaken a candid examination of Theism, found himself reluctantly compelled to pronounce an unfavourable verdict on the Theistic argument. His words sound like the wail of Rachel weeping for her children, and refusing to be comforted because they are not. "Forasmuch as I am far from being able to agree with those who affirm that the twilight doctrine of the 'new faith' is a desirable substitute for the waning splendour of 'the old,' I am not ashamed to confess that with this virtual negation of God the universe to me has lost its soul of loveliness; and although from henceforth the precept to 'work while it is day,' will doubtless but gain an intensified force from the terribly intensified meaning of the words that 'the night cometh when no man can work,' yet when at times I think, as think at times I must, of the appalling contrast between the hallowed glory of that creed which once was mine, and the lonely mystery of existence as now I find it—at such times I shall ever feel it impossible to avoid the sharpest pang of which my nature is susceptible. For whether it be due to my intelligence not being sufficiently advanced to meet the requirements of the age, or whether it be due to the memory of the sacred associations, which to me at least were the sweetest that life has given, I cannot but feel that for me, and for others who think as I do, there is a dreadful truth in those words of Hamilton—Philosophy having become a meditation, not merely of death, but of annihilation, the precept *know thyself* has become transformed into the terrific oracle to Œdipus:

> 'Mayest thou ne'er know the truth of what thou art.'"*

We can imagine men of a different temper, on the other hand, contemplating the abandonment of the Christian name with philosophic serenity, with a sense of relief, or even with passionate delight. To them the name is a synonym for an unintelligible system of supernaturalism, for a spiritual tyranny, and even for a ghastly hypocrisy. Therefore they say Amen to the sentiment of Voltaire, *ecrazez l'infame,* and hail the dawn of the day when the religion of miracle, and of the wearisome life unending with its horrible hell and its almost equally repulsive heaven, and of incredible dogmas to be received under pain of excommunication and damnation, and of priests and sacramental magic and ascetic gloom, shall have become at last a thing of the past. The darkness is past, they exclaim; the true light for which we have so long waited, now shines. The era, so called, of grace has come to an end, and the era of science is being ushered in not with the song of mystic angels, but with the hearty welcomes of rational men.

And who is to be the divinity of the new era; what name or names are to succeed those of Christ? Two claimants to the vacant throne present themselves: the Universe, and Humanity, to us the most important thing in the universe. Perhaps I should have said three, reckoning as the third the unknowable Ultimate Reality from which all existence proceeds. But this recondite deity of evolutionary philosophy,

---

* *A Candid Examination of Theism,* by Physicus, p. 114.

unless inconsistently invested with attributes incompatible with his (or its) character as the unknowable, does not seem fitted to be the object of religious affection. The one feeling the contemplation of it can excite is an awful sense of being in presence of an inscrutable mystery. The ultimate reality, cause of all things, like nothing which it causes, is to the imagination as a boundless sandy desert, monotonous, dreary, awe-inspiring, stupefying. It is *τὸ ὄν*, pure being, of which no affirmations can be made, having no contents for thought, still less, if possible, for the heart. The religion of the unknowable has been called, with a witty reference to Mr. Spencer's theory of the origin of religion, "the ghost of religion." * The name is more than a witticism; it expresses the simple truth. The agnostic has a God without a religion, just as the humanitarian has a religion without a God. Belief in the unknowable can never give rise to a worship, or affect conduct; it must remain for ever barren, till the unknowable be merged in the known universe, and worshipped through its manifestations. Mr. Spencer himself virtually acknowledges this when he says: "Very likely there will ever remain a need to give shape to that indefinite sense of an ultimate existence, which forms the basis of our intelligence. We shall always be under the necessity of contemplating it as some mode of being, that is, of representing it to ourselves in some form of thought, however vague." † The whole history of religion justifies the statement, for wherever the highest God has been conceived of as *τὸ ὄν*, abstract being, there the worship of God under many modes, that is polytheism, has prevailed. The concrete universe, either in detail or as an

---

* Vide *Nineteenth Century*, vol. xv., article on ***The Ghost of Religion***, by Frederic Harrison.

† Vide *First Principles*, p. 113.

organic unity, inevitably takes the place of the hidden ground. The worship of the universe in detail belongs to the prescientific epoch; the worship of the universe as a whole replaces polytheism in our modern epoch of scientific culture.

This new worship goes by various names. Strauss denominates it the worship of the *Universum*, the author of *Ecce Homo natural religion*, and in America it has assumed the title of *Cosmism*. To old-fashioned people it may appear, by whatever name called, little less absurd than the ghostly religion of the unknowable. The universe my God! we can imagine such exclaiming, I cannot love the universe, for it is a thing, and love is for a person. Bless the *universum*, O my soul; how ridiculous the idea! I cannot be thankful to the universe, I can only enjoy my own existence; for however happy my lot may be, I cannot regard the universe as my benefactor; for conferring benefit presupposes intention, and the universe, on the testimony of modern philosophers, has no intentions, but acts blindly. But the apostles of the new religion assure us that the universe can awaken veritable thrills of "cosmic emotion." They declare belief and trust in the universe to be the corner-stone of their faith. Strauss, for once speaking almost with unction, professes to cherish towards the *Universum* a quite tender feeling, a feeling of dependence which does not destroy freedom, a feeling in which pride mingles with humility and joy with resignation. He demands for it from all his fellow-philosophers the same piety which the devout man of the old style demanded for his God. He is, therefore, quite shocked with Schopenhauer's pessimistic view of the world as something that had better not have been, as almost blasphemous, and he cites his pious horror in proof that his feeling for the universe is of the nature of a religion, whose characteristic it is to be unable to bear all irreverences against the object of worship. "Our feeling for the all," he quaintly remarks, "when it is injured, reacts quite religiously." *

What, then, are the aspects or elements in the universe that communicate to its votaries thrills of cosmic religious emotion? They are threefold. First, there is the august order of physical law which calls forth worshipful recognition from the devout man of science; next, there is the moral order which reveals itself, dimly indeed but perceptibly, in history, the power not ourselves working for righteousness, which appeals to the religious feelings of the morally earnest; and lastly, there is the æsthetic order, the revelation of beauty, which awakens raptures in the breast of the poet and the artist. These three aspects of the universe combined, it is claimed, satisfy the wants of man's whole spiritual being. The rational order of the universe, in virtue of which it is interpretable by reason, supplies the intellect with ample materials for devout contemplation. The moral order, through which the idea of the good is at least approximately realised, offers to the conscience a satisfactory substitute for a righteous God, exciting in a Fichte or a Carlyle, essentially the same sentiments as those Hebrew psalmists and prophets cherished towards a personal Jehovah, just in all his ways and holy in all his works The æsthetic order appeals to the sense of the beautiful and the sublime, the unfailing source of manifold gratification to all, and of genial inspiration to the gifted few who can interpret nature's revelation of beauty in song, and music, and painting.

Cosmic religion, it is maintained, does not require us to

---

* *Der Alte und der Neue Glaube*, p. 147.

break away altogether from Christianity, but rather takes up all that is valuable in it; and in the Bible generally, and supplements its one-sidedness. What, it is asked, is Christianity, or Hebrewism, but an emphatic assertion of the supreme importance of conduct? Is it not the persistent, powerful proclamation of that great truth that gives to the Bible its unique, imperishable value? But the message of the Bible finds full recognition in Cosmic religion under its second phase, according to which it consists in an earnest faith in the moral order of the universe, in the deep conviction that there is a tendency ever at work to bring about a correspondence between character and lot, and to fulfil the promise of holy writ that verily it shall be well with the righteous. What is this faith but the creed of Hebrew prophets under a new form, what we may call a "Natural Christianity."*

The cultus of the new religion will certainly differ considerably from that to which Christians have been accustomed. If, as is proposed by the author of Natural Religion, the existing ecclesiastical framework be retained, that the revolution may be achieved with as little disturbance as possible, many of our churches will have to undergo transformation. While some may still be devoted to the preaching of Hebrewism, or the supreme importance of conduct, and the reality of a moral order, others will need to be transformed into lecture-rooms where men of science may expound the rational order of the Cosmos, or into theatres where dramatic representations may be performed, and concert-rooms where the works of the great masters of the musical art may be interpreted, and picture-galleries for the exhibition on canvas of the beauties of earth and sky and sea.

---

* Vide *Natural Religion*, chapter viii.

The clergy of the new era will be the *savants*, the poets, and the painters, with a sprinkling of men of the Carlyle type just to keep the public in mind that a community cannot live on science and art alone, but requires for its preservation and prosperity a certain amount of righteousness What type of devotion is likely to be developed may be partly guessed from the criticisms on the poets and musicians of Germany with which the author of *the old ana the new faith* has favoured his readers.*

The religion of humanity took its rise as a distinct cult with Auguste Comte, who did his best to make it ridiculous. In England it received influential support from John Stuart Mill, who expressed the opinion "that the sense of unity with mankind, and a deep feeling for the general good, may be cultivated into a sentiment and a principle capable of fulfilling every important function of religion and itself justly entitled to the name."† The description here given of this modern religion is somewhat vague, but it is as definite as any definition elsewhere to be found. Mr. Herbert Spencer, a hostile critic, calls it "an ecstatic philanthropy,"‡ an expression which seems justified by the account given of the religion of humanity by its chief interpreter and advocate, Mr. Harrison, who says it "means recognising your duty to your fellow-men on human grounds,' and is "simply morality fused with social devotion, and enlightened by sound philosophy."§ When, in absence of precise authoritative definitions, one tries to conceive how humanity may be the object and provocative of religious affections, various points of view suggest themselves. We

* Vide Appendix to *Der Alte und der Neue Glaube.*

† Vide *Three Essays on Religion,* p. 110.

‡ Vide *Nineteenth Century,* vol. xvi., p. 836.

§ Vide *Nineteenth Century,* vol. xvi., pp. 369–70.

may look upwards to humanity, as represented by choice specimens of the race, with feelings of veneration; or downwards to the many degraded samples, with feelings of compassion. We may think of humanity as an organic whole, and worship it as our great parent or creator who has made us what we are by the law of heredity. We may look back on the past of humanity, and observe the steady, onward progress of civilisation with feelings of devout thankfulness; or forward to the future with high hope of indefinite further progress, finding in the prophetic vision of a perfect social state, to be approximately realised in a good time coming, ample compensation for the loss of that individual future life of bliss which the Christian religion promises its votaries. It is obvious that this is simply a mutilated or transformed Christianity. Instead of one perfect Christ, Lord, and Saviour, we have many imperfect christs, saviours, or benefactors of the race; instead of the Father in heaven we have mother humanity, who through countless generations has poured her blood into our veins; instead of personal immortality we have an impersonal immortality in our posterity, and the cheering hope that their world will be a much better one than ours. In so far as it takes the form of beneficent effort for the poor, the diseased, and the degraded, the religion of humanity is simply Christianity on its philanthropic side, shorn of some of the most powerful motives which stimulate the Christian to benevolent deeds.

Looking now at these two, or let us say, three religions with critical eyes, it may be observed in the first place, that they are all fancy worships of philosophers. They are simply modern science and philosophy coloured by the imagination and touched with a little emotion. They are not indeed idle or gratuitous inventions; they are the best religions that can be had where faith in a living God has died out, and we may not grudge sceptics any solace they yield. By all means let men worship the Unknowable, the Universum, Humanity, if they can discover in the universe no other objects of adoration. We can well understand how the heart of a Strauss may be thankful to have even the universum to love after all other deities have been ruthlessly demolished. The homage of the arch-sceptic to the chosen god of his old age is a pathetic testimony to the need of the human heart for some object of unlimited trust, love, and reverence. Nevertheless it must be acknowledged that the universum is only a makeshift divinity. It is absurd to speak of loving the universe, as reason not less than Scripture teaches God ought to be loved, with all the heart, soul, strength, and mind. The remark applies with increased force to the worship of the unknowable. Psalmists strove to kindle their affections towards the living God, and exquisite lyrics like the 103d Psalm remain to attest their success. It will be a while before the worship of the unknowable produces anything like that. Attempts to stir up religious emotion towards the Ultimate Force must needs be artificial and desperate. The very idea has been ridiculed, as not less absurd than would be a worship of the mathematical symbol x^n. "Where two or three are gathered together to worship the Unknowable, there the algebraic formula may suffice to give form to their emotions: they may be heard to profess their unwearying belief in x^n, even if no weak brother with ritualist tendencies be heard to cry, O x^n, love us, help us, make us one with thee.'"* The writer of these words is a devotee of the religion of humanity, and thinks that in his own religion he has something

* Mr. Harrison, in *Nineteenth Century*, vol. xv., p. 503.

that really can touch the heart and rouse its dormant emotions. And he is right. The religion of humanity is, by comparison with the other two, warm, real, and rational. The worshipper is in presence of something he knows familiarly, is intensely interested in, and can without artificial stimulus become enthusiastic about, if not by way of reverence, at least along the channel of benevolence. The object of his worship may seem unworthy. Mr. Spencer calls humanity a bubble,* and another adverse critic characterizes it, as represented by many samples, as "a half-beast of a creature." † But you can at least pity the bubble that so soon bursts, and try to make the half-beast more of a man, and such pity and effort, if not an integral religion, are at least an essential part of all religions worthy of the name. But this modern religion is not content with being a part; it aspires to be a whole, not needing to borrow from or lean on any other faith. And for this purpose it conjures into existence a purely imaginary deity, the "Great Being Humanity," and offers it the incense of an extravagant rhetoric expressive not of genuine emotion, but of a refined philosophic sentimentalism, fitted to weaken rather than strengthen the philanthropic impulses which are the redeeming feature of the new cultus.

A second legitimate criticism on these modern religions is that their objects of worship, not less than that of Christianity as conceived by naturalism, are far away if not in time, then in another sense not less serious in its practical effect. It may indeed plausibly be claimed for them that they are ever-present sources of inspiration. Humanity, and especially her poor, we have always with us; the universe is all around us; and Mr. Spencer tells us that we are "ever in

* *Nineteenth Century*, vol. xvi., p. 23.

† Sir James Stephen, in *Nineteenth Century*, vol. xv., p. 917.

presence of an Infinite and Eternal Energy, from which all things proceed." * But while humanity as an object of pity and philanthropic service is ever near, humanity as an object of veneration is far away. It is either an ideal to be reached by an effort of abstraction, or an organic growth that can be known only by a wide study of history. The universe also, while near to all as an object of sense, is far away as an object of science. Worship of the universe is possible for the multitude only in detail, in the form of a revived Paganism or polytheism ; worship of the universe as an embodiment on a grand scale of a rational, moral, and æsthetic order is possible only to the elect children of culture. As for "the Infinite and Eternal Energy from which all things proceed," those who can pretend to be in presence of it are a still more select class. Philosophers are not agreed even as to its existence, one school extending their agnosticism so far as not to know whether there be an Unknowable. Speaking to common men we could not say of the God of Evolutionary philosophy what Paul said to the Athenians of the unknown God, whom they ignorantly worshipped, He is not far from every one of you. He is not in all their thoughts, neither are they able to make the effort of mental abstraction necessary to bring them into His presence.

From these observations it follows that whatever value the modern religions may have for philosophers, they are not fitted to take the place of Christianity for popular purposes. It is essentially the religion of the million, not in the sense of pandering to their weakness, but in the sense of coming down to their level that it may exalt them. If, therefore, perchance, the leaven of unbelief in miracle were

---

* *Nineteenth Century*, vol xv., p. 12.

to spread from the inner circle of culture to the wide world of the masses, and Christianity in consequence were to die out for a season, there is reason to believe that like its founder, it would rise again. It might even rise to a more vigorous life than before, and renew its youth like the eagle. One is sometimes tempted to think it might even be to the advantage of the Christian faith if it were to disappear for a while, like a river losing itself in sand to emerge again further down its course. It might thus rid itself of many chronic corruptions, and regain a fresh intuition of the truth as it was in Jesus, clear of benumbing scholasticism and of Evangelicism that caricatures the Evangel, and relearn the almost lost art of commending a lofty faith by a noble life. The author of *Natural Religion* expresses the opinion that an impartial bystander would say that the average scientific man worships just at present a more awful, and, as it were, a greater Deity than the average Christian ; assigning as the reason that in many Christians the idea of God has been degraded by childish and little-minded teaching, whereby the Eternal, Infinite, All-embracing One has virtually been degraded into the head of the clerical interest, and become a sort of clergyman, schoolmaster, or philanthropist.* It might be invidious to say how far this opinion is well founded, but the general admission must be made that the baldest creed associated with a high moral tone is better than a religion theoretically high, but practically low. Even a virtuous atheism of reaction is to be preferred to a debased theism. Buddhism at its commencement was an atheistic religion, but it was a vast improvement on the Brahmanical system against which it rose in revolt. Anything that clears the air of cant and hypocrisy and traditionalism is a matter for thankfulness. It may be—I do not believe it, but I am

* *Natural Religion*, p. 19.

willing to concede—that the popular Christianity of the present time has so much of the evil element in it that a general cessation from profession of the Christian faith for a generation would be a relative good. If, however, such a glacial epoch were to overtake us, it would not, one may predict, be final. The dechristianised world would begin to long for its lost Lord. Men weary of new gods, or of no god, would listen once more to the voice of Jesus saying, Come unto me. Worshippers of the Unknowable might be glad to learn from one who claimed to know, and assured them that the Unknown One was a Father. Worshippers of the universe might welcome rest for an exclusive faith offered by one who is represented in the New Testament as the Eternal Reason of God, gathering up in Himself as a centre the whole meaning of the creation. Worshippers of humanity might at length discover the true justification of their devotion in Him who first taught the worth of human nature, and who realised in Himself the ideal of manhood. Nay, might not even Pessimists, to whom the world is a huge mistake, and its maker, if it had any, an almighty blunderer. to whom life appears not worth living, and humanity an object of contempt—might not even such unhappy mortals be found coming to Jesus for a little alleviation of their misery, perusing wistfully His strange, weird story which seems so fully to justify their poor opinion of mankind, and finding solace in the thought that a man of such inimitable gentleness, goodness, and wisdom once appeared on this earth, perhaps even venturing to hope that He did not appear in vain? When all this happens, Christianity, done to death by unworthy faith and by scientific unbelief abhorrent of the supernatural, will repeat the miracle of the resurrection, and will run a new career fraught with glory to Jesus and with manifold blessing to men.

INDEX.